Verification and Validation in Systems Engineering

T0137816

Mourad Debbabi · Fawzi Hassaïne · Yosr Jarraya ·
Andrei Soeanu · Luay Alawneh

Verification and Validation in Systems Engineering

Assessing UML/SysML Design Models

 Springer

Dr. Mourad Debbabi
Computer Security Laboratory
Concordia Institute for Information
    Systems Engineering (CIISE)
Faculty of Engineering and Computer Science
Concordia University
1455, Boulevard de Maisonneuve West, EV 7-642
Montreal, Quebec, H3G 1M8 Canada
debbabi@ciise.concordia.ca

Dr. Fawzi Hassaïne
Capabilities for Asymmetric and
    Radiological Defence and Simulation
Defence Research and Development
    Canada – Ottawa
3701 Carling Avenue
Ottawa, ON, Canada K1A 0Z4
fawzi.hassaine@drdc-rddc.gc.ca

Dr. Yosr Jarraya
Computer Security Laboratory
Concordia Institute for Information
    Systems Engineering (CIISE)
Faculty of Engineering and Computer Science
Concordia University
1455, Boulevard de Maisonneuve West, EV 7-642
Montreal, Quebec, H3G 1M8 Canada
y_jarray@encs.concordia.ca

Andrei Soeanu
Computer Security Laboratory
Concordia Institute for Information
    Systems Engineering (CIISE)
Faculty of Engineering and
    Computer Science
Concordia University
1455, Boulevard de Maisonneuve West,
EV 7-642
Montreal, Quebec, H3G 1M8 Canada
a_soeanu@ciise.concordia.ca

Luay Alawneh
Department of Electrical and
    Computer Engineering
Faculty of Engineering and Computer Science
Concordia University
1455, Boulevard de Maisonneuve West,
EV 13-173
Montreal, Quebec, H3G 1M8 Canada
l_alawne@encs.concordia.ca

ISBN 978-3-642-42316-1   ISBN 978-3-642-15228-3 (eBook)
DOI 10.1007/978-3-642-15228-3
Springer Heidelberg Dordrecht London New York

ACM Codes: D.2, C.4, K.6

Cover design: KuenkelLopka GmbH, Heidelberg

Printed on acid-free paper

Springer is part of Springer Science+Business Media (www.springer.com)

To our families and friends!

Preface

At the dawn of the 21st century and the information age, communication and computing power are becoming ever increasingly available, virtually pervading almost every aspect of modern socio-economical interactions. Consequently, the potential for realizing a significantly greater number of technology-mediated activities has emerged. Indeed, many of our modern activity fields are heavily dependant upon various underlying systems and software-intensive platforms. Such technologies are commonly used in everyday activities such as commuting, traffic control and management, mobile computing, navigation, mobile communication. Thus, the correct function of the forenamed computing systems becomes a major concern. This is all the more important since, in spite of the numerous updates, patches and firmware revisions being constantly issued, newly discovered logical bugs in a wide range of modern software platforms (e.g., operating systems) and software-intensive systems (e.g., embedded systems) are just as frequently being reported.

In addition, many of today's products and services are presently being deployed in a highly competitive environment wherein a product or service is succeeding in most of the cases thanks to its quality to price ratio for a given set of features. Accordingly, a number of critical aspects have to be considered, such as the ability to pack as many features as needed in a given product or service while concurrently maintaining high quality, reasonable price, and short time -to- market. Consequently, modeling is becoming a key activity in product development since it enables a controlled design process that can allow for design reuse and easy feature integration in a predictable timeline. Also, the economical globalization and multinational cooperation trends are active drivers pushing for standardized modeling and engineering practices. Standardization could potentially facilitate the deployment and adoption of cost-effective verification and validation methodologies that could, in turn, be harmonized with current business goals.

The overall objective in modern product development for maximizing immediate economical gains can cause conflicts between business goals and engineering practices. Consequently, many aspects such as ergonomics, various environmental concerns, thorough verification and validation, or computational efficiency are frequently ignored. This is especially the case in those areas where the effects are not immediately apparent such as in software applications (e.g., operating systems, web browsers, office suites) or in software-intensive systems (e.g., computer and mobile networking, portable/wearable electronics, and pervasive computing).

Although we can observe an ever-increasing awareness regarding ergonomics and environmental issues, the same can hardly be said about the necessity for a thorough verification and validation methodology for modern software and software-intensive systems. Nowadays, most of the systems' verification and validation is usually performed through testing and simulation; these techniques although very convenient for certain categories of systems do not provide necessarily for a complete screening of the possible states of a system.

Thus, it becomes apparent that an appropriate science for conscience setting should always accompany, to some extent, any development initiative. Furthermore, in such a setting, it is not so difficult to acknowledge that the most precious resource that human society benefits from is not any physical or material datum but rather the human resources themselves. As such, one may argue that as human society becomes increasingly technology dependant, the importance of assuring robust, bug-free, and high-quality software and systems is also equally increasing.

Systems engineering has marked an impressive comeback in the wake of the new challenges that emerged in this modern era of complex systems design and development. As the main objective of systems engineers is to enable the realization of successful systems, verification and validation represent an important process that is used for the quality assessment of the engineered systems and their compliance with the requirements established at the origin of the system development. Furthermore, in order to cope with the growing complexity of modern software and systems, systems engineering practices have undergone a fundamental transition to a model-based approach. In these settings, systems engineering community and standardization bodies developed interest in using and/or developing some specific modeling language that supports the cooperative work and the exchange of information among systems engineering practitioners.

This volume investigates the available means that can be employed in order to provide a dedicated approach toward the automatic verification and validation of systems engineering design models expressed in standardized modeling languages. It also provides a bird's eye view of the most prominent modeling languages for software and systems engineering, namely the unified modeling language (UML) and the more recent systems modeling language (SysML). Moreover, it innovates with the elaboration of a number of quantitative and qualitative techniques that synergistically combine automatic verification techniques, program analysis, and software engineering quantitative methods, applicable to design models described in modern modeling languages such as UML and SysML. Here is the way, the rest of this book is organized: Chap. 1 presents an introduction to the verification and validation problem, systems engineering, various related standards, and modeling languages along with the model-driven architecture (MDA) concept. In Chap. 2, we discuss the paradigm of architecture frameworks adopted and extended by defense organizations but also employed in the commercial arena as enterprise architecture frameworks. Moreover, in Chap. 3, we provide an overview of the UML 2.0 modeling language in the historical context leading to its emergence. Then, we present in

Chap. 4 the more recent SysML modeling language, the chronological account of its adoption and the commonalities and specific differences between SysML and UML. Chapter 5 describes the verification, validation, and accreditation concepts. Therein, we review noteworthy assessment methodologies based on software engineering techniques, formal verification, and program analysis. Chapter 6 describes an effective and synergistic approach for the verification and validation of systems engineering design models expressed in standardized modeling languages such as UML and SysML. Moreover, Chap. 7 demonstrates the relevance and usefulness of software engineering metrics in assessing structural system aspects captured by UML class and package diagrams. Chapter 8 details the automatic verification and validation of UML behavioral diagrams. Computational models are derived from state machine, sequence, or activity diagrams and are matched against logical properties that capture verification and validation requirements. The corresponding model-checking verification methodology is also described. Chapter 9 discusses the mapping of SysML activity diagrams annotated with probabilities to Markov decision processes (MDP) that can be assessed by probabilistic model checking procedures. Furthermore, Chap. 10 details the performance analysis of SysML activity diagrams annotated with time constraints and probability artifacts using a discrete-time Markov chain model. Chapter 11 is dedicated to the semantic foundations of SysML activity diagrams. We define a probabilistic calculus that we call activity calculus (AC). The latter algebraically captures the formal semantics of the activity diagrams using the operational semantics framework. In Chap. 12, we establish the soundness of the translation of SysML activity diagrams into PRISM specifications. This ensures that the code generated by our algorithm correctly captures the behavior intended by the SysML activity diagram given as input. Finally, a discussion of the presented work together with some concluding remarks are sketched as conclusion in Chap. 13.

Acknowledgments

We would like to express our deepest gratitude to all the people who contributed to the realization of this work. Initially, our research on the verification and validation of systems engineering design models has been supported thanks to a research contract from the Defence Research & Development Canada, the R&D establishment for Canada's Department of National Defence, under the Collaborative Capability Definition, Engineering and Management (Cap-DEM) project. We also acknowledge support from the Natural Sciences and Engineering Research Council (Discovery Grant) of Canada and Concordia University (Research Chair Tier I). We would like also to express our gratitude to the members of the Computer Security Laboratory of Concordia University who helped in reviewing the preliminary versions of this book.

Contents

List of Figures

List of Tables

Acronyms

AP233	application protocol 233
ATM	automated teller machine
CASE	computer-aided software engineering
CBO	coupling between object classes
CCRC	class category relational cohesion
CPU	central processing unit
CR	class responsibility
CTL	computation tree logic
CTS	configuration transition system
DIT	depth of inheritance tree
DMS	distance from the main sequence
DMSO	Defense Modeling and Simulation Organization
DoD	Department of Defense
DoDAF	Department of Defense Architecture Framework
DTMC	discrete-time Markov chain
EFFBD	enhanced function flow block diagram
EIA	Electronic Industries Alliance
FSM	finite state machine
HDL	hardware description language
ICAM	integrated computer-aided manufacturing
IDEF	integrated definition language
IEEE	Institute of Electrical and Electronics Engineers
INCOSE	International Council on Systems Engineering
ISO	International Organization for Standardization
IT	information technology
LCA	least common ancestor
LTL	linear time logic
MDA	model-driven architecture
ML	modeling language
MOF	MetaObject Facility
M&S	modeling and simulation
NAVMSMO	Navy Modeling and Simulation Management Office

NMA	number of methods added
NMI	number of methods inherited
NMO	number of methods overridden
NOA	number of attributes
NOC	number of children
NOM	number of methods
OCL	object constraint language
OMG	Object Management Group
OMT	object modeling technique
PCTL	probabilistic computation tree logic
PDA	personal digital assistant
PMR	public methods ratio
PRISM	probabilistic symbolic model checker
QA	quality assurance
R&D	research and development
RPG	Recommended Practices Guide
SIX	Specialization Index
SOS	structural operational semantics
SoS	systems on top of systems
SMV	symbolic model verifier
SPT	schedulability performance and time
STEP	standard for the exchange of product model data
SysML	system modeling language
TCTL	timed computation tree logic
TeD	telecommunications description language
TOGAF	The Open Group Architecture Framework
UML	unified modeling language
V&V	verification and validation
VV&A	verification, validation, and accreditation
WebML	Web modeling language
XML	extensible markup language

Chapter 1
Introduction

In this day and age, various forms of programming and computation are common-place in our immediate urban surroundings, often embedded in sensors, traffic and other driving-related assistance, public advertisements, hotspots, smart elevators, and many other micro-controller or CPU-based systems. Moreover, wearable electronics, like mobile phones, PDAs, and the likes, are more popular than ever. Thus, in modern engineering fields, especially those related to software-intensive systems, the solution space available to the designers and engineers is significantly increased due to the presence of the programmable aspect. In this context, mere intuition and ingenuity, though still playing a significant role, can hardly ensure strong, flaw-free, and cohesive designs, especially after reaching a high level of complexity. Moreover, the programmable aspect allows for a broader specialization range of a given design, inevitably inviting engineers to benefit from design reuse. Hence, various aspects such as understandability, extensibility, and modularity are becoming increasingly important in modern system design, along with general requirements such as those of cost and performance. Consequently, there is a clear trend toward the systematization and standardization of systems engineering design practices and methodologies.

Systems can depend on many components, including people, hardware, and/or software, all working together in order to accomplish a set of common specific objectives. The design and realization of successful systems, as well as the effective management of engineering projects, represent the prime concerns of systems engineering (SE) [229]. Notably, the critical aspect in system development consists in the difficulty to ensure specification compliant products. This is due to many factors including, among others, the increased complexity of the engineered systems, the effectiveness of the applied methods, as well as the presence of budgeting constraints.

Along with the increased system size and complexity, quality assurance methods also need to be extended accordingly. Given this context, the usual methodologies, based on testing and simulation, become tedious, lengthy, and, more importantly, hardly thorough. Additionally, real-life systems may exhibit stochastic behavior, where the notion of uncertainty is pervasive. Uncertainty can be viewed as a probabilistic behavior that models, for instance, risks of failure or randomness. Well-known examples include lossy communication channel systems [213] and dynamic

M. Debbabi et al., *Verification and Validation in Systems Engineering*,
DOI 10.1007/978-3-642-15228-3_1, © Springer-Verlag Berlin Heidelberg 2010

power management systems [16]. Consequently, taking into account this aspect leads to more accurate models. The integration of probabilistic aspects in V&V is relevant from many perspectives. For instance, many quality attributes such as performance, reliability, and availability are probabilistic in nature. Thus, performance can be expressed by means of expected probability. Also, reliability can be defined by the probability of successful system operation. Availability is given by the probability that a system operates satisfactorily when needed for a particular mission or application [75]. Finally, performing quantitative assessment of systems after successful integration is generally the industry norm. However, quantitative system assessment performed early in the development life cycle may reveal important information that qualitative assessment might miss.

As part of the SE, verification and validation (V&V) aims at providing a significant level of confidence in the reliability of a system. Thus, attention is focused on applying an effective and timely V&V task at a reasonable cost. Obviously, the anticipated evaluation and correction of potential errors during the early stages of development produces many benefits, such as that of a higher return on investment, since it allows for a decrease in maintenance time, effort, and cost.

That was confirmed by Bohem [25], stating that "fixing a defect after delivery can be one hundred times more expensive than fixing it during the requirement and the design phases." Therefore, early V&V reduces the risk involved in the engineering of complex systems. Furthermore, it improves the quality of systems and shortens their time to market.

V&V spans over the life cycle of the system. In this respect, most of the efforts are traditionally focused on testing, a technique that has been used extensively in software engineering. Testing involves exercising various test scenarios, developed by engineers on different testbeds ranging from simulators to actual hardware [171], and comparing the results with the anticipated or expected ones. However, this approach is usually prone to *"late in the game"* error discovery and some types of errors may remain virtually transparent. Consequently, this technique exhibits a specific limitation since it can only reveal the presence of faults but not guarantee their absence [70], as much as it is limited to the specified testing scenarios.

In the following, we present the core concepts involved in the SE discipline and an overview of the related standards and modeling languages.

1.1 Verification and Validation Problem Statement

Existing verification methodologies are rarely supported by formal foundations and proofs of soundness. Ideally, an efficient V&V approach needs to comply with the following guidelines:

- Enable automation as much as possible. This optimizes the V&V process and prevents potential errors that may be introduced by manual intervention.
- Encompass formal and rigorous reasoning in order to minimize errors caused by subjective human judgment.

- Support the graphical representation provided by modeling languages, for the sake of conserving the usability of the visual notation, and hide the intermediate transformations underlying the mechanisms involved.
- Combine quantitative as well as qualitative assessment techniques.

In the field of verification of systems and software, we pinpoint three well-established techniques recommended in order to build a comprehensive V&V framework. On the one hand, automatic formal verification techniques, namely model checking, is known to be a successful approach for verifying the behavior of software and hardware applications. Many model checkers can generate counterexamples for failed qualitative properties in support of debugging activities. Also, in the stochastic world, probabilistic model checkers are becoming widely applied to quantitatively analyze specifications that encompass probabilistic information about systems behavior [172]. On the other hand, static analysis, that is usually applied on software programs [32], is used prior to testing [21] and model checking [232]. For example, static slicing [232] yields smaller programs, which are less expensive to verify. Furthermore, empirical methods, specifically software engineering metrics, have proved to be successful in quantitatively measuring quality attributes of object-oriented design models. As the absence of measurement precludes any relevant comparison [66], metrics provide valuable means to evaluate the quality of proposed design solutions and can help in reviewing various design decisions.

1.2 Systems Engineering

Systems engineering (SE) is, as its name stands, the engineering discipline that is concerned with systems through their entire life cycle, which encompasses their conception, design, prototyping, implementation/realization, fielding, and disposal. Throughout these phases, SE is seen as a multidisciplinary approach, focused on the system as a whole. The most common definition used for a system is "a set of interrelated components working together toward some common objective" [138]. Although SE has been applied for a long time [229], it is sometimes referred to as an emerging discipline [62]. This can be understood in the sense that its importance has been recognized in the context of the increased complexity of today's problems. Systems have changed significantly in the last few decades, becoming increasingly large and complex, integrating various components such as software, electronics, and mechanics. This has triggered new challenges for the design and development of successful systems.

As many other engineering disciplines, SE is supported by a number of organizations and standardization bodies. One of the most active organizations is the International Council on Systems Engineering (INCOSE) [50]. Its primary mission is "to advance the state of the art and practice of systems engineering in industry, academia, and government by promoting interdisciplinary, scalable approaches to produce technologically appropriate solutions that meet societal needs" [120].

INCOSE [50] describes SE as an "interdisciplinary approach that enables the realization of successful systems" by using the "systems" approach in order to design complex systems such as systems of systems (SoS). Ubiquitous systems such as hi-tech portable electronics, mobile devices, ATMs, as well as many other advanced technologies such as aerospace, defence, or telecommunication platforms represent important application fields of systems engineering. The mission of SE is summarized in this statement by IEEE [113]: "to derive, evolve, and verify a life cycle balanced system solution that satisfies customer expectations and meets public acceptability." In other words, aside from deriving an effective system solution, SE's duty is to ensure that the engineered system meets its requirements and its development objectives and performs successfully its intended operations [138]. To this end, systems engineers attempt to anticipate and resolve potential problems as early as possible in the development cycle.

The design aspect in systems engineering focuses on finding feasible solutions to given problems in the context of a generic solution domain. This can involve many tasks relating to the subsystem decomposition, the targeted hardware platform, the data storage, and the like. As well as describing the proposed solution, the design model usually details the required or existing structural and behavioral aspects identified during a prerequisite analysis phase. It is often difficult to pinpoint the exact boundary between analysis and design. In general terms, the analysis phase is concerned with the description of the problem and the user requirements, whereas the design phase concentrates on the construction of a solution that satisfies the identified requirements.

Today, the critical aspect of system design is no longer found in conceptual difficulties or technical shortcomings but rather in the increasing difficulty to ensure appropriate and bug-free designs. Currently, systems engineering is clearly shifting away from traditional document-based one to model-based design and development, thus enabling and promoting the use of tool-assisted design. One important advantage of modeling is that it allows for various types of analysis. The analysis of a model is helpful in providing a deeper understanding of the attributes and/or operations described by the model in the context of the required or existing structure and behavior of the envisioned product (e.g., system or application). Furthermore, the analysis of the model provides a base for assessment by analysts and experts in the application domain that can, in turn, provide relevant information to the stakeholders.

Modeling and simulation (M&S) is an approach widely used by systems engineers to gain insight into the system structure and behavior prior to effectively producing it. This allows for the management of failure risks to meet the system's mission and performance requirements [230]. Modeling is defined in [69] as "the application of a standard, rigorous, structured methodology to create and validate a physical, mathematical, or otherwise logical representation of a system, entity, phenomenon, or process." With respect to simulation, it is defined by Shannon [220] as "the process of designing a model of a real system and conducting experiments with this model for the purpose of understanding the behavior of the system and/or evaluating various strategies for the operation of the system." Generally, it is the subject matter experts that develop and validate the models, conduct the simulations, and analyze the results [230].

A model may be used to represent the system, its environment, and its interactions with other enabling and interfacing systems. M&S is an important tool for decision making, giving the engineer the means of predicting a system's characteristics such as performance, reliability, and operations. The predictions are used to guide decisions regarding the system design, construction, and operation and also to verify its acceptability [230]. That said, simulation is experiencing ever-increasing difficulties in keeping up with the rapidly growing complexity of modern system design. Indeed, the number of simulation cycles required in the verification process is continuously rising and simulation-based methodologies require time-consuming test input creation.

In order to cope with the advancements in model-driven SE and fulfill related requirements to correctly represent systems, standardized modeling languages and graphical representations have emerged (e.g., UML 2.x [185, 186], SysML 1.0 [187]).

1.3 Systems Engineering Standards

Many software and systems engineering modeling languages have emerged in response to the continuous advancements in the field. These languages, created for an abstract, high-level description of a design and the components thereof, allow the designers to successfully cope with increasing complexities. Systems engineers have been using different documentation approaches to capture systems requirements and also various modeling techniques to express the complete design. Unfortunately, this diversity of techniques and approaches limited both cooperative work and information exchange. In order to ensure worldwide SE technologies compatibility and interoperability, international standards are needed. Hence, various international standardization bodies are involved in SE, providing standard frameworks and modeling languages for SE. The Object Management Group (OMG)[1], the INternational Council On Systems Engineering (INCOSE)[2], and the International Standard Organisation (ISO)[3] are the main pertinent standardizing organizations.

OMG [183] is an international computer industry consortium founded in 1989 whose role is to develop and maintain computer industry specifications. The OMG task force develops enterprise integration standards for a wide range of technologies including real-time, embedded and specialized systems, analysis and design. Among their standards, of note is the unified modeling language (UML) and the model-driven architecture (MDA) [178] that provide capabilities such as powerful visual design, execution, maintenance of software and other processes. Moreover, OMG

---

[1] http://www.omg.org

[2] http://www.incose.org

[3] http://www.iso.org

has developed UML profiles, which are specializations of UML designed to support specific domains based on built-in extension mechanisms. It has also established a number of widely used standards such as Meta-Object Facility (MOF) [175] and XML Metadata Interchange (XMI) [176], to name just a few.

INCOSE [120] is an international organization formed in 1992 whose mission is to "foster the definition, understanding, and practices of world-class SE in industry, academia, and government" [148]. A collaborative effort between INCOSE and OMG has resulted in a modeling language dedicated to SE, namely SysML. In September 2007, the first specification document for SysML [187] was issued by the OMG.

Finally, ISO [116] is the world's largest developer of standards used by industrial and business organizations of all types, from governments and other regulatory bodies down to end users. One of the standards issued by ISO related to product data representation and exchange is ISO 10303 [122], known as the STandard for the Exchange of Product model data (STEP) [121]. It has been constructed as a multipart standard, one of the most relevant parts of it being the AP233 (Application Protocol 233 also known as ISO 10303-233) entitled *Systems engineering data representation*. It is designed as a neutral information model for the exchange of data between SE and related tools in order to ensure interoperability [244].

1.4 Model-Driven Architecture

Model-driven architecture (MDA) is an OMG architectural framework and standard whose goal is to "lead the industry towards interoperable, reusable, portable software components and data models based on standard models" [178]. MDA stemmed from the concept of separating the specification of the operation of a given system from the details related to the way the system uses the underlying capabilities of its platform [178]. In essence, MDA's approach is to use models in software development, which includes both the specifications and the actual development of applications, independently of the platform supporting them. This enables the application to be easily ported from one environment to another by first creating one or more platform-independent models (PIM) and subsequently translating the PIM into one or more platform-specific models (PSM). Thus, the three primary goals of MDA are portability, interoperability, and reusability, these being attained through architectural separation of concerns [178]. The MDA paradigm is being developed in order for it to be successfully applied to virtually all software development projects, including such major fields as electronic commerce, financial services, health care, aerospace, and transportation. It uses metamodeling, which encompasses the analysis, construction, and development of the frames, rules, constraints, models, and theories applicable for modeling in a predefined class of problems.

As shown in Fig. 1.1, MDA is based on the four-layer metamodeling architecture [180], as well as several complementary standards of the OMG. These standards are the meta-object facility (MOF) [175], unified modeling language (UML), and XML metadata interchange (XMI). Specifically, the layers comprise (1) meta-metamodel layer, (2) metamodel layer, (3) model layer, and (4) instance layer. The

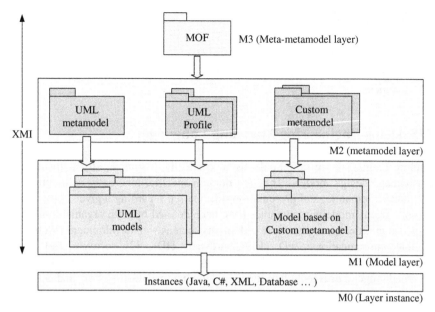

Fig. 1.1 MDA layers (source [71])

main objective of having four layers within a common meta-metamodel architecture is to support and enable the extensibility and integration of multiple metamodels and models.

In the context of SE, model-based systems engineering (MBSE) is defined by INCOSE as "the formalized application of modeling to support system requirements, design, analysis, verification and validation." It starts during the conceptual design phase and continues throughout the development and later life cycle phases [117]. MBSE for systems engineering is what MDA is for software engineering. Both paradigms target the use of a model-based approach to development, where the functionality and the behavior of the developed system are separated from the implementation details. In MBSE, the principal artifact is a coherent model of the system being developed. It is intended to support activities of systems engineering that have traditionally been performed with a document-based approach. The goal of MBSE is to enhance communications, specification and design precision, system design integration, and reuse of system artifacts [85]. Among the benefits of MBSE, the most relevant ones are the following [86]:

- Vendor/contractor-independent understanding of system requirements
- Requirements validation
- Common basis for analysis and design
- Enhanced risk identification
- Separation of concerns by using multiple views
- Traceability through hierarchical system models
- Support for impact analysis of requirements and design changes
- Support for incremental development

- Improved design quality
- Support for early V&V
- Enhanced knowledge capture

Prominent visual modeling languages such as UML and SysML support MBSE methodologies.

1.5 Systems Engineering Modeling Languages

Modeling languages are commonly used to specify, visualize, store, document, and exchange design models. They are domain-specific, inherently containing all the syntactic, semantic, and presentation information regarding a given application domain. Various modeling languages have been defined by both organizations and companies in order to target different domains such as web development (WebML) [41], telecommunications (TeD) [169], hardware (HDL) [2], software, and, most recently, systems (UML) [184]. Other languages such as IDEF [154] were designed for a broad range of uses including functional modeling, data modeling, and network design.

Although SE has been in existence for more than five decades, up until recently, there has been no dedicated modeling language for this discipline [255]. Traditionally, systems engineers have relied heavily on documentation to express systems requirements and, in the absence of a specific standard language [177], have had to use various modeling languages in order to express a complete design solution. This diversity of techniques and approaches has limited cooperative work and information exchange. Among existing modeling languages that have been used by systems engineers, one can cite HDL, IDEF, and EFFBD [106, 107, 147]. In order to provide a remedy, OMG and INCOSE, along with a number of experts from the SE field, have been collaborating toward building a standard modeling language for SE. UML, being the modeling language *par excellence* for software engineering, was the language of choice destined for customization with regard to systems engineers needs. However, UML 1.x was found to be inadequate for such a use [73, 256] and so the evolving revision of UML (i.e., UML 2.0) was issued, with features of special interest to systems engineers. In April 2006, a proposal for a standard modeling language for systems modeling, namely SysML, was submitted to the OMG, with the goal of achieving a final standardization process.

In the subsequent sections, we provide a brief description of the core concepts behind the UML 2.x [188], SysML 1.0 [187], and IDEF [154] modeling languages. The UML 2.x [188] and SysML 1.0 [187] concepts are detailed in Chaps. 3 and 4, respectively.

1.5.1 UML 2.x: Unified Modeling Language

The unified modeling language (UML) [198, 207] is a general-purpose visual modeling language whose maintenance has been assumed by OMG since 1997. It is a result of the merging of three major notations: Grady Booch's methodology for describing a set of objects and their relationships, James Rumbaugh's object-modeling technique (OMT), and Ivar Jacobson's use case methodology.

Although UML was originally designed for specifying, visualizing, and documenting software systems, it can also be applied to various other areas such as company organization and business processes. UML has many advantages; it is widely accepted by numerous industry leaders, is non-proprietary and extensible, and is also commercially supported by many tools and textbooks. The UML standard has been revised many times and many versions have been issued. In August 2003, a major revision was issued (UML 2.0 [181]) to correct the shortcomings discovered in UML 1.x [35, 184]. The recently released UML 2.1 [186] consists of specific updates, the same number of diagrams having been preserved.

The OMG issues a set of four specifications [200] for UML features: the diagram interchange specification, the UML infrastructure, the UML superstructure, and the object constraint language (OCL). The diagram interchange specification provides a way to share UML models between different modeling tools. The UML infrastructure defines low-level concepts in UML and represents a metamodel. The UML superstructure addresses the definition of UML elements. The superstructure document contains the description of the UML syntax, including the diagrams' specifications. It defines 13 diagrams that can be classified into two main categories: structural diagrams and behavioral diagrams. In Chap. 3 dedicated to the detailed presentation of UML, we further elaborate the UML diagrams and describe their features and characteristics. Finally, the OCL specification defines a language for writing constraints and expressions in UML models.

1.5.2 SysML: Systems Modeling Language

The SysML initiative can be traced back to a decision made at the *Model Driven Systems Design* workgroup meeting with INCOSE, held in January 2001, to pursue an extension of UML for systems engineering. This language is intended to provide core capability for modeling a broad spectrum of domains that may include software-intensive, information-intensive, hardware-intensive, people-intensive, or natural systems. The system modeling language (SysML) [187] is the SE-specific language developed in response to the request for proposals (RFP) UML for SE [177], issued by the OMG in 2003. The goal of designing SysML is to satisfy basic requirements of the SE community. SysML is a joint effort between INCOSE and OMG. Numerous industries are involved in the development process of SysML including BAE Systems, Boeing, Deere & Company, EADS Astrium, and Motorola. Some government institutions, such as NASA/Jet Propulsion Laboratory, National Institute of Standards and Technology (NIST), and DoD/Office of the Secretary of Defense (OSD), are also involved. In addition, tool vendors such as ARTISAN Ware Tools, IBM, I-Logix, Telelogic, and Vitech are present in this project. In addition to new diagrams, SysML [187] introduces the concept of allocation. The latter is defined by the standard as "...the term used by systems engineers to describe a design decision that assigns responsibility...or implementing a behavior to structural elements of the system." [187]. Allocations are used especially in the early stages of a systems design in order to show, in an abstract or even tentative way, the mapping of elements within the structures or hierarchies of a design model. Allocations can be used for assessing user model consistency or for directing future design activity. Moreover, the allocation establishes cross-associations that can be used for navigating the model and facilitate the integration of component parts of the model. In Chap. 4 dedicated to the detailed presentation of SysML, we further elaborate on the corresponding diagrams and describe their characteristics and features.

1.5.3 IDEF: Integration Definition Methods

IDEF [154, 242] is a compound acronym for ICAM DEFinition, where ICAM stands for Integrated Computer-Aided Manufacturing. IDEF, also known as integration definition methods, provides techniques and standard languages of communication for the engineering discipline. The family of ICAM definition languages was initiated during the 1970s and finalized in the 1980s. Its development was prompted by the numerous, but mostly incompatible, methods for storing computer data available at that time.

These "definition languages" were intended to be used as standard modeling techniques and to cover a broad spectrum of uses ranging from function modeling and simulation to object-oriented analysis and design and even knowledge acquisition.

The first generation of IDEF methods (IDEF0 Function Modeling Method, the IDEF1 Information Modeling Method and the IDEF2 Simulation Modeling

Table 1.1 IDEF methodologies

IDEF methodology	Description
IDEF0	Function modeling
IDEF1	Information modeling
IDEF1X	Data modeling
IDEF2	Simulation model design
IDEF3	Process description
IDEF4	Object-oriented design
IDEF5	Ontology description
IDEF6	Design rationale
IDEF7	Information system auditing
IDEF8	User interface modeling
IDEF9	Business constraint discovery
IDEF10	Implementation architecture
IDEF11	Information artifact
IDEF12	Organizational design
IDEF13	Three schema mapping design
IDEF14	Network/distribution design

Method) emerged from the U.S. Air Force's Integrated Computer-Aided Manufacturing (ICAM) program in the late 1970s [153]. IDEF methods were designed for tasks such as information requirements definition, process knowledge capture, and object-oriented systems design. Each IDEF method addresses a unique aspect or perspective of engineering.

IDEF can be used in many fields for performing need analysis, requirements definition, functional analysis, systems design, as well as documentation for business processes. It consists of a set of 16 methods from IDEF0 to IDEF14, including IDEF1X. Table 1.1 lists the different methods along with the perspective they provide. IDEF0 and IDEF1X (the successor to IDEF1) are the methods most extensively used in various government and industry settings. The most significant benefit in using the IDEF1 data modeling technique is its ability to represent data structures independently from how they are to be stored. In contrast, IDEF2 is no longer used to any significant extent [114].

1.6 Outline

The remainder of this book is organized as follows:

- In Chap. 2, we discuss the paradigm of architecture frameworks. Though initially stemming from research conducted by industry leaders such as IBM, the concept was adopted and extended by defense organizations, mainly the US Department of Defense. The latter tailored the paradigm based on the specific needs of defense systems' procurement and capability engineering, providing guidelines for its major contractors toward interoperability achievement and a common methodology usage. The concept of architecture framework is also present in the commercial arena, where it is known as enterprise architecture framework. The latter is generally used by large businesses and corporations that undertake long-term projects involving many design and development teams who are often spread over a large geographic area. This maintains a commonality of views and promotes a homogeneous understanding of the design concepts, thus enabling effective information sharing and communication. As a result, the emergence of standardized systems engineering modeling languages like SysML demands that they employ their features in the context of architecture frameworks. In this respect, we will also detail the corresponding features of interest.
- In Chap. 3, we provide an overview of the UML 2.0 modeling language, describing the historical context that led to its emergence, followed by a presentation of its corresponding structural and behavioral diagrams. Moreover, the UML profiling mechanism is also introduced.
- In Chap. 4, we present the newly adopted SysML modeling language along with a chronological account of its adoption process. The commonalities as well as the specific differences between SysML and UML are then discussed followed by a description of the features of SysML's structural and behavioral diagrams. We also detail the informal syntax and semantics of the most relevant UML 2.0

behavioral models, namely, the state machine, sequence, and activity diagrams, focusing on the control flow aspect.

- Chapter 5 describes the verification, validation, and accreditation concepts, including a review of the most relevant V&V methodologies along with specific verification techniques for object-oriented designs such as software engineering techniques, formal verification, and program analysis. A number of useful techniques and relevant research initiatives are also presented, such as the state of the art in verification and validation research targeting UML and SysML design models. Finally, we examine various tools for specific areas of the V&V process, including formal verification environments and static program analyzers.

- Chapter 6 proposes an effective and synergistic approach for performing V&V on systems engineering design models expressed in standardized modeling languages, mainly UML and SysML. Moreover, we submit a number of established results that make the case for the proposed synergistic verification and validation methodology, which can be applied on systems engineering design models in a highly automated manner.

- Chapter 7 demonstrates the usefulness of software engineering metrics in the assessment of structural aspects of a system captured by UML class and package diagrams. To that effect, a set of 15 metrics is discussed within a relevant example.

- Chapter 8 presents the proposed verification methodology for the considered behavioral diagrams. In this context, we detail the computable model concept of the configuration transition system (CTS) and show how this model can be used as a semantic interpretation of design models expressed as state machine, sequence, or activity diagrams. We also describe the corresponding model-checking verification methodology by using an appropriate model checker, namely, NuSMV, that can be used for the assessment of the proposed semantic model. We also show how model checking can have a great potential for verifying systems engineering design models expressed in the considered behavioral diagrams. In this respect, the temporal logic used by NuSMV, namely CTL, is introduced along with an illustrative description of its temporal operators and their corresponding expressiveness as well as a helpful CTL macro notation. Then, a number of relevant case studies exemplifying the assessment of the state machine, sequence, and activity diagrams are presented and discussed in the context of the proposed methodology.

- Chapter 9 presents the probabilistic verification of SysML activity diagrams. Therein, we explain the translation algorithm that maps these types of diagrams into an asynchronous probabilistic model, namely MDP, which is based on the input language of the probabilistic model checker PRISM. Next, we present a case study that demonstrates the proof of concept of the V&V approach for the performance analysis of asynchronous SysML activity diagram models.

- Chapter 10 details a transformation procedure of SysML activity diagram annotated with time constraints and probability artifacts to a network of discrete-time Markov chains. These can be analyzed by the PRISM probabilistic model checker in order to assess various performance aspects such as time-bounded reachability.

- Chapter 11 describes our probabilistic calculus, namely activity calculus (AC). It is a dedicated heretofore unattempted calculus that captures the essence of SysML activity diagrams. First, we present AC language syntactic definition and summarize the mapping of activity diagram's graphical notation into AC terms. Afterward, we elaborate the definition of its corresponding operational semantics. Finally, we illustrate the usefulness of such a formal semantics on a SysML activity diagram case study.
- Chapter 12 examines essentially the soundness of the translation procedure described in Chap. 9. To this end, we first explain the methodology that we applied. Then, we present a formal description of the translation algorithm using a functional core language. After that, we propose an operational semantics for the specification language of the probabilistic model checker PRISM. Finally, we present a simulation pre-order upon Markov decision processes that we use for formulating and proving the correctness of the translation algorithm.
- Chapter 13 is dedicated to closing remarks and final conclusions.

Chapter 2
Architecture Frameworks, Model-Driven Architecture, and Simulation

With the introduction and rapid success of the personal computer (PC) in the late 1970s, numerous computer applications were marketed to support the users in various domains. In the SE domain particularly, along with these software applications, several languages both formal and informal like VHDL [246], Petri Net family [4], IDEF [154, 242], UML [184], and SysML [255] were created to support developers in capturing essential aspects of the systems being engineered. The system properties usually reflect structural, temporal, or functional aspects and could be related to various areas such as processes, information infrastructures, internal systems/components, interoperability with other systems, and user interactions.

Along with the advent of design languages, the complexity of systems' design also increased. This was reflected in both the internal structure and the system's behavior as well as in the interaction with other, often very large, systems. In this context, significant difficulties arose and impeded the development and life cycle of large systems aggregations. Consequently, large organizations specifically needed a systematic approach for the description of a system where all the information related to the requirements, design, architecture, development, fielding, and disposal of the system were captured. This had to be performed for all the systems at the enterprise level in a consistent and comprehensive manner. In return, the organizations would benefit from such efforts since the results consist in well-documented and structured common views of all the structures and systems the enterprise is dealing with. Additionally, this would guarantee that all contracting parties would have a common layout for the description of the delivered systems. This approach is often described as an enterprise architecture framework (or architecture framework).

In this chapter, Sect. 2.1 presents the concept of architecture frameworks as well as the most relevant initiatives in this field. Section 2.2 provides an overview of the standard for data exchange, namely AP233. Section 2.3 discusses executable architectures and their role in modeling and simulation. Finally, Sect. 2.4 relates DoDAF[243] to SE field and SysML.

M. Debbabi et al., *Verification and Validation in Systems Engineering*,
DOI 10.1007/978-3-642-15228-3_2, © Springer-Verlag Berlin Heidelberg 2010

2.1 Architecture Frameworks

The concept of architecture framework often supports and is applied within a paradigm called enterprise architecture. Initially developed in the information technology (IT) domain, the enterprise architecture concept has evolved since to encompass a much broader scope. Nowadays, it is employed within multiple industries including automotive and IT or governments such as defense and accountability domains. Although most of what enterprise architectures refers to is related only to enterprise business structures and processes, current definitions incorporate a much more general understanding as defined, for instance, by the General Accountability Office (GAO) of the US federal government [104]: "An enterprise architecture is a blueprint for organizational change defined in models that describe (in both business and technology terms) how the entity operates today and how it intends to operate in the future; it also includes a plan for transitioning to this future state."

Thus, the concept of enterprise architecture appears to be exhaustive enough to include both the enterprise structures and the operation blueprints for current and future business, with respect to business, technology, and human beings and, in addition, the transformational roadmaps, the related execution plans, and the processes and programs. Architecture frameworks are used within enterprise architectures to capture, by way of graphical artifacts, domain-specific views. Such views can be related to a specific system or platform and provide all the necessary architectural information to its stakeholders, i.e., users, developers, sponsors, etc.

In the following, we present a chronological overview of the most relevant initiatives in the architecture frameworks field. A comparative study of the most relevant architecture frameworks can be found in [42].

2.1.1 Zachman Framework

In 1987, J.A. Zachman published an article[1] in the *IBM Systems Journal* entitled "A framework for information systems architecture" [259]. Although the actual term "enterprise architecture framework" is not literally mentioned in this paper, it is commonly recognized that this work paved the ground for the development of the architecture framework paradigm.

Zachman identified, often with a resulting description of step-by-step processes, a deficiency in the information system modeling area where classic approaches were applied. He introduced a more diverse approach toward the description of the systems by borrowing commonly used architectural representations for design and development from other engineering disciplines such as architecture, construction, and manufacturing. He also clearly defined three potential users of these representations for a given system: namely, the owner, the designer, and the builder. In modern architecture frameworks, these representations are now called views and correspond

---

[1] This paper is one of the most highly cited papers ever published in the *IBM journals*.

Table 2.1 Three different description types for the same product (source [259])

	Description I	Description II	Description III
Orientation	Material	Function	Location
Focus	Structure	Transform	Flow
Description	WHAT the thing is made of	HOW the thing works	WHERE the flows (connections) exist
Example	Bill-of-materials	Functional specifications	Drawings
Descriptive model	Part–relationship–part	Input–process–output	Site–link–site

Table 2.2 Information systems analogs for the different types of descriptions (source [259])

	Description I (material)	Description II (function)	Description III (location)
Information systems analog	Data model	Process model	Network model
I/S descriptive model	Entity–relationship–entity	Input–process–output	Node–line–node

to the various perspectives that should be brought to the attention of each stakeholder of a system.

With the notion of building different perspectives (i.e., architectural representations) for each stakeholder, Zachman also identified the need to provide different representations to capture various aspects of a system. He proposed considering three parameters of an object: the material, the function, and the location. These are, respectively, mapped into a matrix in the "WHAT," "HOW," and "WHERE" columns (see Table 2.1). Later, he extended his matrix by adding the "WHO," "WHEN," and "WHY" descriptions (see Table 2.2). These elements provide for the people and organizations involved, respectively, the events that trigger business activities and the motivations and constraints that determine how the business behaves.

2.1.2 Open Group Architecture Framework

Various organizations in the information technology domain have realized the importance of an enterprise architecture framework. Consequently, a joint venture was pursued under the Open Group Architecture Forum [194], with the objective of developing an open industry standard for information systems architecture. This is now called The Open Group Architecture Framework (TOGAF) [195]. The formal user requirements for the framework were gathered in 1994 and the first version of TOGAF, as a proof of concept, was revealed in 1995. The original underlying concept was to develop a comprehensive architecture framework that would fit specific domains' requirements. However, later on, TOGAF evolved as a methodology for modeling and analyzing the overall business architecture of organizations. The actual version of the framework is composed of three components:

- The architecture development method (ADM) captures the TOGAF methodology, which lies in the use of architecture views captured throughout the iterative execution of the nine following phases:

  1. Preliminary phase: Framework and principles. Stakeholders' agreement with the overall plan and principles
  2. Phase A: Architecture vision. Define scope, focus, and requirements
  3. Phase B: Business architecture. Determine current and future architectures using business process models and specific diagrams
  4. Phase C: Information system architectures. Develop target architectures (i.e., applications, data models)
  5. Phase D: Technology architecture. Create the overall target architecture that will be implemented in future phases (i.e., systems)
  6. Phase E: Opportunities and solutions. Develop the overall strategy toward the architecture described in step 5 (D) (i.e., implementation)
  7. Phase F: Migration planning
  8. Phase G: Implementation governance
  9. Phase H: Architecture change management. Review current system(s) and implement adjustments if necessary; iterate the process

- The enterprise continuum captures the output of the execution of the architecture development method steps. It is essentially a virtual repository at the enterprise level for architectural assets (data, models, patterns, architecture descriptions, and other artifacts). It may also contain assets from external organizations.
- The resource base is a collection of resources in the form of examples, techniques, templates, guidelines, and background information, whose main purpose is to support the architects through the architecture development method.[2]

2.1.3 DoD Architecture Framework

The US Department of Defense (DoD) Architecture Framework (DoDAF) [243] is the DoD Deputy Chief Information Officers (CIO) Enterprise Architecture & Standards Directorate endorsed architecture framework. In 2003, DoDAF 1.0 superseded the former US Command, Control, Communications, Computers, Intelligence, Surveillance and Reconnaissance (C4ISR) architecture framework that was created in 1996, in response to the passage of the Clinger-Cohen Act. The latter required the DoD CIOs to use established system architecture documentation-based techniques for any new business process implementation, as well as for migrating existing systems.

With multiple iterations, DoDAF [243] has evolved toward supporting the DoD transformation for network-centric warfare (NCW) also known as network-centric operations (NCO) [68]. The latter is a new combat paradigm that enables various

---

[2] The resulting output architectures are used to populate the enterprise continuum.

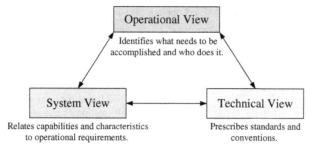

Fig. 2.1 DoDAF views and corresponding areas of concern (source [63])

geographically dispersed actors to engage in operations supported by the effective use of data exchanges through robust network links. Additionally, in order to fully achieve the compliance of the DoD systems with the NCO concept, the approach of service-oriented architecture (SOA) [68] has also been adopted. The SOA approach has influenced the development of DoDAF, by placing the data at the core of the architectures thanks to the core architecture data model (CADM). The latter, like several other architecture frameworks (TOGAF, MODAF, etc.), represents a shared repository for holding products that are compliant with a standardized taxonomy in the form of views that fall into four categories: operational view (OV), systems view (SV), technical standards view (TV), and all views (AV). Each of the operational, systems, and technical views correspond to a specific area of concern, as depicted in Fig. 2.1. Each view encompasses a set of architecture data elements depicted in graphical, tabular, or text-based products. The architectural aspects related to all the three (OV, SV, TV) views, without representing a distinct view of the architecture, are captured in the all views (AV) products.

An architecture view is different than an architecture product in that a view represents a perspective of a given architecture whereas a product is a specific representation of a particular aspect of that perspective. It should be noted that a common practice in DoDAF utilization is to generate only a subset of the full DoDAF views to specify or describe a system's architecture. Below we present a description of the views in DoDAF 1.5 [243].

2.1.3.1 Operational View (OV)

The operational view (OV) products are intended to provide the description of the performed tasks, activities, and the operational elements as well as the exchanged information (e.g., type, frequency, nature) required in order to accomplish established goals or missions. Table 2.3 presents a summary of the OVs that are described as follows:

- The OV-1 provides a high-level perspective that graphically depicts the overall concept of the architecture, usually describing a mission and highlighting the main operational nodes related to OV-2. Moreover, it provides a description of

Table 2.3 DoDAF 1.5 operational view (source [243])

Framework product	Framework product name	General description
OV-1	High Level Operational Concept Graphic	High-level graphical and textual description of operational concept
OV-2	Operational Node Connectivity Description	Operational nodes, activities within nodes, connectivity, and information exchange between nodes
OV-3	Operational Information Exchange Matrix	Information exchanged between nodes and the relevant attributes of that exchange
OV-4	Organizational Relationships Chart	Organizational, role, or other relationships among organizations
OV-5	Operational Activity Model	Operational activities, relationships among activities, inputs, and outputs; overlays can show cost, performing nodes, or other pertinent information
OV-6a	Operational Rules Model	One of three products used to describe operational activity; identifies business rules that constrain operation
OV-6b	Operational State Transition Description	One of three products used to describe operational activity; identifies business process responses to events
OV-6c	Operational Event-Trace Description	One of three products used to describe operational activity; traces actions in a scenario or sequence of events
OV-7	Logical Data Model	Documentation of the system data requirements and structural business process rules of the operational view

the interactions between the subject architecture and its environment as well as between the architecture and external systems.

- The OV-2 depicts the operational node dependencies associated with the information flow. It describes the operational nodes, their connectivity, and the information exchange needlines between them and represents an important tool in translating concepts into capability gaps and linking organizations to activities. According to the DoDAF specification, "a needline represents an aggregation of information flows between two operational nodes, where the aggregated information exchanges are of a similar information type or share some characteristic."
- The OV-3 tracks and details the information exchanges and identifies "who exchanges what information, with whom, why the information is necessary, and how the information exchange must occur." The construction of this product requires significant knowledge capture effort. This can be effectively achieved by conducting selected interviews during model construction, followed by validation.
- The OV-4 illustrates organizational relationships and various command and control characteristics among human roles, organizations, or organization types that are the key players in a given architecture.

- The OV-5 is used to describe functional activities and tasks and can be used to relate tasks to capability areas and mission requirements and also to demarcate lines of responsibility. It covers the capabilities, operational activities, relationships among activities, inputs, and outputs. Moreover, annotations can be used to show the cost, the performing nodes, and other pertinent information.
- The OV-6 series covers the business rules that govern operational activities. For existing operational elements, the doctrine and standard operating procedures (SOPs) can provide the basis for constructing the OV-6. The OV-5 operational activities diagram provides the "sequencing" reference for developing OV-6s. In sum these three products are describing how the current state of a process or activity is changing over time in response to external and internal events and they are as follows:

  - The OV-6a specifies operational or business rules that represent constraints on an enterprise, a mission, operation, or a business and can be used to map scenario tasks to operational activities in order to indicate how operational activities are driven by scenario tasks. Also, it extends the capture of business requirements and concept of operations for the use cases of OV-5.
  - The OV-6b represents a graphic depiction of event-driven state transition and it is used for describing how an operational node or activity responds to various events by changing its state.
  - The OV-6c is one of three products used to describe operational activity. It traces actions in a scenario or sequence of events and includes a time-ordered examination of information exchanges.

- The OV-7 is relevant to modeling information systems that deal with storage, retrieval, and updates of persistent data. It describes the structure of the data types used in the architecture domain systems as well as structural business process rules that govern the system data, the latter being defined in the corresponding OV-6a product of the architecture. Moreover, it provides a definition of architecture domain data types along with their attributes or characteristics and their interrelationships.

2.1.3.2 Systems View (SV)

The systems view (SV) products provide descriptions of the system, services, and underpinning system/component interconnections that support the enterprise business, knowledge, and infrastructure. The SV functions are aimed at directly supporting the operational activities. Thus, there is a direct link between the artifacts of the SVs and those of the OVs. The SV views are summarized in Tables 2.4 and 2.5. A description of each SV product and its relation with the OV products is provided in the following:

- The SV-1 identifies system nodes and interfaces, relates these to the operational nodes reflected in the OV-1 and OV-2, and depicts the systems resident nodes

Table 2.4 DoDAF 1.5 systems and services – part 1 (source [243])

Framework product	Framework product name	General description
SV-1	Systems/Services Interface Description	Identification of systems nodes, systems, system items, services, and service items and their interconnections, within and between nodes
SV-2	Systems/Services Communications Description	Systems nodes, systems, system items, services, and service items and their related communications lay-downs
SV-3	Systems-Systems/Services-Systems/Services-Services Matrices	Relationships among systems and services in a given architecture; can be designed to show relationships of interest, e.g., system-type interfaces, planned vs. existing interfaces.
SV-4a	Systems Functionality Description	Functions performed by systems and the system data flows among system functions
SV-4b	Services Functionality Description	Functions performed by services and the service data flow among service functions
SV-5a	Operational Activity to Systems Function Traceability Matrix	Mapping of system functions back to operational activities
SV-5b	Operational Activity to Systems Traceability Matrix	Mapping of systems back to capabilities or operational activities
SV-5c	Operational Activity to Services Traceability Matrix	Mapping of services back to operational activities
SV-6	Systems Data Exchange/Services	Data exchange matrices provide details of system or service data elements being exchanged between systems or services and the attributes of that exchange
SV-7	Systems Performance Parameters/Services Performance Parameters Matrices	Performance characteristics of systems and services view elements for the appropriate time frame(s)
SV-8	Systems Evolution/Services Evolution Description	Planned incremental steps toward migrating a suite of systems or services to a more efficient suite or toward evolving a current system to a future implementation
SV-9	Systems Technology/Services Technology Forecast	Emerging technologies and software/hardware products that are expected to be available in a given set of time frames and that will affect future development of the architecture

that support organizations/human roles. It also identifies the interfaces between collaborating or interacting systems.

- The SV-2 depicts pertinent information about communications systems, communications links, and communications networks. SV-2 documents the kinds of communications media that support the systems and implements their interfaces

Table 2.5 DoDAF 1.5 systems and services – part 2 (source [243])

Framework product	Framework product name	General description
SV-10a	Systems/Services Rules Model	One of three products used to describe system and service functionality; identifies constraints that are imposed on systems/services functionality due to some aspect of systems design or implementation
SV-10b	Systems/Services State Transition Description	One of three products used to describe system and service functionality; identifies responses of a system/service to events
SV-10c	Systems/Services Event-Trace Description	One of three products used to describe system or service functionality; identifies system/service-specific refinements of critical sequences of events described in the operational view
SV-11	Physical Schema	Physical implementation of the logical data model entities, e.g., message formats, file structures, physical schema

as described in SV-1. Thus, SV-2 shows the communications details of SV-1 interfaces that automate aspects of the needlines represented in OV-2. Although SV-1 and SV-2 are strictly speaking two DoDAF products, there is a lot of cross-over and, such as, they are often represented as one diagram. These products identify systems, systems nodes, system items, and their interconnections.

- The SV-3 provides the architecture with a matrix representation detailing the interface characteristics described in SV-1. In this context, it depicts the logical interface properties.
- SV-4 describes the characteristics and the functions performed by systems and the system data flows among system functions. It can be used during the capability assessment to support analysis as system functions are mapped to operational activities. Usually, system characteristics can be captured by conducting interviews with subject matter experts (SMEs).
- SV-5 specifies the relationships between the set of operational activities applicable to an architecture and the set of system functions applicable to that architecture. The matrix can be produced from OV-5 and SV-4 diagram and element annotations.
- SV-6 provides the details of system data elements being exchanged between systems along with the attributes of that exchange.
- SV-7 represents the system-level performance by specifying the quantitative characteristics of systems and hardware or software items, their interfaces (system data carried by the interface as well as communications link details that implement the interface), and their functions. Performance parameters include

all technical performance characteristics of systems for which requirements can be developed and specification defined usually during an interaction with SMEs.

- SV-8 captures the evolution plans that describe how the system, or the architecture in which the system is developed, will evolve over a typically long-term predictable time interval.
- SV-9 defines the underlying current and expected supporting technologies. The expected supporting technologies include those categories that can be reasonably forecast given the current state of technology and expected advancements. The new technologies should be coupled to specific time periods which can be correlated against the time periods considered in the SV-8 milestones.
- The SV-10 product suite is used for describing the system functionality and identifying the constraints that are imposed on the systems, including the response of a system to events and system-specific refinements of critical sequences of events described in the operational view:

  - The SV-10a product describes the rules that govern the behavior of the architecture or its systems under specified conditions. At lower levels of granularity, it may consist of rules that specify the pre- and post-conditions of system functions.
  - The SV-10b is a graphical method of describing the state change of the system or the response of a system function to various events.
  - The SV-10c provides a time-ordered examination of the system data elements exchanged between participating systems (external and internal), system functions, or human roles in the context of a given scenario.

- The SV-11 is the closest one to actual system design in the context of the architecture framework. It defines the structure of the different kinds of persistent system data utilized by the systems in the architecture.

2.1.3.3 Technical Standards View (TV)

The purpose of TV is to ensure that the architecture is well "governed" by provisioning a comprehensive set of technical systems implementation guidelines in the form of technical standards, implementation conventions, standards options, and business rules. The TV views are summarized in Table 2.6 and defined as follows:

Table 2.6 DoDAF 1.5 technical standards (source [243])

Framework product	Framework product name	General description
TV-1	Technical Standards Profile	Listing of standards that apply to systems and services view elements in a given architecture
TV-2	Technical Standards Forecast	Description of emerging standards and potential impact on current systems and services view elements within a set of time frames

- The TV-1 product collects the systems standards rules that implement – and possibly constrain – the possible choices in the design and implementation of an architecture description.
- The TV-2 contains the expected changes in technology-related standards and conventions documented in TV-1. The evolutionary changes forecast for the standards must be correlated to the time intervals mentioned in the SV-8 and SV-9 products.

2.1.3.4 All Views (AV)

The AV products provide overarching aspects of the architecture that can be related to the OVs, SVs, and TVs, but not specific to any of them as such. These products also define the scope (subject area and time frame) and context of the architecture. The AVs are shown in Table 2.7 and they are defined as follows:

- AV-1 provides executive-level summary information in a consistent form and allows for quick reference and comparison of architectures. It is concerned with the assumptions, constraints, and limitations that might have an impact in the high-level decision processes involving the architecture.
- The AV-2 consists of definitions of terms that are used in the described architecture. It contains textual definitions presented as a glossary corresponding to a repository of architecture data along with the corresponding taxonomies and metadata information of the architecture data associated with the architecture products developed.

2.1.4 UK Ministry of Defence Architecture Framework

The UK Ministry of Defence (MOD) Architecture Framework (MODAF) [165] represents a variant of DoDAF adapted for the MOD. MODAF 1.2 primarily extends DoDAF with the addition of three viewpoints: strategic, acquisition, and the service-orientated aspect while adding the human dimension to the systems view.

2.1.5 UML Profile for DoDAF/MODAF

Although DoDAF does neither require nor advocate specific methodologies, notations, or semantic models, substantial efforts have been made in producing DoDAF

Table 2.7 DoDAF 1.5 all views (source [243])

Framework product	Framework product name	General description
AV-1	Overview and Summary Information	Scope, purpose, intended users, environment depicted, analytical findings
AV-2	Integrated Dictionary	Architecture data repository with definitions of all terms used in all products

product views using UML and/or IDEF notations. In order to standardize these
efforts, a relatively recent initiative called the UML profile for DoDAF/MODAF or
UPDM [191] was launched within the OMG [183]. This effort is now undertaken by
the UPDM Group [241], a new standardization consortium that includes industrial
and governmental partners (e.g., DOD, MOD). The UPDM group is continuing the
past efforts of OMG, while also ensuring that all new developments are aligned with
the North Atlantic Treaty Organization (NATO) Architecture Framework (NAF).
The latter is based on MODAF but has specific extensions for service-oriented
architecture (SOA).

The objectives of UPDM are as follows:

- Provide an industry standard representation that fully supports DoDAF and
  MODAF
- Build on UML, UML dialects such as SysML and other OMG standards
- Make use of the NAF architecture framework
- Ensure interoperability of architecture data among various tool vendors
- Facilitate reuse and maintainability of architecture data

2.2 AP233 Standard for Data Exchange

The relatively rapid proliferation of commercial off-the-shelf SE modeling applications and environments has gone ahead without an adequate development of accompanying standards. This led to a situation where very few development environments
achieved interoperability. The reason for this deficiency is twofold. First, there is a
lack of a common semantic of the derived architecture product data. Second, there is
a lack of a common data representation format. However, both aspects are required
for data exchange between different tools.

The AP233 [244] initiative was specifically initiated to address this deficiency
within the STEP's System Engineering Project[3]; STEP, also known as the ISO
10303, is an international standard for computer-interpretable representations and
exchange of product data. AP233 development is aligned with other initiatives in the
computer-aided design (CAD), structural and electrical engineering, analysis and
support domains and is achieved through collaboration with the OMG and INCOSE.

2.3 Executable Architectures or from Design to Simulation

For a long time, engineers have entertained the idea of executing their architectures
and have indeed achieved this objective in some cases. For instance, several modeling tools can execute their models (TAU [127], Simulink [59], etc.). Alternatively,
appropriate code generation techniques (Simulink RTW [205], TAU [127], etc.) may

---

[3] STEP is the STandard for the Exchange of Product.

be used to produce the corresponding source code in specific target programming languages (C, C++, Java, etc.). Thus, executable behavioral models are obtainable. Using these techniques, a control model designed in a tool such as Simulink would have its equivalent C program generated, built, and then directly embedded on the target hardware to be controlled.

In some areas, particularly in the case where control theory is applied to dynamic systems, this practice is very common. However, it has not reached all branches of SE with a similar success. While several aspects (views) of a given design within an architecture framework are static by nature (e.g., a vehicle CAD model), there are often dynamic aspects (e.g., behavioral engine models) that could be executed over time to produce an execution/simulation of some of the aspects of the architected system. Furthermore, data from the static design is often embedded or provided as input to the execution. For example, in order to accurately represent the target model, a vehicle chassis structure should be taken into account during a simulation of the vehicles motion.

2.3.1 Why Executable Architectures?

Engineers can draw several benefits from the paradigm that is now known as "executable architecture." First, an executable version of a model could be used for V&V purposes. By running the model, one can detect unwanted behaviors that the diagrammatic models would not otherwise reveal. Moreover, one can use an executable model to stress test the system or to explore "what if" situations. This is particularly compelling nowadays due to the ever-growing complexity of systems whose components are often designed individually and brought together subsequently. In this respect, a means to observe the dynamics of the "whole" provides a much more insightful capability than just a few individual static design views/diagrams.

Second, there are special circumstances encountered with other parallel developments in the SE field such as the AP233, the various architecture frameworks (DoDAF, MODAF, etc.), UML 2.x [181], and SysML [187] and with the wide acceptance of the extensible markup language (XML) [257]. The latter enables the use of metalanguages containing rules for constructing specialized markup languages beyond the IT-related Web applications domain, and specifically aimed at the SE field. This is particularly reflected by the model-driven architecture (MDA) paradigm [178]. All these developments have the potential to further empower the concept of executable architectures by providing the foundations on which commercial tool vendors can build and articulate their applications as "executable architectures" capable.

Third, frequent user intervention in the development of the system from the architecture blueprints induces higher risk of errors. This is mostly caused by the developer's own interpretation in translating the architecture models,[4] along with

---

[4] Often times, the design and architecture team is different than the developers team.

the addition of implementation details that were not provided in the architecture. Therefore, automating or merely semi-automating the process of systems development/production can alleviate such risks by putting human intervention out of the loop or at least minimizing it. Also, generating an executable version of the architectures (especially if it is coupled to a virtual simulation environment, nowadays commonly called synthetic environment) could provide the means by which communication and exchange would be stimulated among the various project stakeholders, for technical and non-technical purposes (e.g., early concept presentation, visualization).

Finally, if the architecture models are to be used directly to generate the systems, more focus is required during the design and architecture phases. In return, the benefit of minimizing the risks of design flaws during the development of real systems – which undoubtedly involves more engineers and developer teams as well as additional financial expenditure – is significant in this context, since the more V&V is performed during the design and architecture phases, the less it is to be performed after the system generation. This confirms again Bohem's findings [25].

2.3.2 Modeling and Simulation as an Enabler for Executable Architectures

Due to the diversity and multiplicity of the views related to a system's architecture, it is highly unlikely that the aggregation of all the views into a single executable application will meaningfully represent the whole architecture. Nonetheless, it is most probable that the whole architecture can be mapped to several applications that may be networked into a single execution environment or federation. In the modeling and simulation domain, the federation concept is often defined as: "A set of interacting simulations (also called federates) participating to a common objective, and interoperating through a predefined communication protocol."

The federation concept is frequently adopted in ad hoc constructs. However, only with the distributed interactive simulation (DIS) [118] protocol and the high level architecture (HLA) [119] was this concept fully formalized and technically articulated, in terms of the federation constituents, data exchanged,[5] publish and subscribe mechanisms, run-time infrastructure, and various services (e.g., time management, objects managements). We will focus in the following on the high-level architecture and explain how it can support the concept of executable architecture.

2.3.2.1 High-Level Architecture

The United States Department of Defense (DoD) high-level architecture (HLA) [60] for modeling and simulation (M&S) was developed under the supervision of the Defense Modeling and Simulation Office (DMSO). The main objectives of the HLA

---

[5] Object models, derived from an object-oriented description approach.

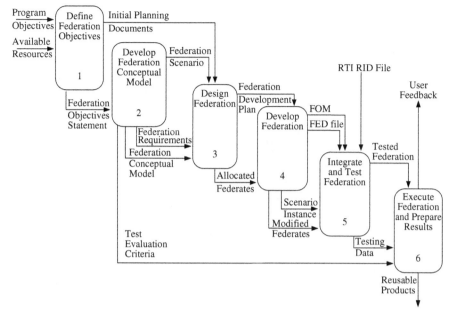

Fig. 2.2 DMSO HLA FEDEP (source [237])

were to increase interoperability among simulations and to promote reuse of simulations and their components. After going through several development iterations, the HLA was defined by a series of documents that specified

- Basic concepts and a set of rules that defined general principles to be met
- The Federation Development and Execution Process (FEDEP), which is a six-step process for developing distributed simulations (see Fig. 2.2)
- The federate interface specification, which specifies the interface between federates and a run-time infrastructure (RTI), the latter being the software that manages data distribution between federates and provides various services to them, such as simulation time management
- The HLA object model template (OMT) specification, which defines the format for specifying a federation object model (FOM), and the federate (simulation – related) object model (SOM). A FOM specifies the set of objects, attributes, and interactions that are created and shared during a federation execution. A SOM describes the federate in terms of the types of objects, attributes, and interactions it will provide to future federations. It is not intended to be an internal description of the federate (simulation), but rather a description of its capability in the form of an interface.

Receiving broader recognition in 2000, the Institute of Electrical and Electronics Engineers extended HLA, leading to the adoption of the following IEEE standards:

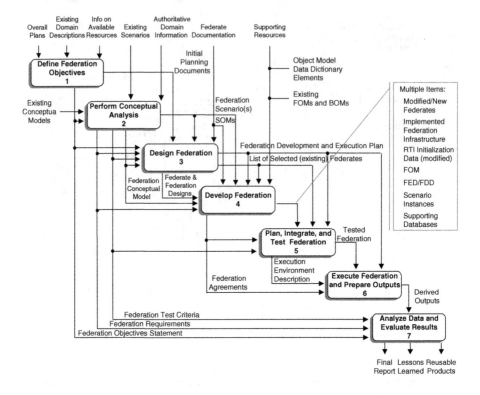

Fig. 2.3 IEEE 1516.3 seven-step HLA FEDEP (source [237])

- IEEE 1516-2000: IEEE Standard for Modeling and Simulation (M&S) high-level architecture (HLA) – Framework and Rules
- IEEE 1516.1-2000: IEEE Standard for Modeling and Simulation (M&S) high-level architecture (HLA) – Federate Interface Specification
- IEEE 1516.2-2000: IEEE Standard for Modeling and Simulation (M&S) high-level architecture (HLA) – object model template (OMT) specification
- IEEE 1516.3-2003: IEEE Recommended Practice for high-level architecture (HLA) Federation Development and Execution Process (FEDEP) (see Fig. 2.3)

Thanks to the various rules and services along with the federation and federates object descriptions and an RTI, one may envision a federation as a set of applications (i.e., federate) running concurrently, providing own object updates and consuming other federation objects (owned by other simulations/federates). All the interactions are happening exclusively between the applications and the RTI; no communication is allowed between the federates. Also, no constraint is imposed on the nature of a federate, thus it can be a pure mathematical simulation, a simulator (e.g., a flight simulator), or a real system (e.g., aircraft) interacting with the other virtual or real assets in the federation. This is depicted in Fig. 2.4.

Fig. 2.4 Conceptual view of
an HLA federation

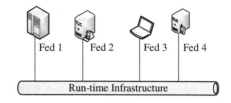

2.3.2.2 Achieving Executable Architectures Through HLA

In order to realize an executable architecture, the following prerequisites should be
met by the architecture products (DoDAF, MODAF, etc.):

1. The architecture products to be executed should be described with an unambiguous and consistent (formal) representation (language)
2. There should be a mechanism to translate these architecture products into time-dependant executable software packages, usually through automatic code generation techniques or dedicated execution environments (TAU, Simulink, etc.)
3. The resulting software should be wrapped as HLA federates
4. Selection or development of specific federation FOM and federates SOM
5. Specification and development of a simulation scenario
6. Specification of starting states for all applications with initial states, inputs, parameters, etc.

2.4 DoDAF in Relation to SE and SysML

The DoDAF views and products are useful when classifying and presenting the
operational and system descriptions along with the relations between them. This
is depicted in Fig. 2.5. In the context of SE, SysML can be used as the modeling
notation, backed by the semantics of its metamodel. Moreover, AP233 can provide

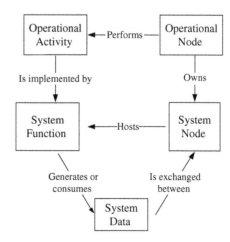

Fig. 2.5 DoDAF element
relations (source [63])

Table 2.8 The AV products mapping

Framework product	UML	AP233	SysML
AV-1	Diagram and element annotations	Most of the elements are covered by view definition context, project, person, and organization	Diagram and element annotations on applicable descriptions
AV-2	Diagram and element annotations	Reference data libraries to support standard terms and product or property types	Diagram and element annotations, and associated model repository

a neutral data exchange [192] format for the data presented within the architecture framework.

DoDAF suggests products based on the intended use of the architecture and specifies that a minimum set is required for the architecture to qualify as an "integrated architecture." It largely aims at enhancing the user friendliness while better explaining the applicability of the architectures. Moreover, given the increasing popularity of the unified modeling language (UML), various types of UML representations can be used for describing DoDAF architectural products. An "integrated architecture" is realized when the data are properly shared across the operational, systems and technical views. According to the DoDAF: "An architecture description is defined to be an integrated architecture when products and their constituent architecture data elements are developed such that architecture data elements defined in one view are the same (i.e., same names, definitions, and values) as architecture data elements referenced in another view." [261]. SysML provides the capabilities of UML and other models and representations that are required for DoDAF. In this context, the SysML and DoDAF specifications are supported by metamodels that define the meaning of the elements in the specification and provide relationships between these elements. Since the contents of the metamodels are required to be comparable with the AP233 specification, the metamodels represent key aspects in the development of the AP233 standard, which is independent of any systems modeling approach. Consequently, the AP233 format can be used as a bridge for model exchange between tools that use different notations.

Thus, it is possible to use AP233 as a neutral format in order to convert data from existing systems engineering tools into SysML models and use these in the context of DoDAF architecture products. For example, an IDEF0 activity diagram can be exported to AP233 and then imported into a UML-based tool as a SysML activity diagram. This allows collaborating partners to use their own preferred notations while still being able to exchange information and prepare their DoD architecture framework in one common notation such as SysML. Moreover, since DoDAF acknowledges the suitability of UML for many of its products as per the UPDM [191] initiative, the enhanced capabilities of SysML may help in reducing ambiguity while adding an enriched semantics and expressiveness to many DoDAF products. The mapping of DoDAF products into systems engineering field is presented in Tables 2.8 (AV products), 2.9 (OV products), 2.10 and 2.11 (SV products), and 2.12 (TV products) [63].

Table 2.9 The OV products mapping

Framework product	UML	AP233	SysML
OV-1	No complete equivalent but covered by use case diagrams	No complete equivalent, but covered by view definition context, project, person, and organization	Free form iconic class diagrams or utilizing use case diagrams describing the usage of the system (subject) by its actors (operational nodes)
OV-2	Interaction (collaboration) diagrams	Person and organization module; needlines represented by the organization relationship entity	Operational nodes represented as packages that group operational activities; needlines represented by item flows showing the information exchange along a needline
OV-3	Not available	Person and organization module. Needlines might be represented using the organization relationship entity	No complete equivalent; information exchange attributes may be described by decomposition and specification of the item flows identified in OV-2. These item flows may also correspond to object nodes in OV-5
OV-4	Class diagram	Person and organization module. The organization relationship entity might be used, classified by the appropriate reference data	Block definition diagram. Class relationships may be used to show the relations among organizations
OV-5	Use case and activity diagrams	Activity method and scheme module	Use case diagrams, activity diagrams, and activity hierarchies
OV-6a	Not available	Activity method, requirement assignment, requirement identification, and version	Requirements diagram and parametric diagram to specify constraints. Parametric diagrams can depict constraints among the properties of the operational use cases of OV-5
OV-6b	Statechart (state machine) diagrams	State definition, state observed, and state characterized	State machine diagrams
OV-6c	Sequence and activity diagrams	Activity, activity method, scheme, and person and organization modules	Sequence and activity diagrams
OV-7	Class diagram	Not available	Block definition diagram

Table 2.10 The SV products mapping – part 1

Framework product	UML	AP233	SysML
SV-1	Deployment and component diagrams	System breakdown and interface modules	Packages represent grouping of systems. Systems are represented by block definition diagrams; internal block (composite structure) diagrams are used to recursively decompose the system
SV-2	No exact equivalent but deployment diagrams can be used to some extent	System breakdown and interface modules. Generic interfaces can be used to represent connections in SV-1 and SV-2	Internal block diagrams and allocation relationships that maintain traceability between logical and physical connectors. Allocation relationships can be used for traceability between logical and physical connectors (i.e., between SV-1 logical connectors and SV-2 physical connectors)
SV-3	Not available	System breakdown and interface modules	No exact equivalent. Attributes can be specified for connectors while reference data (e.g., project status) can be added to item flows or connectors in SV-1
SV-4	Use case, class, and package diagrams	System breakdown, functional breakdown, and interface modules	Activity diagrams with object nodes to represent data flows
SV-5	Not available	Covered in part by activity method, method assignment, system breakdown, functional breakdown, and interface modules	No exact equivalent. The matrix can be produced from diagram and element annotations corresponding to the OV-5 and SV-4 products
SV-6	Not available	System breakdown interface modules. The matrix representation is out of the scope of AP233, which seeks to model just the underlying semantics of the system of systems	No exact equivalent. Systems data exchange can be represented as item flows over an interface described in SV-1. It may also correspond to object nodes in SV-4
SV-7	Not available	System breakdown and property assignment modules	Parametric diagrams that identify critical performance parameters and their relationships
SV-8	Not available	Scheme, system breakdown, product version, date time assignment	No exact equivalent. A timeline construct may be defined in SysML or UML 2.x to show use case capabilities over time
SV-9	Not available	Covered in part by system breakdown and date time assignment modules	No exact equivalent. One might use a tabular form or a timeline with the technology forecast showing a property (technology standards forecast) with respect to time

Table 2.11 The SV products mapping – part 2

Framework product	UML	AP233	SysML
SV-10a	Not available	Requirement identification, requirement assignment, system breakdown, and rules	Requirements diagram depicting constraints among the properties of the systems
SV-10b	Statechart (state machine) diagrams	State definition, state observed, state characterized	State machine diagrams
SV-10c	Sequence diagrams	State definition, state observed, state characterized, functional behavior	Activity and sequence diagrams
SV-11	Class diagram	Not available	Block definition diagram

Table 2.12 The TV products mapping

Framework product	UML	AP233	SysML
TV-1	Not available	Document identification, document assignment, system breakdown	Requirements diagram
TV-2	Not available	Document identification, document assignment, system breakdown, date time assignment	No exact equivalent. May be represented either in a tabular form or as a timeline showing property (technology forecast) versus time

2.5 Conclusion

The wide availability of increased computing power, faster network connectivity, and large data storage solutions facilitates the use of simulation in synthetic environments exhibiting a high level of realism while allowing the interaction of real and virtual systems. In this respect, systems engineering methodologies provide the separation of design from implementation, thus promoting design reuse and allowing the construction of synthetic environments and virtual systems based on systems engineering designs of real entities.

In this setting, the topics presented in this chapter have addressed the general paradigm encompassed by architecture frameworks and discussed the benefits of executable architectures and the related concepts of modeling and simulation. The DoD architecture framework (DoDAF) was emphasized along with its noteworthy modeling features and capabilities in relation to architectures, synthetic environments, and systems engineering modeling languages and methodologies. Furthermore, a mapping of DoDAF products to corresponding SysML/UML design diagrams was presented in the context of the AP233 neutral format.

Chapter 3
Unified Modeling Language

The unified modeling language (UML) [185, 186] is a standardized general-purpose modeling language that lets one to specify, visualize, build, and document the artifacts of software-intensive systems. The goal of such a language is to model software systems prior to construction and concurrently automates the production, improves the quality, reduces the inferred costs, and shortens time to market. The resulting models represent systems at different levels of detail prior to their actual implementation.

The UML notation, based on a set of diagrams, is very rich. Each diagram provides a view of the element being modeled in its specific context. Although models and diagrams might appear to be similar, they are actually two different concepts. A model uses UML (or some other notation) to describe a system at various levels of abstraction. It often contains one or more diagrams representing graphically a given aspect or a subset of the model's elements. Diagrams, on the other hand, describe visually quantifiable aspects such as relationships, behavior, structure, and functionality. For example, a class diagram describes the structure of the system, while a sequence diagram shows the interaction based on message sending between objects over time. Thus, UML diagrams can be classified into two separate categories: structural and behavioral. This chapter provides an overview of the UML modeling language to introduce the readers to its notation and meaning. Section 3.1 briefly presents the history of the definition of UML. Section 3.2 describes the syntax of each UML diagram and its meaning according to the OMG specifications [186]. Finally, Sect. 3.3 presents the UML profiling mechanisms.

3.1 UML History

In the early 1990s, several object-oriented modeling languages developed by the software engineering community proved to be unsatisfactory for the software community at large. Hence, the need for a united solution was crucial. In late 1994, Grady Booch [30] (Rational Software Corporation), seeking to create a rich modeling language, introduced the idea behind UML. In the fall of 1995, a merging of Booch's methodology for describing objects and their relationships and

M. Debbabi et al., *Verification and Validation in Systems Engineering*,
DOI 10.1007/978-3-642-15228-3_3, © Springer-Verlag Berlin Heidelberg 2010

Rumbaugh's object modeling technique (OMT) [182] resulted in a modeling language designed specifically to represent object-oriented software: the unified modeling language (UML 0.8). In June 1996, UML 0.9 was released with the inclusion of Ivar Jacobson's object-oriented software engineering (OOSE) method [123], which consisted of the use case methodology. Thereafter, the standard progressed through versions 1.1, 1.3, and 1.4.

Although UML 1.x was widely accepted in the community, some shortcomings were signaled, namely, the lack of support for diagram interchange [136], its increased complexity, its limited customizability, and also its inadequate semantics definition. Moreover, UML 1.x was not fully aligned with MOF [175] and MDA [178]. Consequently, a major revision was required to address these problems [35] and so OMG adopted officially a new major revision of UML: UML 2.0 [181]. Many improvements to the language have since been applied to UML 2.0 in the form of minor revisions [186].

3.2 UML Diagrams

UML diagrams are classified into two main categories: structural and behavioral. The latter category includes a subset category called the interaction diagrams. The diagram taxonomy is depicted in Fig. 3.1.

The structural diagrams model the static aspects and structural features of the system, whereas the behavioral diagrams describe the dynamic behavior of the system. Structural diagrams include the class, component, composite structure, deployment, object, and package diagrams. Behavioral diagrams include the activity, use case, and state machine diagrams. The interaction diagrams are part of the behavioral diagrams category since they emphasize the interaction between the modeled components; they include the communication, interaction overview, sequence, and timing diagrams. The new diagrams proposed in UML 2.x are composite structure, interaction overview, and timing. Also, other diagrams have been extended and modified since UML 1.x, namely, the activity, state machine, sequence, and communication diagrams.

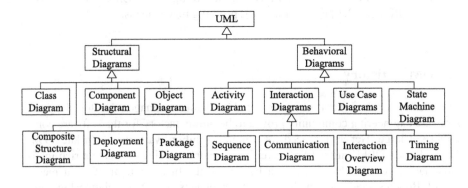

Fig. 3.1 UML 2 diagram taxonomy (source [186])

3.2.1 Class Diagram

The class diagram represents the principal building block in object-oriented modeling. It depicts the static view of either a specific area of model or its entirety, describing the structural elements and their relationships. It is mainly used to build a system's architecture. It captures and defines classes and interfaces and the relationship between them. Moreover, classes are abstract templates from which the runtime objects are instantiated. A class diagram describes the relationships between classes rather than those between specific instantiated objects. Classes relate to each other through different relationships such as association, aggregation, composition, dependency, or inheritance.

As a basic building block, the class diagram defines the essential resources needed for the proper operation of the system. Each resource is modeled in terms of its structure, relations, and behaviors. In general, a class diagram consists of the following features:

- **Classes**. Each class is composed of three compartments: the class name, the attributes, and the methods. The attributes and methods can be public, private, or protected. Abstract roles of the class in the system can also be indicated.
- **Interfaces**. Titled boxes represent interfaces in the system, providing information about the name of the interface and its methods.
- **Generalization relationships**

  - **Inheritance** is represented by a solid line with a solid arrowhead that points from the child class (or interface) to its parent class (or interface).
  - **Implementation** is represented by a dotted line with a solid arrowhead that points from a class to its implemented interface.

- **Association relationships** represent a "has a" relationship. An association relationship is represented by a solid line and an open arrowhead. The arrow points from the containing class to the contained one. Composition and aggregation, two special types of association relationships, are defined as follows:

  - **Composition** is represented by a solid line with a solid black diamond at its tail end. Composition models a class "owning" another class, therefore being responsible for the creation and destruction of objects of the other class.
  - **Aggregation** is represented by a solid line with a hollow white diamond at its tail end. Aggregation models a class "using" another class without being responsible for the creation and destruction of the other class' objects.

- **Dependency** is represented by a dotted line with an open arrowhead. It shows that one class "entity" is dependent on the behavior of another entity. It is useful for showing that a class is used to instantiate another or that it uses the other as an input parameter.

Figure 3.2 shows a class diagram example for a residence rental system that includes a reservation facility. It shows that the two types of residences that are available are apartment and house. The *Apartment* and *House* classes are inheriting from the class *Residence*. A class *customerProfile* is contained in the class

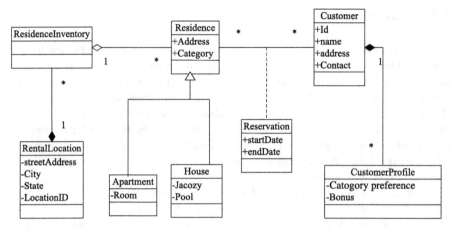

Fig. 3.2 Class diagram example

Customer via a composition relationship. The latter means that one class (*Customer-Profile*) cannot exist without the other (*Customer*). The same composition relationship exists between the *ResidenceInventory* and *RentalLocation* classes. There is also an aggregation relationship between the *Residence* and *ResidenceInventory* classes, as a residence inventory might be made up of several residence, but the *Residence* class continues to exist even if the *ResidenceInventory* class is destroyed. Moreover, when a reservation is made, both the *Residence* and *Customer* classes are used.

3.2.2 Component Diagram

The component diagram describes software components and their dependencies among each other. It shows the definition, internal structure, and dependencies among the systems' components. A component is a modular and deployable part of the system. Components are depicted as boxes in the diagram and are generally interrelated to each other through connectors. A component diagram has a higher level of abstraction than a class diagram, it usually being implemented by one or more classes (or objects) at runtime. A component diagram allows the capturing of relationships among the major building blocks of the system without having to dig into the functionality and/or implementation details.

The purpose of the component diagrams is to

- model the real software or system in the implementation environment;
- reveal the software or system configuration issues through dependency analysis;
- depict an accurate picture of the system prior to making changes or enhancements;
- reveal bottlenecks in an implementation without having to examine the entire system or code;
- define physical software modules and their relationships to one another.

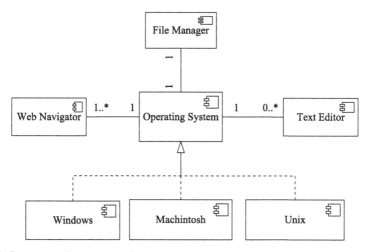

Fig. 3.3 Component diagram example

Figure 3.3 shows a component diagram example representing operating systems and a subset of their applications. The diagram shows that an operating system is able to run software applications such as *Text Editor*, *Web Navigator*, and *File Manager*. Moreover, *Windows*, *Unix*, and *Macintosh* operating systems, in this example, inherit the behavior of the *Operating System* component.

3.2.3 Composite Structure Diagram

A composite structure diagram is a static structure diagram that shows the internal structure of a classifier such as a class, component, or collaboration. It can also include internal parts such as ports through which the classifiers interact with each other or with external entities and their underlying connectors. Moreover, it shows the configuration and relationship of different parts of the system that perform, as a whole, the behavior of the containing classifier. The elements of a composite structure diagram are as follows:

- **Containing classifier** is the class, component, or collaboration that represents the composite structured element. As shown in Fig. 3.4, *Car* is the diagram's containing classifier.
- **Part** is an element that comprised a set of one or more instances owned by the containing classifier. For example, Fig. 3.4 shows that *Vehicule* owns the instances of the three parts, namely *Engine*, *Axle*, and *Wheel*.
- **Port** is an element that represents the visible parts of a containing classifier. It defines the interaction between a classifier and its environment. Ports may exist on the boundary of the contained classifier or on the boundary of the composite structure itself. Moreover, ports may specify the services offered by the containing classifier as well as those offered by the environment to the classifier.

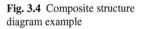

Fig. 3.4 Composite structure
diagram example

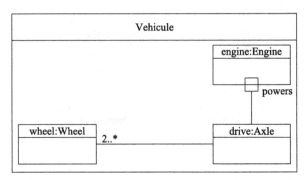

- **Interfaces** are similar to classes but with some restrictions. Its attributes are all constants and their operations are abstract. They can be represented in composite structure diagrams. When interfaces are owned by classes, they are referred to as "exposed interfaces" and can be of type "provided" or "required." In the former, the containing classifier supplies the operations defined by the named interface and is linked to the interface through a realization association. In the latter, the classifier communicates with another classifier, which provides operations defined by the named interface.

Figure 3.4 is an example of a composite structure diagram describing the main elements of a vehicle. More precisely, a vehicle should contain an engine, two or more wheels, and an axle. A port is located on the boundary of the engine part through which the engine powers the drive. In this context, *powers* represent a service provided by the engine to the axle.

3.2.4 Deployment Diagram

UML deployment diagrams depict both the hardware architecture of a system and the components that run on each piece of hardware. A deployment diagram is needed for applications that run on several devices since it shows the hardware, the software, and the middleware used to connect the hardware devices in the system.

Hardware components are depicted using boxes. Component diagrams may be embedded into deployment diagrams. More precisely, the same boxes used to model the UML component diagram are used inside the hardware boxes to represent the software running on a specific piece of hardware. Moreover, nodes in the deployment diagram can be interconnected through lines (connectors) to represent interdependencies.

Figure 3.5 depicts an example of a deployment diagram for a communication network architecture. It describes the relationships between three different hardware components connected through a *TCP/IP* network. An *Application Server* can connect to one or more *Web Servers*. Each hardware component runs one or more software applications. For example, the *Web Server* deploys *Windows XP* and other

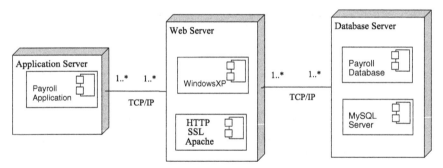

Fig. 3.5 Deployment diagram example

services such as *Http*, *SSL*, and *Apache*. In summary, a deployment diagram is used to depict an abstract view of the hardware's and software components' architecture in a designed system.

3.2.5 Object Diagram

The object diagram shows how specific instances of a class are related to each other at run-time. It consists of the same elements as its corresponding class diagram. While a class diagram defines the classes of the software with their attributes and methods, an object diagram assigns values to the corresponding classes' attributes and methods' parameters. Object diagrams support the study of requirements by modeling examples from the problem domain. Moreover, they may be used to generate test cases that can later serve for the validation of class diagrams.

An object consists of two compartments: the first one has the name of the object and its corresponding class in the class diagram, the second one shows the attributes of the object and its values. Objects in the object diagram are linked using connectors. These connectors are instances of the associations in the class diagram. Note that these connectors are not labeled with multiplicity values as it is the case for class diagrams.

Figure 3.6 shows an object diagram example along with the class diagram wherefrom it was derived. The diagram shows that a faculty in a university may have more than one student while a student can belong to one faculty only. The object diagram shows that two instances of the class *Student* exist with only one instance of the class *Faculty*.

3.2.6 Package Diagram

Package diagrams are used to organize different packages in the system's model. A package is used to group model elements and other diagrams in an aggregation. Since the number of use case and class diagrams tend to grow, making their

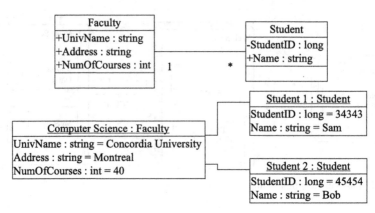

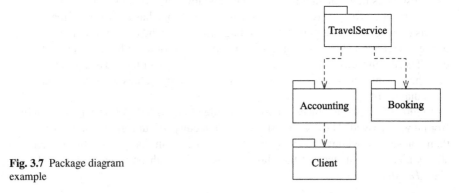

Fig. 3.6 Class diagram (*top*) and object diagram (*bottom*)

management difficult, these diagrams are grouped. Thus, packages help structuring a project into manageable parts. A package is depicted by a rectangle with a small tab at the top showing the package's name. A package diagram may contain several packages organized into a hierarchy. Similar to classes in class diagram, packages are related to each other using different types of connectors, such as association, dependency, and generalization connectors.

An element in a package may depend on another element in another package in different ways. For example, a class in one package may inherit the properties of a class in another package; in this way a generalization relationship should be established between the two containing packages. Figure 3.7 shows an example of a package diagram subset of a travel service system.

Fig. 3.7 Package diagram example

3.2.7 Activity Diagram

Activity diagrams are generally used to depict the flow of a given process by emphasizing the input/output dependencies, sequencing, and other conditions (e.g., synchronizations) required for coordinating the process behavior. Moreover, UML activity diagrams [207] can capture the behavior of a process or system in a wide variety of domains for use cases detailing computational, business, and other work-flow processes as well as modeling in general. A number of activity diagrams might be needed in order to describe a given system; each diagram may focus on a different aspect of the system or show a specific aspect of the model.

An activity diagram is composed of a set of actions related by control flow paths in a specific order of invocation (or execution). The input and the output dependencies can be emphasized using dataflow paths.

An action represents the fundamental unit of a behavior specification and cannot be further decomposed within the activity. An activity may be composed of a set of actions coordinated sequentially and/or concurrently. Furthermore, the activity may also involve synchronization and/or branching. These features can be enabled by using control nodes including fork, join, decision, and merge. These nodes support various forms of control routing. Additionally, one may specify hierarchy among activities using call behavior action nodes, which may also reference another activity definition. In the following, we provide a detailed description of the activity diagram's modeling elements.

3.2.7.1   Activity Actions

Activity actions are used to specify the fine-grained behavior, similar to the kind of behavior of executable instructions in ordinary programming languages. In essence, an action can be understood as the value transformation of a set of inputs into a set of outputs. For a given action, the inputs are specified by the set of incoming edges and the outputs by the set of outgoing edges. Note that, in the case of elementary action nodes, only one incoming and one outgoing edge are likely to be specified. The run-time effect of a given action is described by the difference in the state of the system from the pre-condition of the action versus its post-condition. The pre-condition holds immediately before the action is executed and the post-condition holds immediately after the execution of the action completes. In this context, the UML specification does not make any restrictions on the duration of the actions. Therefore, in accordance with the requirements and constraints, both instantaneous (i.e., zero time) and timed execution semantic models can be employed.

3.2.7.2   Activity Flows

It is usually necessary to combine a number of transforming actions in order to get an overall desired effect; this is accomplished by using activity flows. These are used to combine actions that perform primitive (basic) state transformations. Thus, it is with activity flows that actions and their effects are combined to produce complex transformations and serve the conditions and execution order of the combined actions. The UML standard supports both control flows and dataflows (object flows). In this volume we are concentrating on control flows since they represent one of the main targets of our verification and validation efforts. Control flows are the most conventional and natural way of combining actions. Indeed, a control flow edge between two actions is understood as starting the execution of the action at the target end of the edge, immediately after the executing action at the source of the edge has completed its execution. In most cases, the processes that use activity diagrams require various alterations of the execution flow done with, for example, conditional branches and loops. In order to support the aforementioned constructs, a number of specific control nodes, including standard control constructs such as fork and join, are used in a similar manner to those used in the state machine diagrams. Likewise, the control flow can be adjusted by specifying guards (in essence, side effect-free boolean predicates) that label the flows, which are used for conditional transfer of control.

3.2.7.3 Activity Building Blocks

An activity diagram might contain object nodes for capturing corresponding object flows.[1] However, since the control flow aspect represents the point of interest in the behavioral assessment, in the following paragraphs we will discuss the corresponding subset of control flow artifacts.

The building blocks of an activity diagram consist of the control flow elements depicted in Fig. 3.8 and are described as follows:

- **Initial node** indicates the beginning (e.g., initial entry point) of the activity diagram.
- **Final node** indicates when the execution of the whole diagram terminates.
- **Flow final** node is meant to stop the execution of a specific flow of actions.

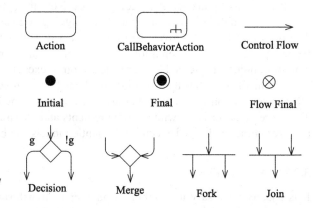

Fig. 3.8 Activity control flow artifacts

---

[1] Dataflows connect actions in a different manner than control flows. They are used to connect input and output pins on actions while allowing certain actions to be started before finishing the activity wherefrom the dataflow stems. Consequently, dataflow dependencies tend to be highly fine-grained compared to the control flow, as the actions might have multiple inputs and outputs connected in sensitive and intricate ways.

- **Action nodes** are processing nodes. Actions can be executed sequentially or concurrently. Furthermore, an action represents an elementary execution step that cannot be further decomposed into smaller actions.
- **Fork node** is a control node that triggers concurrent processing in parallel execution paths.
- **Join node** is a control node that synchronizes different concurrent execution paths into one execution path.
- **Activity edge** (transition) is used to transfer the control flow in the diagram from one activity node to another. If specified, a guard controls the firing of the edge.
- **Decision node** (branch node) is used to select between different execution flows in the diagram by specifying an execution path depending on the truth value of a guard.
- **Merge node** is a construct that merges (without synchronization) several alternative paths into a common activity flow.

An aggregation of action nodes and edges represents an executable block. An executable block is usually conceived as a structured activity node which corresponds, in general, to the concept of a block in some structured programming languages. They are useful for constructing arbitrarily complex activity node hierarchies.

3.2.8 Activity Diagram Execution

The execution semantics of the UML activity diagram is similar to Petri net token flow. In this respect, according to the specification, each activity action is started as soon it receives a control flow token. Once an action is completed, subsequent actions receive a control flow token and are triggered immediately while the tokens are consumed.

There are several basic control flow patterns defining elementary aspects of process control as depicted in Fig. 3.9:

- Sequencing provides the ability to execute a series of activities in sequence
- Parallel split (fork connector) provides the ability to split a single thread of control into multiple threads of control, which execute in parallel
- Synchronization (join connector) allows the convergence of multiple parallel sub-processes/activities into a single thread of control thus synchronizing multiple threads
- Exclusive choice (branch connector) provides the ability to choose one of several branches at a decision point
- Multiple choice provides the ability to split a thread of control into several parallel threads on a selective basis
- Simple merge (merge connector) is a point in the workflow process where two or more alternative branches merge together without synchronization

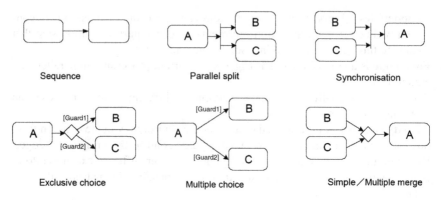

Fig. 3.9 Activity control flow patterns

- Multiple merge (merge connector) allows the convergence of two or more distinct branches in an unsynchronized manner. If more than one branch is active, the activity following the merge is started for every activation of each incoming branch.

3.2.9 Use Case Diagram

A use case diagram describes a set of scenarios that expose the interaction between the users and a system. A user can be either a person or another system. A use case refers to the actions that the system can perform by interacting with its actors. Therefore, the use case diagram shows a series of actions as well as the actors that can perform those actions. Use cases are employed in the initial phase of the development process. They are useful in eliciting the software and system's requirements. Most use cases are defined in the initial stages, while new ones might be necessary during the development process. Moreover, use cases are employed to identify the expectations of a system, its specific features, and the shared behavior among its components.

In general, use case diagrams consist of the following three entities:

- **Actor** is the role that a user, subsystem, or device can play when interacting with the system. Actors are drawn as stick figures.
- **Use case** provides actors with a sequence of actions that can be performed. Use cases are drawn as horizontal ellipses.
- **Association** is a semantic relationship between two or more classifiers; they specify the connections that are allowed among their instances. They are drawn as solid lines. When necessary, the lines can be arrows indicating the directions of the connections.

Figure 3.10 shows an example of a use case diagram. It models an online customer ordering system. A sales person is responsible for registering new customers.

Fig. 3.10 Use case diagram
example

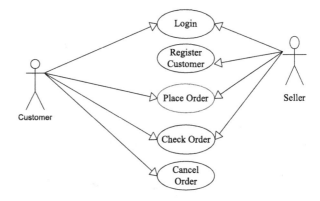

The user will log in to the system and check different items. He can place an order, which will later be checked by the salesperson. The diagram shows the functions that each actor can perform in the system.

3.2.10 State Machine Diagram

The primary motivation underlying the development of hierarchical state machines in general and their UML formalism in particular was driven by the necessity to overcome the limitations of the conventional state machines when describing large and complex system behavior.

The UML state machines are hierarchical in nature and support orthogonal regions (i.e., concurrency). They can be used in order to express the behavior of a system or its components in a visual, intuitive, and compact manner. The state machine evolves in response to a set of possible incoming events dispatched one at a time from an event queue. These events can trigger the state machine transitions which, in turn, are generally associated with a series of executed actions.

Some of the key features of UML state machines include the ability to cluster states into composite (OR) super-states and to refine abstract states into substates, thus providing a hierarchical structure. Moreover, concurrency can be described by orthogonal (AND) composite concurrent states that contain two or more concurrently active regions, each of which is a further clustering of states, as depicted in Fig. 3.11. Hence, when a system is in an "AND" state, then each of its regions will contain at least one active state. Furthermore, as there can be more than one state active at a time, the state machine dynamic is configuration based rather than state based. A configuration denotes a set of active states and represents a stable point in the state machine dynamics while proceeding from one step to the next. A number of state machine diagrams are sometimes needed in order to describe the behavior of a given entity and each diagram can focus on a different aspect of the entity's behavior.

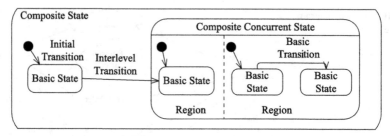

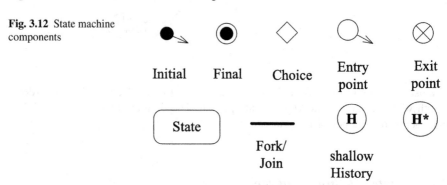

Fig. 3.11 State machine hierarchical clustering

Fig. 3.12 State machine components

State machines are basically a structured aggregation of states and transitions as well as a number of other pseudo-state components. The building blocks of a state machine are depicted in Fig. 3.12. The states are either simple or composite (i.e., clustering a number of substates). Moreover, the states are nested in a containment hierarchy so that the states contained inside a region of a composite state are denoted as the substates of that composite state.

3.2.10.1 Regions

A region is a placeholder that contains the substates of a composite state. Composite states may contain one or more regions, where the different regions are separated by a dashed line and each region is said to be orthogonal to other(s) within the same composite state. Hence, concurrency is present whenever a composite state contains more than one region.

3.2.10.2 States

Each state has a unique name or label that represents either the source or target for a transition. States may also have "entry," "exit," and "do" associated actions. Final states can only be a target of transitions and have no substates or associated actions. Once reached, the parent region needs to be completed.

Simple or basic states represent the leaves of the state hierarchy tree and, as such, do not contain substates or regions. Conversely, the composite states are represented by all the other non-leaf nodes and, as such, have at least one region containing substates. Moreover, whenever a composite state is active, all of its regions have exactly one active nested substate. A single region composite state is called a non-orthogonal composite state or sequential (OR) state, whereas a multi-region composite state is called an orthogonal (AND) composite state.

3.2.10.3 Pseudo-states

The UML state machine formalism draws a distinction between states and pseudo-states in that the latter are not included in configurations; their main function serves to model various forms of compound transitions. Moreover, pseudo-states have no names or associated actions and are used as an abstraction for various types of intermediary vertices that are used to link different states in the state machine hierarchy tree. The following itemized list presents the different types of pseudo-states:

- **Initial** is used to indicate the default active state of a particular region upon entry. Moreover, only one initial vertex can be present in each region of a composite state.
- **Fork** signifies that the incoming transition originates from a single state and has multiple outgoing transitions occurring concurrently, requiring the targets to be located in concurrent regions.
- **Join** combines two or more transitions emanating from multiple states located in concurrent regions into a compound synchronized transition with a single target state.
- **ShallowHistory** is used to represent the entry point to the most recently active substate within the region of a composite state. This entry point corresponds to the state configuration that was established when the composite state was last exited. In the case where the composite state has never been visited before, a single transition is allowed to indicate the default shallow history state.
- **DeepHistory** is an extension or generalization of a shallow history and is used to represent the entry point to the most recently active configuration enclosed in the region of a composite state. Consequently, the configuration is established by descending recursively into the most recently active substate, activating at each containment level the most recently active descendant(s).

3.2.10.4 Transitions

Transitions are relating pairs of states used to indicate that a dynamic element (e.g., an object) is changing state in response to a trigger (event) once some specified condition (guard) is satisfied. The guard is evaluated after the event is dispatched, but prior to the firing of the corresponding transition. If the guard is evaluated as *true*, the transition is enabled; otherwise, it is disabled. Each transition allows for an optional action (e.g., issuing a new event) to be specified and, if applied, results in the effect of the transition.

Transitions from composite states are called high-level or group transitions. When triggered, all the substates of a given composite state are exited. Furthermore, a compound transition is an acyclic chain of transitions linked by various pseudo-states and represents a path from a set (possibly a singleton) of source states to a set (possibly a singleton) of destination states. When the source and the destination sets are both singletons, the transition is said to be basic or simple. Moreover, if the intersection of the source states belonging to two or more enabled transitions is not empty, the transitions are said to be "in conflict." In this case, it is possible that one has higher priority than the other(s). Thus, in the case of simple transitions, the UML standard assigns higher priority to the transition having the most deeply nested source state.

Furthermore, UML specifies a number of transition constraints:

- The set of source states of a transition involving a join pseudo-state is a set of at least two orthogonal states.
- A join vertex must have at least two incoming transitions and exactly one outgoing transition.
- All transitions incoming a join vertex must originate in different regions of an orthogonal state.
- The transitions entering a join vertex cannot have guards or triggers.
- A fork vertex must have at least two outgoing transitions and exactly one incoming transition.
- All target states of a fork vertex must belong to different regions of an orthogonal state.
- Transitions from fork pseudo-states may not target pseudo-states
- Transitions outgoing pseudo-states may not have a trigger.
- Initial and history transitions are restricted to point only to their default target state.
- Transitions from one region to another, in the same immediate enclosing composite state, are not allowed and in fact require that the two regions be part of two different composite states.

3.2.10.5 State Configurations

In the UML state machine, thanks to the containment hierarchy and concurrency, more than one state can be active at a time. If a simple substate of a composite state is active, then its parent and all the composite states that transitively contain it are also active. Furthermore, some of the composite states in the hierarchy may be orthogonal (AND) and hence potentially concurrently active. In that case, the currently active states of the state machine are represented by a sub-tree of the state machine hierarchy tree and, consequently, the states contained in such a sub-tree denote a configuration of the state machine.

3.2.10.6 Run-to-Completion Step

The execution semantics of the UML state machine is described in the specification as a sequence of run-to-completion steps. Each step represents a move from one active configuration to another in response to the dispatched events stored in an event pool.

The UML specification is silent regarding the kind of order imposed on the event pool, leaving it to the discretion of the modeler. However, the events are required to be dispatched and processed one at a time. Consequently, the run to completion means that an event can be popped from the event pool and dispatched only if the processing of the previously selected event is completed. Thus, the processing of a single event in a run-to-completion step is achieved by firing the maximal number of enabled and non-conflicting transitions of the state machine. This results in a consistent change in the currently active set of states along with the execution of the corresponding actions, if any, and ensures that before and after each run-to-completion step the state machine is in a stable active configuration.

Furthermore, multiple transitions can be fired in an arbitrary order provided that they reside in mutually orthogonal regions. In the case where an event is not triggering any transitions in a particular configuration (i.e., there is an empty set of enabled transitions), the run-to-completion step is immediately completed, though with no configuration change. In this case the state machine is said to stutter and the event is discarded.

3.2.11 Sequence Diagram

Sequence diagrams describe the interactions within a system using communicating entities represented by a rectangle from which lifelines descend. An interaction is a communication based on the exchange of messages in the form of operation calls or signals arranged in a temporal order [255]. Objects assume the role of such communicating entities. The body of a lifeline represents the life cycle of its corresponding object.

A message is used for passing information and it can be exchanged between two lifelines in two possible modes: synchronous and asynchronous. There are four types of messages: operation call, signal, reply, and object creation/destruction. This is symbolized by a labeled arrow pointing from the sender to the receiver. Moreover, the diagram may contain timing requirements, placed on the left of the diagram, which allows specifying how much time an operation needs to complete its execution.

Aside from lifelines and messages, sequence diagrams can define other constructs in order to organize the modeled interactions. The abstraction of the most general interaction unit is called "interaction fragment" [186], which represents a generalization of a "combined fragment." The latter defines an expression of the former and consists of an interaction operator and interaction operands [186]. Combined fragments allow for compact illustration of traces of exchanged messages. They are represented by a rectangular frame with solid lines and a small pentagon in the upper left corner showing the operator with dashed lines separating the operands [255]. On the one hand, an interaction operand contains an ordered set of interaction fragments. On the other hand, the interaction operators include, but are not limited to, conditional execution operator (denoted by "alt"), looping operator (denoted

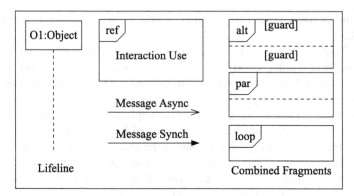

Fig. 3.13 Syntax of sequence diagrams

by "loop"), and parallel execution operator (denoted by "par"). Finally, sequence diagrams define interaction use constructs in order to reference other interactions. This allows for a hierarchical organization of interactions and its decomposition into manageable units. Figure 3.13 illustrates a subset of sequence diagrams syntax. The primary interaction operators are as follows:

- **Ref name** is used to reference a sequence diagram fragment defined elsewhere
- **opt [condition]** contains a fragment that is executed based on a condition or state value
- **alt** has two or more parts out of which only one executes, based on a condition or state value. The complementary operand fragment labeled "[else]" can be used in order to provide an execution path if no other condition is true
- **par** has two or more parts that execute concurrently. Concurrence in this context does not require simultaneousness and can signify an undetermined order. On a single execution unit the behavior could be either sequential or interleaving
- **loop min..max [escape]** represents an execution that has at least a minimum number of iterations and at most an optional maximum number of executions. Moreover, an optional escape condition can be used
- **break [condition]** has an optional guard condition. When evaluated to true, the contents (if any) are executed while the remainder of the enclosing operator is not executed

Figure 3.14 shows an example of a sequence diagram of an elevator. The example shows the steps that are executed when a floor's button in an elevator is pressed by the passenger. The elevator button will illuminate until the requested floor is reached. After reaching the floor, the *Elevator_Controller* will send a message to the button to turn off its light. Afterward, the *Elevator_Controller* will send a message to the *Elevator* to open its door. At the end, the *Elevator_Controller* will send a message to the elevator to close its door in order to be able to serve another request. The time needed for the elevator to wait after opening the door can be specified on

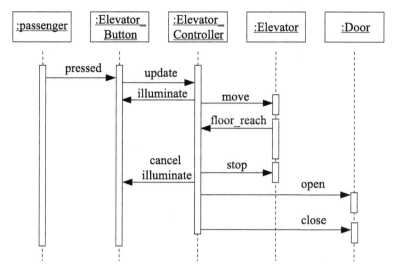

Fig. 3.14 Sequence diagram example (source [72])

the sequence diagram by an appropriate annotation. In this respect, UML profile for schedulability, performance, and time (SPT) [179] can be used for such annotation.

3.2.12 Communication Diagram

A communication diagram, previously called a collaboration diagram in UML 1.x, represents another interaction diagram in UML 2.x. Similar to the sequence diagram, in that it shows interactions between objects, it is also responsible for showing the relationships among objects. Mainly, communication diagrams are used to

- identify the interface requirements of the participating classes
- identify the structural changes required to satisfy an interaction
- explicitly identify the data that are passed during interactions. This may help in finding the source of the data and reveal new interactions
- reveal the structural requirements for completing a given task

In communication diagrams, objects are depicted as rectangles containing the object name and its related class. Relationships among objects are shown using association connectors. Numbered messages are added to the associations with an arrow indicating the direction of the message flow.

An example of a communication diagram is shown in Fig. 3.15. It illustrates the interaction between several objects that are part of an elevator system when serving an elevator button. The interaction is initiated by the passenger after pressing a floor button. Then, the *Elevator_Button* interacts with the *Elevator_Controller* by sending a request. Later, the *Elevator_Controller* sends the *illuminate* message

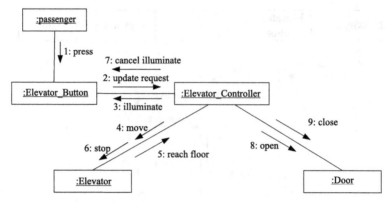

Fig. 3.15 Communication diagram example (source [72])

to the specific *Elevator_Button* object. A *move* message is then sent to the *Elevator* to reach the requested floor. When the requested floor is reached, a *stop* message is sent to the *Elevator*, which opens its door after a specific amount of time. Finally, the *Elevator_Controller* sends a *close* message to the *Elevator* to close its door.

3.2.13 Interaction Overview Diagram

The purpose of the interaction overview diagram is to provide a high-level view of the logical progression of the execution of the system through a set of interactions. UML 2 interaction overview diagrams are variants of UML activity diagrams. They use the syntax and semantics of an activity diagram to model the flow of logic in a series of interactions. They are mainly used to show interactions among systems that are combined together to produce a specific function. While sequence, communication, or timing diagrams describe the details of an interaction, the interaction overview diagram describes a high-level overview of how one or more interactions can be performed to carry out a higher order task.

The nodes within the diagram are either interaction frames, depicting another UML interaction diagram (such as sequence, communication, timing, or interaction overview diagram), or interaction occurrence frames, indicating an activity or operation to invoke. The lines that connect the frames are control flows. Control nodes, such as decision, merge, fork, and join, can be used to coordinate the flow between frames.

Figure 3.16 shows an example of an interaction overview diagram of an elevator system. The diagram starts at the initial state. After pressing the button, the system will check whether or not the requested floor is in the opposite direction of the movement. If it is, the controller will send a message to turn off the button, otherwise the flow will continue to the next step.

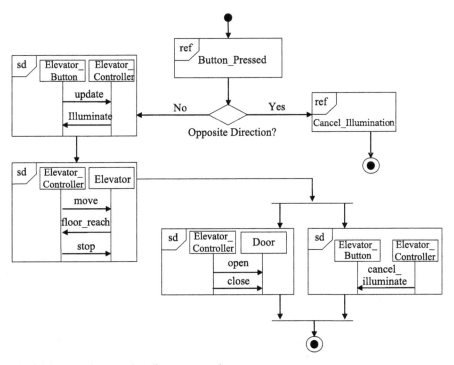

Fig. 3.16 Interaction overview diagram example

3.2.14 Timing Diagram

Timing diagrams are one of the new artifacts added to UML 2. They offer a different way of presenting sequence diagrams, explicitly showing the behavior of one or more elements of the system according to a timeline.

They display the change in state or value of one or more elements over time and can also show the interaction between timed events and the corresponding time and duration constraints. Moreover, they are used to document timing requirements that control the changes in the state of the system. They can also be used with the state machine diagram when the timing of events is considered critical for the proper operation of the system.

A timing diagram contains state lifelines. A state lifeline displays the modification of an element's state over time. The X-axis displays the elapsed time, while the Y-axis is labeled with a given list of states. At the bottom of the diagram, a timeline shows how time goes by while element states change. Furthermore, messages can be exchanged between different interacting elements in order to specify the triggers of the changes in the states.

Figure 3.17 shows an example of a timing diagram for a door-locking mechanism.

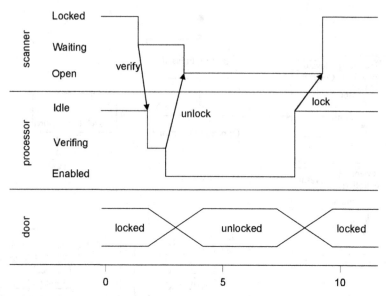

Fig. 3.17 Timing diagram example

The example contains three different state lifelines. The scanner has three states: "idle," "waiting," and "open." The processor also has three states: "idle," "verifying," and "enabled." Finally, the door has only two states, namely "locked" and "unlocked." The last state lifeline is represented differently (value lifeline). Two lines are shown to represent each state. When the door is in the unlocked state, the unlocked term is written between the two lines. When the door changes its state, the lines cross each other and continue to move in the timeline direction, while presenting the new state (lock) in between the lines.

3.3 UML Profiling Mechanisms

UML defines a specific profile concept that provides a generic extension mechanism for building UML models within a particular domain. UML profiling allows a refining of the semantics of standard UML elements in a strictly additive manner and without introducing semantical contradictions.

The main UML profiling mechanisms are stereotypes and tagged values. These mechanisms are applied to specific model elements such as classes, attributes, operations, and activities in order to adapt them for different purposes. The mechanisms are defined as follows:

- UML stereotypes are used in order to extend the UML vocabulary by creating new model elements derived from existing ones. Stereotypes add specific properties suitable for a specific problem domain and are used for classifying or marking the UML building blocks.

- The tagged values are used for specifying keyword values. They allow the extending of a UML building block's properties and the creation of new information in the specification of an element defined for existing model elements or for individual stereotypes. Moreover, tagged values can be used in order to specify properties that are relevant to code generation or configuration management.

Various UML profiles have been issued by the OMG in order to customize UML for particular domains (e.g., aerospace, healthcare, financial, transportation, systems engineering) or platforms (e.g., J2EE, .NET). Examples of UML profiles include the OMG systems modeling language (OMG SysML) [187] for systems engineering applications, the UML profile for schedulability, performance, and time (SPT) [176] for modeling of time, schedulability, and performance-related aspects of real-time systems, and its successor, namely the UML profile for modeling and analysis of real-time and embedded systems (MARTE) [189].

3.4 Conclusion

UML strives to be a rich and expressive powerful language for specifying complete systems across a broad spectrum of application domains. In many cases, models require more than modeling software and computation. This is the case with many designs of real-time and embedded systems, where it may be necessary to model the behavior of diverse real-world physical entities, such as hardware devices or human users. The physical components of a system certainly tend to be highly heterogeneous and much more complex than most mathematical formalisms can capture. Moreover, it is often the case that, for a given entity, different viewpoints or perspectives related to various sets of concerns are required in the process of modeling and design (e.g., dissimilar sets of concerns are considered in modeling the performance of the system when compared to modeling the same system from the viewpoint of human–machine interaction). This may be one of the reasons behind the informal semantics of UML, as one of its primary objectives is to unify a set of broadly applicable modeling mechanisms in one common conceptual framework – a task that any specific concrete mathematical formalism would likely restrict. Indeed, the commonality of UML is a characteristic that underpins the use of the same tools, techniques, knowledge, and experience in various domains and situations. Notwithstanding, the community generally acknowledges that there is a compelling need for the formalization of many of the UML features [219].

Chapter 4
Systems Modeling Language

Systems modeling language (SysML) [187] is a modeling language dedicated to systems engineering applications. It is a UML profile that not only reuses a subset of UML 2.1.1 [186] but also provides additional extensions to better fit SE's specific needs. These extensions are mainly meant to address the requirements stated in the UML for SE request for proposal (RFP) [177]. It is intended to help specify and architect complex systems and their components and enable their analysis, design, and verification and validation. These systems may consist of heterogeneous components such as hardware, software, information, processes, personnel, and facilities [187].

SysML encompasses modeling capabilities that allow representing systems and their components using

- structural components composition, classification, and interconnection;
- behaviors including activity flows, interaction scenarios, and message passing as well as state-dependent reactive behaviors;
- allocation of one model element to another, such as functions to components, logical to physical components, and software to hardware;
- constraints on system property values such as performance, reliability, and physical properties;
- requirement hierarchies and derivations as well as their relations to other model elements.

In this chapter, we first present the history of SysML in Sect. 4.1. Then we expose the relationships between UML and SysML in Sect. 4.2. Finally, in Sect. 4.3, we present the SysML diagram taxonomy and describe each diagram by using an illustrative example.

4.1 SysML History

The SysML initiative started in January 2001 with a decision made by the Model-Driven Systems Design workgroup of the International Council on Systems Engineering (INCOSE) in order to customize the UML for systems engineering

M. Debbabi et al., *Verification and Validation in Systems Engineering*,
DOI 10.1007/978-3-642-15228-3_4, © Springer-Verlag Berlin Heidelberg 2010

applications. At that point, OMG [183] and INCOSE [120], with a number of experts from the SE field, collaborated in order to build a standard modeling language for SE. The OMG Systems Engineering Domain Special Interest Group (SE DSIG),[1] with the support of INCOSE and the ISO AP233 workgroup, developed the requirements for the envisioned modeling language. These requirements were subsequently issued by the OMG as part of the UML for systems engineering request for proposal [177] in March 2003. Being the modeling language *par excellence* for software engineering, UML has been selected to be customized for systems engineers' needs. However, the old UML 1.x version was found to be inadequate for systems engineering use [73, 256]. Meanwhile, an evolving revision of UML (i.e., UML 2.0) was issued with features of interest for systems engineers. In 2003, the SysML Partners, an informal association of industry leaders and tool vendors, initiated an open-source specification project to develop SysML in response to the UML for SE RFP, submitted to the OMG for adoption. Later on, a proposal for OMG SysML was submitted to the OMG and finally adopted. Consequently, the OMG SysML 1.0 [187] specification was issued by the OMG as an Available Specification in September 2007. The current OMG SysML 1.1 [190] was issued by the OMG in November 2008.

4.2 UML and SysML Relationships

SysML reuses a subset of UML 2.1 [186], called "UML4SysML," which represents approximately half of the UML language. An important portion of the UML concepts was discarded since they were not considered relevant for SE's modeling needs. Some of the reused diagrams were included as is in UML 2.1.1 [186]. These include state machine, sequence, and use case diagrams. Other diagrams were extended, such as activity diagrams, in order to tackle specific SE's needs. Additionally, SysML omitted some UML diagrams, namely object, component, deployment, communication, timing, and interaction overview. Class and composite structure diagrams were fundamentally modified and replaced by block definition and internal block diagrams, respectively. These extensions are based on the standard UML profiling mechanism, which include UML stereotypes, UML diagram extensions, and model libraries. The profiling mechanism was chosen over other extension mechanisms in order to leverage existing UML-based tools for systems modeling. Furthermore, SysML adds two new diagrams, those being requirements and parametric diagrams, and integrates new specification capabilities such as allocation. The relationship between UML and SysML is illustrated in Fig. 4.1.

The correspondence between SysML and UML diagrams is summarized in Table 4.1.

---

[1] Systems Engineering Domain Special Interest Group, http://syseng.omg.org/

Fig. 4.1 UML and SysML
relationship

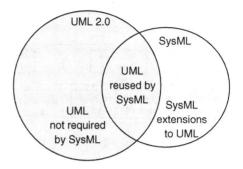

Table 4.1 Correspondence between SysML and UML (source [227])

SysML diagram	Purpose	UML analog
Activity	Shows system behavior as control flows and dataflows. Useful for functional analysis	Activity
Block definition	Shows system structure as components along with their properties, operations, and relationships	Class
Internal block	Shows the internal structures of components, including their parts and connectors	Composite structure
Package	Shows how a model is organized into packages, views, and viewpoints	Package
Parametric	Shows parametric constraints between structural elements	N/A
Requirement	Shows system requirements and their relationships with other elements	N/A
Sequence	Shows system behavior as interactions between system components	Sequence
State machine	Shows system behavior in terms of states that a component experiences in response to some events	State machine
Use case	Shows systems functions and the actors performing them	Use case

4.3 SysML Diagrams

SysML diagrams define a concrete syntax that describes how SysML concepts are visualized graphically or textually. In the SysML specification [187], this notation is described in tables that show the mapping of the language concepts into graphical symbols on diagrams.

SysML completely reuses some diagrams from UML 2.1:

- Use case
- Sequence
- State machine
- Package

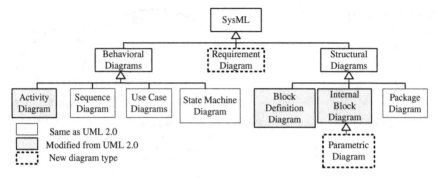

Fig. 4.2 SysML diagram taxonomy (source [187])

In addition, two new diagrams are added:

- Requirements
- Parametric

Furthermore, some other UML diagrams are reused in extended form:

- Activity (extends UML activity diagram)
- Block definition (extends UML class diagram)
- Internal block (extends UML composite structure diagram)

Figure 4.2 depicts the SysML diagram taxonomy.

4.3.1 Block Definition Diagram

SysML defines block definition diagrams (BDD), which contain UML 2.0 class diagrams as their legacy. This diagram is used to define block characteristics in terms of their structural and behavioral features, as well as the relationships between the blocks. These relationships include associations, generalization, and dependencies.

A block in SysML is the fundamental modular unit of structure used to define the type for a logical or conceptual entity. It can be a physical entity (e.g., a system component), a hardware part, a software, or a data component, a person, a facility, an item that flows through the system (e.g., water) or an entity in the natural environment (e.g., the atmosphere or ocean) [85]. Blocks have defining features that can be classified into structural features, behavioral interaction features, and constraints. Properties are the primary structural feature of blocks and they are used to capture the structural relationships and values of a block [85]. The three important categories of properties are as follows:

- The part properties, which describe the decomposition hierarchy of a block.
- The reference properties, which describe the relationships between blocks that are weaker than the previous ones.
- The value properties, which describe the quantifiable characteristics of a block.

In addition to the aforementioned properties' categories, ports are a special class of property used to specify allowable types of interactions between blocks [187]. A given port enables the behavior of a block (or part of it) to be accessed. A block may have many ports, each specifying a different interaction point. Though ports are defined on blocks, they can only be connected to one another by connectors on internal block diagrams.

The behaviors associated with a block define how the block responds to stimuli [85]. The three main behavioral formalisms that are used for specifying the behavior of blocks are activity, state machine, and sequence diagrams:

- Activity diagrams transform inputs to outputs (e.g., energy, information).
- State machine diagrams are used to describe how a block reacts to events.
- Sequence diagrams describe how the parts of a block interact with each other via message passing.

An example of a block definition diagram is provided in Fig. 4.3.

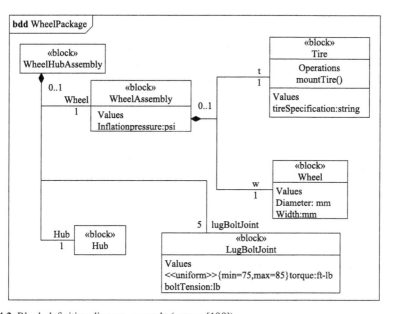

Fig. 4.3 Block definition diagram example (source [190])

4.3.2 Internal Block Diagram

The SysML internal block (IBD) diagram is similar to the UML 2.x composite structure diagram. Its main purpose is to describe the internal structure of a block in terms of interconnections between its parts. Connectors are used to bind different parts or ports so they can interact. The interaction between the parts of a block is

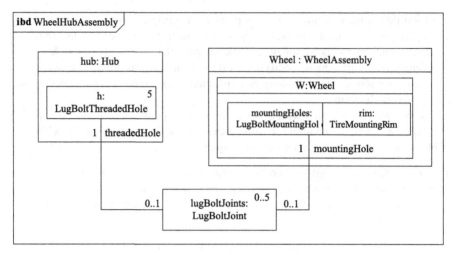

Fig. 4.4 Internal block diagram example (source [190])

specified by the behavior of each part. It may include input and output flow, services invocation, messages sending and receiving, or constraints between properties of the parts at either end. Figure 4.4 shows an example of an internal block diagram.

4.3.3 Package Diagram

The package diagram is reused by SysML and it is mainly designed for organizing the model by grouping the model elements. Consequently, models can be organized in various ways (e.g., by domain, by relationship). Figure 4.5 depicts an example of a SysML package diagram [190].

4.3.4 Parametric Diagram

Parameters are very important concepts that need to be modeled in a system design. A parameter (e.g., temperature, pressure) is essentially a measurable factor that can vary in an experimental setup. Consequently, a parameter variation can alter the system's behavior.

In SysML, parametric diagrams are commonly used in order to model properties along with their relationships. Moreover, this diagram is also used for representing complex mathematical and logical expressions or constraints. Its purpose is to bring more interaction capabilities, with various domain-specific modeling and analysis tools (e.g., equation solvers), by defining a set of quantifiable characteristics and relations that can be used and analyzed by such tools. Moreover, the parametric diagram shows how changing a value of a property impacts the other properties in the system. Therefore, this diagram can be used to perform simulations on models

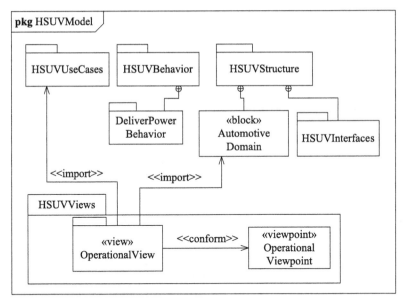

Fig. 4.5 SysML package diagram example (source [190])

by modifying parameter values and observing the resulting impact on the whole system. Additionally, parametric diagrams are useful for analyzing the performance and reliability of a system by identifying the conditions that might make the system unreliable or malfunctioning.

A parametric constraint specifies the dependency between one structural property of a system and another. Usually, such constraint properties show quantitative characteristics of a system. However, parametric models may be used on non-quantitative properties as well. Such constraint specifications can mainly be used for defining dependencies between the system's parameters and are typically used in combination with block diagrams. Moreover, this information can also be used when performing trade-off analysis.

An example of a parametric diagram for a power subsystem is depicted in Fig. 4.6. It shows the constraints on the FuelFlow Rate, which depends on FuelDemand and FuelPressure variables. This example involves aspects related to causality and dependent/independent variables and provides the capability to express parametric relations between different properties. Equation solvers can then be used on the parameters in order to determine particular solutions when specific variables are given values, the benefit being that one can use the set of equations differently, depending on what the established known and unknown variables are.

4.3.5 Requirement Diagram

A requirement represents a feature, property, or behavior that a system has to provide or comply with. The task of defining and listing the requirements is done in the

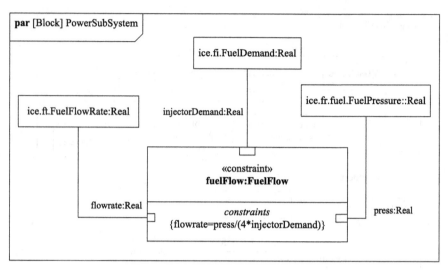

Fig. 4.6 Parametric diagram example (source [190])

very first steps of the system designing process. Requirements allow the designer to explicitly state what is expected from the future system. Moreover, requirements form a cornerstone of the verification and validation process, since they are the key ingredient for stating exactly what the engineered system should do and how it is supposed to do it. SysML introduced the requirement diagram, being absent in UML. This new diagram provides the means to depict requirements and to relate them to other specification, design, or verification models. The requirements can be represented in graphical, tabular, or tree structure formats. The strength and usefulness of the requirement diagram consist in the fact that it allows one to easily understand the relations between the requirements and their environment. The semantics of these relationships and other diagram elements are explained in Table 4.2.

A requirement can be decomposed into sub-requirements in order to organize multiple requirements as a tree of compound requirements. Moreover, a requirement can be related to other requirements as well as to other elements, such as analysis, implementation, and testing elements. Therefore, a requirement can be generated or extracted from another requirement by using the *derive* relationship.

Furthermore, requirements can be fulfilled by certain model elements using the *satisfy* relationship. The *verify* relationship is used to verify a requirement by applying different test cases. All of these stereotypes are actually specializations of the UML *trace* relationship, which is used to trace requirements and changes across the model.

Figure 4.7 shows a requirement diagram for the hybrid system vehicle and focuses mainly on the `Acceleration` requirement with respect to other requirements and model elements. Therein, a `refine` relation shows how the acceleration requirement is refined by a use case named `Accelerate`. Moreover,

Table 4.2 Requirement diagram syntax elements

Node name	Concrete syntax	Definition
Requirement	<<requirement>> R101 Id: 101 text: The system shall provide acceleration. criticality: H	Includes properties to specify texts, identifiers, and criticality
Rationale	<<rationale>> reference: analysis report	Attached to any requirement or relationship
Test case	<<testcase>> verdict = pass	Links requirements to a verification procedure (TestCase)
Containment relationship	⊕——	Indicates that a requirement is a composition of other sub-requirements
Satisfy dependency	- - - - - - - - - → <<satisfy>>	Indicates that a requirement is fulfilled by a model element
Verify dependency	- - - - - - - - - → <<verify>>	Links a requirement to a verification procedure
Trace dependency	- - - - - - - - - → <<trace>>	Links a requirement to other requirements
Derive dependency	- - - - - - - - - → <<derive>>	Links two requirements in which a client requirement can be derived from a supplier requirement
Copy dependency	- - - - - - - - - → <<copy>>	Links a supplier requirement to a client requirement, specifying that the text of the client requirement is a read-only copy of the supplier requirement
Refine dependency	- - - - - - - - - → <<refine>>	Links a requirement to another model element for clarification

the diagram shows that the `PowerSubsystem` block has to satisfy the `Power` requirement which is derived from the `Acceleration` requirement. Additionally, a `Max Acceleration` test case verifies the `Acceleration` requirement.

4.3.6 Activity Diagram

The activity diagram illustrates the behavior of the system and can be conceived as a process, a function, or a task occurring over time with known results. It helps one understand the system behavior by clearly defining inputs, outputs, and coordinations between behaviors or functions. Activity represents an important diagram for systems modeling due to its suitability for functional flow modeling commonly used by systems engineers [23]. Compared to other diagrams, its syntax and semantics have been significantly extended and its expressive power has also been enhanced. The major extensions that have been made are as follows:

- **Control as data:** The first major extension made by SysML to activity diagrams is the support of disabling actions that are already executing within a given

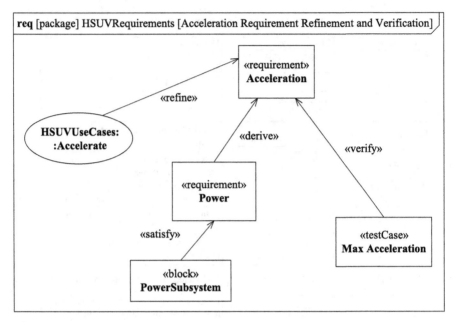

Fig. 4.7 Requirement diagram example (source [190])

activity diagram. In UML 2.1.1 activities, control can only enable actions to start. This extension is accomplished using a type for control values that are treated like data. Graphically, control operators, which are activities that accept and emit control values, are called behavior actions extended with a stereotype "control operator." Control operator and control values are mostly relevant in the case of streaming applications, where activities run until disabled by other activities; otherwise, they might run forever or at an inappropriate time.

- **Continuous systems:** SysML activity diagrams added that extension to allow continuous object flows. For this type of flows, the expected rate of flow is infinite, which means that the time between token arrivals is zero. This is especially helpful in modeling systems that manipulate continuous data such as energy, information, or physical material. SysML added two options to continuous feature extension; one describes whether to replace values that are already in the object nodes with newly arriving values (Overwrite), and the other one states whether to discard values if they do not immediately flow downstream (NoBuffer).

- **Probability:** SysML extends activity diagrams with probabilities in two ways: on edges outgoing from a decision node and also on output parameter sets (the set of outgoing edges holding data output from an action node). According to SysML specification, probability on a given edge expresses the likelihood that a token traverses this edge.

- **Enhanced functional flow block diagrams (EFFBD):** The activity diagram has been updated in order to support mapping into EFFBD since the latter is a widely used model in systems engineering.

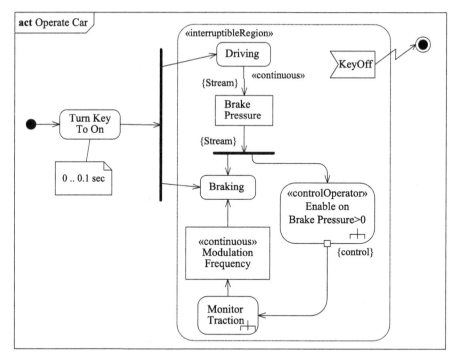

Fig. 4.8 SysML activity diagram example (source [190])

Section 3.2.7 is dedicated to a more detailed description of UML4SysML concepts in activity diagrams. Figure 4.8 is an example of the usage of some new features in activity diagrams. This example shows the model of an operating car, which engine is turned on by a key and that runs until disabled by turning the key off. The "interruptible region" shows that all the included activities will continue to occur until the key is turned off. The diagram also shows that driving sends continuous information to the braking subsystem.

4.3.7 State Machine Diagram

The UML 2 state machine diagram is reused as it is by SysML specification [187].

However, the UML concept of protocol state machines is excluded since it is found to be unnecessary in the case of systems modeling. This significantly reduces the complexity of the language. The only relevant new feature is related to the behavior of the invoked activity while in a given state (specified as "do activities"), which can be either continuous or discrete, thanks to the extension made by SysML to UML activity diagrams.

Figure 4.9 shows the high-level states or modes of the HybridSUV including the events that trigger states modifications.

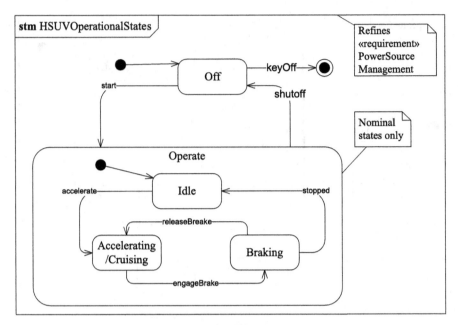

Fig. 4.9 SysML state machine example (source [190])

4.3.8 Use Case Diagram

SysML completely reuses the use case diagram, which describes the usage of a system (subject) by its actors (environment) to achieve a goal [187]. Use case diagrams include the use case and actors as well as the associated communications between them. Interacting actors are generally external to the system and may correspond to users, systems, or other environmental entities. They may interact directly or in a mediated manner with the system. The association relation between the actors and the use case represent the communications between the actors and the subject in accomplishing the functionality associated with the use case. The use cases enclosed in the system boundary represent functionality realized by behaviors such as activity, sequence, and state machine diagrams. Figure 4.10 depicts an example of SysML use case diagram corresponding to the "operating a vehicle" use case.

4.3.9 Sequence Diagram

Regarding interaction diagrams, SysML only includes sequence diagrams; both the interaction overview and communication diagrams were excluded because of their overlapping functionalities and also due to the fact that they do not offer any additional capabilities compared to sequence diagrams for system modeling applications. Furthermore, the timing diagram was also excluded due to its limited

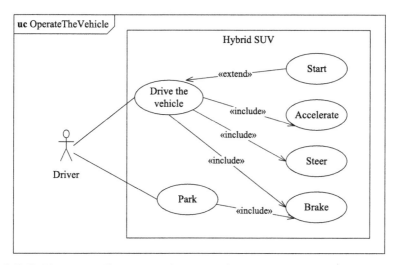

Fig. 4.10 SysML use case diagram example (source [187])

suitability for systems engineering needs [187]. Sequence diagrams can capture highly complex interactions that are described along lifelines corresponding to inter-acting actors in various usage scenarios. These actors may represent users, subsys-tems, blocks, or parts of a system.

4.4 Conclusion

UML has been widely used in the world of software engineering and its utilization in systems engineering was quite successful for many years. However, the need to have a tailored version of UML that meets the emerging requirements of today's systems engineering professionals has emerged. Consequently, the SysML model-ing language has been developed as a UML profile.

SysML is an essential enabler for model-based systems engineering as it allows a system's model to store design decisions at the center of the systems' development process. This offers an enhanced development paradigm that improves the develop-ment speed, communication, and efficiency. Currently, SysML is gaining increased popularity and many companies from various fields, such as defense, automotive, aerospace, medical devices and telecoms industries, are either already using SysML or are planning to switch to it in the near future [255]. This trend is catalyzed by two important factors. First, SysML is aligned with the ISO AP233 data interchange standard and it inherits the XMI interchange from its predecessor (UML). Second, an increased number of tools already offer support for the still young modeling language that is SysML.

4.3 Conclusion

Chapter 5
Verification, Validation, and Accreditation

There exist many definitions for the terms verification and validation, depending on the group concerned or the domain of application. In the SE world, the most widely used definitions of these terms are provided by the Defense Modeling and Simulation Organization (DMSO) [67, 168]. On the one hand, verification is defined as "the process of determining that a model implementation and its associated data accurately represent the developer's conceptual description and specifications" [67]. On the other hand, validation is defined as "the process of determining the degree to which a model and its associated data provide an accurate representation of the real world from the perspective of the model's intended use" [67].

Because the absence of a consensual definition for V&V raises ambiguities leading to incorrect use and misunderstanding [52, 94], the following illustrative example (inspired by Cook and Skinner [52]) strives to clarify exactly how we intend to use the two terms in this book. For instance, if a developer designs a system that complies with the specifications, but presents logical bugs, the system would fail the verification but successfully pass the validation. Conversely, if the system design is bug free but does not behave as expected, the model would fail the validation even though it passes the verification. In more common terms, the main purpose of V&V is to answer two key questions: (1) "Are we building the system right?" (verification) and (2) "Are we building the right system?" (validation).

At the start of system life cycle, the end users and the developers have to identify the system's needs then translate them into a set of specifications. Within this process, a collection of functional and non-functional requirements are identified. Functional requirements specify what functions the system must perform, whereas the non-functional ones define how the system must behave, in which case they might impose constraints upon the systems behavior such as performance, security, or reliability.

The collection of requirements represents a highly iterative process that ends when the requirements reach a level of maturity sufficient in order to initiate the development phase. Then, throughout the system development phase, a series of technical reviews and technical demonstrations are held in order to answer the questions related to V&V [254]. At the end of the V&V process, the results are inspected in order to make an official decision on whether to accept the system or not for a

M. Debbabi et al., *Verification and Validation in Systems Engineering*,
DOI 10.1007/978-3-642-15228-3_5, © Springer-Verlag Berlin Heidelberg 2010

specific usage. This is known as accreditation and it is commonly performed by an accreditation authority. Accreditation (also known as certification) is defined as "the official certification that a model, a simulation or a federation of models with simulations, and the associated data, is acceptable for use for a specific purpose" [67]. For example, a flight simulator to train pilots must be certified or accredited prior to its actual production/deployment.

Generally, the V&V process spans over the system's life cycle and its main objective is the assessment of a given system done by identifying possible defects. Moreover, it has to ensure that it conforms to the requirements predefined by the stakeholders (i.e., the solution solves the right problem) [115]. This process can be a major bottleneck in the development life cycle of any complex software or systems engineering product, since it can represent about 50–80% of the total design effort [116]. Additionally, many engineering solutions are required to meet a very high level of reliability, security, and performance, especially in safety-critical areas. The V&V techniques mainly include testing, simulation, model checking, and theorem proving. Despite the efforts toward improving the development process, CASE tools, testing and simulation techniques, significant systems, and software failures are still occurring. Some examples of these shortcomings include Intel's Pentium^{TM} microprocessor floating point division error in 1994 [124], the Ariane 5 crash in June 1996 [49], and the blackout in parts of the United States and Canada in August 2003 [249]. This highlights the relevance and importance of researching and developing more comprehensive and enhanced V&V approaches in the area of SE.

Hereafter, we present an overview of relevant V&V techniques, including testing and simulation, reference model equivalence, and theorem proving. Though broader in scope, the noteworthy methodologies involving model checking and program analysis are detailed as part of the presentation of the verification techniques V&V technique for object oriented designs. This is because object orientation readily allows for automating the procedure of generating the semantic model to be assessed by model checking or, respectively, the related code to be subjected to program analysis.

5.1 V&V Techniques Overview

According to the Recommended Practices Guide (RPG) [64] published by the Defense Modeling and Simulation Office (DMSO) in the United States Department of Defense, verification and validation techniques can be classified into the four following categories:

- Informal: These techniques rely solely on human interpretation and subjectivity, without any underlying mathematical formalism. Even though they are applied with structure and guidelines, and by following standard policies and procedures, these techniques are tedious and not always effective. Among this category, we can enumerate audit, desk checking (called also self-inspection), inspection, and review.

- Static: These are applied to assess the static model design and the source code (implementation), without executing the model with a machine. They aim at checking the structure of the model, the dataflow and control flow, the syntactical accuracy, and the consistency. Therefore, in order to provide a full V&V coverage, they have to be applied in conjunction with dynamic techniques defined in the next category. As examples, we can cite cause–effect graphing, control flow analysis, dataflow analysis, fault/failure analysis, interface analysis, syntax analysis, and traceability assessment.
- Dynamic: In contrast to the static techniques, dynamic ones are based on the machine execution of the model in order to evaluate its behavior. They do not simply examine the output of an execution but also watch the model as it is being executed. Consequently, the insertion of additional code into the model is needed to collect or monitor the behavior during its execution. Debugging, execution testing, functional testing, and visualization/animation are examples of dynamic techniques. Simulation turns out to be included in this category.
- Formal: These techniques are based on formal mathematical reasoning and proofs. Among them are model checking and theorem proving.

5.1.1 Inspection

Inspection is a coordinated activity that includes a meeting or a series of meetings directed by a moderator [22]. Therein, the design is reviewed and compared with standards. It is based on human judgment and so the success of such an activity depends on the depth of planning, organization, and data preparation preceding the inspection [94]. Unfortunately, this technique is based on documented procedures and policies that are somewhat difficult to manage. It also requires the training of the involved people. Furthermore, the increasing size and complexity of the design models make this task more tedious and sometimes downright impossible.

5.1.2 Testing

Testing consists of conducting specific actions in order to verify the operability, supportability, or performance capability of an item when subjected to real or simulated controlled conditions [230]. The results obtained are then compared with the anticipated or expected ones [171]. It often involves the use of special test equipment or instrumentation in order to obtain accurate quantitative data for analysis. Even though testing is well known and has been used extensively in software engineering, it allows only the late discovery of errors, and some types of errors may actually remain transparent.

5.1.3 Simulation

Simulation is, to a large extent, the workhorse of today's design verification and validation techniques. However, despite the increases in simulation speed and computer performance, simulation is hardly able to keep up with the rapidly increasing complexity of system design witnessed during the last decade. For example, the verification of the 64 bit Sun UltraSparc^{TM} processor required a large server clustering in order to simulate thousands of tests corresponding to a figure of 2 billion instruction cycles [159]. Moreover, the future prospects of simulation are not very encouraging since the number of simulation cycles required in the verification process is growing at an alarming rate (e.g., hundreds of billions of cycles are required for modern CPU-based systems, whereas only hundreds of million were needed a mere decade ago). An additional issue with simulation-based methodologies is that they require the time-consuming step of creating test inputs. The most commonly used test generation method relies primarily on the manual generation of test vectors. As the design size increases, the complexity and laborious nature of manual test generation make it highly impractical.

5.1.3.1 Random Test Generation

The huge search spaces associated with large designs have led to the adoption of random test generation. This approach has the typical undesired side effect of generating a very large number of inefficient test vectors, resulting in a very lengthy simulation even when directed or constraint-driven random test generation techniques are used. For example, many months of simulation using large "computer farms" consisting of hundreds of workstations are typically required to validate today's microprocessor designs.

Pure random test generation has severe limitations. Despite the large number of patterns generated, the effectiveness in detecting design flaws is rather limited. This is typically caused by a large percentage of the tests not being useful, especially in the absence of appropriate constraints. This situation can even result in generating invalid test vectors. To address the problems associated with pure random test generation, weighting or biasing is generally used to attempt to constrain the test generator to interesting areas of the design space with the intention of attempting to cover the "corner cases." The problem with this technique is that the design verification engineer may not always know or be able to determine the direction in which to guide the test generator.

5.1.3.2 Monitoring Internal Nodes

Because of the very low ratio of system ports to internal nodes and interfaces, the ability to observe the internal system logic is typically very low. It can usually be increased by using monitors and assertions. Monitors inspect and log the state of internal nodes or interface signals, while assertions are "self-checking" monitors that assert the truth of certain properties and trigger warning or error messages if these properties are violated. The use of monitors and assertions may help in boosting the coverage achieved during test generation. However, the construction of assertion checkers and monitors is still generally done manually and is particularly labor intensive. The emergence of libraries containing application-specific assertion monitors is providing some hope in alleviating this problem.

5.1.4 Reference Model Equivalence Checking

A widely used verification technique is reference model equivalence checking, which allows two behavioral models to be compared. In general, one of the two is taken as the reference model and represents the so-called golden model. Model equivalence checking can work well and is often used in the design process in order to verify the results of employing various design techniques and/or applying different optimization and tuning procedures. It verifies that the behavior of two models is the same for the exercised scenarios. Note that it does not actually verify that the design is bug free. Also, when a variance is encountered, the error diagnosis capability of the model equivalence checking tools is in most cases rather limited, making it difficult to determine the exact cause(s) of the difference.

5.1.5 Theorem Proving

Theorem proving involves verifying the truth of mathematical theorems that are postulated or inferred throughout the design using a formal specification language [214]. The procedure followed when proving such theorems usually involves two main components, namely a proof checker and an inference engine. However, while the former can be completely automated in most cases, the latter may require occasional human guidance, thus impeding the automation of the whole process. Moreover, there may be rare cases where, due to the formalism involved (e.g., hidden circular references leading to a logical paradox), a given theorem conjecture cannot be neither proven nor disproven (refuted). The aforementioned issues represent some of the main reasons why presently is not currently widely adopted for performing verification and validation.

5.2   Verification Techniques for Object-Oriented Design

Object-oriented design is characterized by its corresponding structural and behavioral perspectives. Thus, when analyzing a given design, both perspectives have to be assessed with appropriate techniques. Moreover, object-oriented design models exhibit specific features, such as modularity, hierarchical structure, inheritance, encapsulation. These features are reflected in various related attributes such as complexity, understandability, reusability, maintainability. Consequently, based on the evaluation of the aforementioned attributes, one can determine the quality of an object-oriented system design.

In this setting, empirical methodologies, such as those involving software metrics, can help assess the quality of the structural architecture of the design. In addition, complementary automatic verification techniques based on formal methods such as model checking can achieve a comprehensive behavioral assessment of the model (or the components thereof) against a set of specification properties. These specifications capture the intended behavior of the system. However, such exhaustive techniques are generally accompanied by corresponding scalability shortcomings (e.g., state explosion).

In this context, techniques like program analysis, particularly dataflow and control flow analysis, have the potential to address, among other things, some of the scalability issues. In turn, this renders the model-checking procedure more efficient.

5.2.1 Design Perspectives

The process of system modelling typically involves an analysis phase followed by a subsequent design phase. In the analysis phase, the key aspects are represented by questions such as "What is the problem space? What are the envisioned components and how are they related to each other? What are the attributes and the operations of the components and how are they interacting in order to accomplish the intended result? etc." In this context, the design of a system usually involves a structural representation of the components and their relations, along with a behavioral specification that captures the system dynamics.

Consequently, when modeling a system using languages like UML, the design can be viewed generally from two main design perspectives, namely the structural description and the exhibited behavior. The structural perspective can be captured in a visual, diagrammatic notation by specifying the distinctive attributes of the system and its components. Alongside, we can specify their respective relations with respect to each other. The behavioral perspective can be encoded by appropriate diagrams that capture the dynamics of various state parameters in the system or the underlying components. Furthermore, such diagrams must also reflect different internal or external interactions of the system. Both perspectives have an accompanying complexity degree that can be the subject of different analysis and assessment processes. Moreover, structural analysis can be used in order to evaluate numerous quality attributes and may be used as a feedback in many tuning and optimization mechanisms. In contrast, the behavioral analysis is usually much more demanding and involves intense rigor and preciseness. As point in fact, it is well known that a relatively short encoding of a behavioral model may have a very complex associated dynamics as is the case with some forms of automata (e.g., cellular automata).

5.2.2 Software Engineering Techniques

A significant number of metrics from the software engineering field [143, 167] are suitable for assessing the quality attributes of various structural design models. Certain literature supports the usefulness of metrics in systems engineering. For instance, Tugwell et al. [236] outline the importance of metrics in systems engineering, especially in relation to complexity measurement. Therefore, a potential synergy can be achieved by applying the metric concept to behavioral specifications. Accordingly, in addition to applying metrics on the structural diagrams such as class diagrams, they can also be applied on the semantic model derived from different behavioral diagrams. For example, the cyclomatic complexity and the length of critical path can be applied on semantic models as various forms of automata. Thus, the assessment of design's quality can combine both the static and the dynamic perspectives.

5.2.3 Formal Verification Techniques

Formal verification techniques, such as model checking, establish a solid confidence in a reliable V&V process. Model checking is an automated and comprehensive verification technique that can be used to verify whether the properties specified for a given design or its components are satisfied for all legal design inputs. Temporal logics allow the users to express the properties of the system over various trajectories (state paths). Model checking is primarily useful in verifying the control parts of a system, which are often the critical areas of concern. Model checking is generally impractical for a thorough dataflow analysis, since it suffers from the well-known state explosion problem. In a worst-case scenario, the state space of the design that must be explored can grow exponentially with the number of state variables. Model checking can also be performed on the design components, but in this case it requires the specification of precise interfaces for those components in order for only legal inputs to be considered. Note that a potential issue in this case consists in the fact that, in practice, the interface specifications of the design component modules are subject to change during the design process.

Model checking can be fully automated for design verification. In fact, it has been successfully used in the verification of real applications, including digital circuits, communication protocols and digital controllers. It yields results much more quickly than theorem proving [139]. In order to use it, one first has to map the design to a formal model that is accepted by the model checker (semantic model, which is usually some sort of a transition system). Second, one needs to express, in temporal logic formulas, the properties (derived from the requirements) that the design must satisfy. Then, by providing these two ingredients, the model checker exhaustively explores the state space of the transition system during the verification stage and checks automatically whether or not the specifications hold. One of the benefits of many model checkers (e.g., SPIN [109], SMV [157], and NuSMV [45]) is that, if a specification is violated, a counterexample is produced.

In the absence of tools that can be used to simplify the specification of design properties, model-checking technique is heavily dependent on experienced users that are able to properly encode the properties of the design or its components into temporal logic formulas. In this respect, the need to rely on experienced design engineers with strong background in temporal logics has restricted the adoption of this technology. However, various forms of macro-notation can be used to simplify the specification of properties.

An additional issue consists of the limited ability to find a well-suited metric that can be used to evaluate the design property coverage and, thus, it is relatively difficult to determine if all design properties have been specified and verified. Notwithstanding, this issue may be circumvented by performing appropriate requirements analysis especially in the cases where it is possible to clearly express design model requirements by using specific diagrams belonging to modelling languages like UML or SysML.

5.2.4 Program Analysis Techniques

Program analysis techniques [170] are used to analyze software systems in order to collect or infer specific information about them to evaluate and verify system properties such as data dependencies, control dependencies, invariants, anomalous behaviors, reliability, and compliance with certain specifications. The gathered information is useful for various software engineering activities, such as testing, fault localization, and program understanding. There are two approaches in program analysis techniques, namely static and dynamic analysis. Static analysis is performed before program execution, while dynamic analysis focuses on a specific execution. The former is mainly used to determine the static aspects of a program and it can be used to check whether the implementation complies with the specifications. The latter, although less reliable, can achieve greater precision in showing the presence of errors by dynamically verifying the behavior of a program on a finite set of possible executions selected from a possibly infinite domain. Static program analysis techniques can also be used in order to slice (decompose) a program or a transition system into independent parts that can be then analyzed separately.

The efficiency and accuracy of the analysis performed by static analyzers vary from a limited scope, wherein only individual statements and declarations are considered, to those that include the complete source code of a program in their analysis. The resulting information obtained from the analysis may vary from highlighting possible coding errors to rigorous methods that prove properties about a given program. In a broader sense, software metrics and reverse engineering can also be considered in the field of static analysis. A static code analyzer tool automates the code inspection process and offers all kinds of intrinsic quality information to the developer. Automated code inspection enables the automation of many tasks that are usually carried out during the code reading and reviewing sessions in order to check the source code against a coding standard. The automation procedure implies that certain parts of the inspections will be done by means of a tool as part of the software development process. A direct result of this approach is that the time required to perform the code reviewing is decreased. Furthermore, because of the automation, all codes can be subjected to inspection. Such a level of coverage is practically never reached with manual inspections. For this purpose, an essential requirement of the static analyzer is its ability to parse and "understand" the target source code. In this respect, it is important to mention that the term "static analysis" is usually applied to the analysis performed by an automated tool, while human analysis is called "program understanding" or "program comprehension."

5.3 V&V of Systems Engineering Design Models

In this section we review the V&V approaches targeting SE design models according to their usability, reliability, automation, rigor, thoroughness, and scalability.

A large number of initiatives conducting research in the V&V of software engineering design models are focusing on designs expressed in UML 1.x [29, 65, 80, 135, 155, 212]. Recently, there has been a greater interest in UML 2.x design models, such as in [15, 79, 93, 98]. Aside from initiatives proposing monolithic approaches (using a single technique), other research initiatives propose a cumulative approach based on model checking and theorem proving [131] or model checking and simulation [173, 174].

Kim and Carrington [131] propose a V&V framework for UML 1.0 that integrates multiple formalisms such as the Symbolic Analysis Laboratory (SAL) [18], CSP, and Higher Order Logic (HOL) [162] via the object-oriented specification language Object-Z [221]. However, a developer's intervention is required in order to choose the formalism to be applied, and this constitutes a major inconvenience. The initiatives [173, 174] emerged in the context of the *IST Omega* project.[1] Ober et al. [174] describe the application of model-checking and simulation techniques in order to validate the design models expressed in the *Omega* UML profile. This is achieved by mapping the design to a model of communicating extended timed automata in IF [31] format (an intermediate representation for asynchronous timed systems developed at *Verimag*). Properties to be verified are expressed in a formalism called UML observers. In [173], Ober et al. present a case study related to the validation of the control software of the Ariane-5 launcher. The experiment is done on a representative subset of the system, in which both functional and architectural aspects are modeled using *Omega* UML 1.x profile. The IFx, a toolset built on top of the IF environment, is used for the V&V of both functional and scheduling-related requirements using both simulation and model-checking functionalities.

SysML is relatively young and thus there are still very few initiatives concerned with the V&V of SysML design models [39, 112, 125, 197, 250, 253]. Most of the proposals on SysML are rather concerned with the use of simulation, either directly or via Petri net formalism. As earlier on, when systems engineers adopted the UML modeling language for describing and documenting their design models, UML 2.x turns out to be a more adequate version than the previous ones [106]. However,

---

[1] http://www-omega.imag.fr/

along with more recent efforts on the V&V of design models targeting UML 2.x and SysML, some relevant ones on UML 1.x are also worthy of mention.

A large body of research proposals target the analysis of UML-based design models. Various research works focus on the analysis of UML diagrams from consistency and data integrity viewpoints. The consistency issue is related to the fact that various artifacts representing different aspects of the system should be properly related to each other in order to form a consistent description of the developed system. Although these aspects are important, the present material focuses on an equally important issue: the verification of the conformance of design models to their stated requirements. Some of the initiatives propose V&V approaches that jointly consider a set of diagrams, whereas the majority focus on a single diagram and particularly on a subset of its semantics. For example, the state machine diagrams have gained significant attention. In addition, a single V&V technique is generally proposed (e.g., automatic formal verification, theorem proving, or simulation). Furthermore, some initiatives propose a formalization of the semantics of a considered diagram, which is subjected to formal verification. However, other proposals prefer a direct mapping into the specification language of a particular verification tool.

Some of the works [51, 54] propose the simulation of UML design models for performance analysis while others [110, 133, 211] target model execution and debugging. For instance, Hu and Shatz [110] propose to convert UML statecharts into Colored Petri Nets (CPN). Collaboration diagrams are used for connecting different model objects, so one obtains a single CPN of the whole system. The design/CPN tool is then used to perform simulation. Sano et al. [211] propose a mechanism where model simulation is performed on four behavioral diagrams, namely statechart, activity, collaboration, and sequence diagrams.

Though the community interest is shifting toward UML 2.0, also worthy of mention are other related works [135, 141, 161] that address UML 1.x statecharts (renamed to state machines in UML 2.0). Latella et al. [141] as well as Mikk et al. [161] propose a translation of subsets of UML statecharts into SPIN/PROMELA [109] using an operational semantics as described in [142]. That approach consists of translating the statechart into an extended hierarchical automaton (EHA). The latter is then modeled into PROMELA and subjected to model checking. Some proposals concentrate only on ascribing a formal semantics to the selected UML diagram.

An extensive survey on the formal semantics of UML state machine can be found in Crane and Dingel [57]. Of note, Fecher et al. [81] present an attempt to define a structured operational semantics for UML 2.0 state machine. Similarly, Zhan and Miao [260] propose a formalization of its semantics using the Z language. This allows the transformation of the diagram into the corresponding flattened regular expression (FREE) state model that is used to identify inconsistency and incompleteness and also to generate test cases. However, pseudostates such as fork/join and history are not considered. Gnesi and Mazzanti [93] provide an interpretation of a set of communicating UML 2.0 state machine diagrams in terms of doubly labeled transition system (L^2TS). The state/event-based temporal logic μUCTL [91] is used for the description of the dynamic properties to be verified. A prototype environment is developed around the UMC on-the-fly model checker [92].

Some researchers, such as van der Aalst [247] and Ellis and Nutt [76] propose Petri nets as the formalism for capturing activity diagrams semantics. Thus, activity diagrams for workflow systems are described using interval-timed colored Petri nets [126], which are Petri nets [206] extended with colored tokens required to model data and timing intervals for transitions. Eshuis [78] uses a mapping of activity diagrams to equivalent activity hypergraphs by flattening the structure of the former. The activity hypergraph of a given diagram is then mapped to a clocked labeled Kripke structure (CLKS), which is an extension of Kripke systems with real variables. Vitolins and Kalnins [251] consider a subset of the activity diagram that is suitable for business process modeling. The semantics is based on the token flow methodology that employs the concept of activity diagram virtual machine. In the context of V&V, the authors consider the defined virtual machine as a basis for UML activity diagram simulation engines.

Guelfi and Mammar [98] propose to verify UML activity diagrams extended with timed characteristics. This is based on the translation of activity diagrams into PROMELA code, the input language of the SPIN model checker [109]. Eshuis [79] proposes two translations of UML activity diagrams into finite state machines which are input to the NuSMV model checker [46]. Both translation approaches are inspired by statechart semantics. The first is a requirement-level translation and the second is an implementation-level translation. The latter is inspired by the OMG statechart semantics. The resulting models are used in model-checking data integrity constraints in activity diagrams and in a set of class diagrams specifying the manipulated data. Activity diagrams are first transformed into activity hypergraphs through transformation rules. The translation rules are then defined for activity hypergraphs resulting in the NuSMV code. However, that activity semantics excludes multiple instances of activity nodes. Beato et al. [15] propose the verification of UML design models consisting of state machine and activity diagrams by means of formal verification techniques using the symbolic model verifier (SMV) [158]. The diagrams are encoded into the SMV specification language via the XML metadata interchange (XMI) format. Mokhati et al. [166] propose the translation of UML 2.0 design models consisting of class, state machine, and communication diagrams into Maude language [152]. Properties expressed using linear temporal logic (LTL) [248] are verified on the resulting models using Maude's integrated model checker. Only basic state machine and communication diagrams with the most common features are considered. Xu et al. [259] propose an operational semantics for UML 2.0 activity diagrams by transforming it into communicating sequential processes (CSP) [105]. The resulting CSP model is then used for analysis with the model-checker FDR. Kaliappan et al. [129] propose the conversion of UML state machines into PROMELA code and mapping sequence diagrams into temporal properties for the verification of communication protocols using SPIN model checker [109]. Engels et al. [77] propose the dynamic meta modeling (DMM) technique, which uses graph transformation techniques to define and analyze the semantics of UML activity diagrams based on its metamodel. The considered activity diagrams are limited to workflow modeling, thus imposing some restrictions on their expressiveness and their semantics. This is because workflows have to adhere to specific syntactic and semantic requirements. DMM is used to generate the transition systems underlying the semantic model of activity diagrams. The analysis is limited to the verification of the soundness property of workflows. The latter is expressed using CTL [48] temporal logic and then inputs into the graphs for object-oriented verification (GROOVE) tool [95] in order to apply model checking over the generated transition systems.

Concerning sequence diagrams, Grosu and Smolka [97] propose non-deterministic finite automata as their semantic model. A given diagram is translated into a hierarchical automaton and both safety and liveness Büchi automata are derived from it. These automata are subsequently used to define a compositional notion of refinement of UML 2.0 sequence diagrams. Li et al. [145] define a static semantics for UML interaction diagrams to support the well-formedness verification of the interaction diagrams. The dynamic semantics is interpreted as a trace-based terminated CSP process that is used to capture the finite sequence of message calls. Cengarle and Knapp [40] propose a trace-based semantics for UML 2.0 interactions. Störrle [223] presents a partial-order semantics for time-constrained interaction diagrams. Korenblat and Priami [137] present a formalization of sequence diagrams based on the π-calculus [164]. The state machine diagrams of the interacting objects are considered in order to identify feasible occurrence of sequences of messages. Accordingly, objects in a sequence diagram are modeled as π-calculus [164] processes and the exchanged messages as communications among these processes. The semantics of sequence diagram is defined based on the structured operational semantics of π-calculus [164]. The corresponding semantic model is a labeled transition system (LTS) that is used to generate the input of the model checker.

As far as SysML is concerned, Viehl et al. [250] present an approach based on the analysis and simulation applied to a system-on-chip (SoC) design specified using UML 2.0/SysML. Time-annotated sequence diagrams, together with UML structured classes/SysML assemblies, are considered for describing the system architecture. However, the SysML version considered therein differs from the one standardized by the OMG. Huang et al. [112] propose to apply simulation based on a mapping of SysML models into their corresponding simulation metamodels. The latter is used to generate the simulation model. Similarly, Paredis and Johnson [197] propose to apply a graph transformation approach to map the structural descriptions of a system into the corresponding simulation models. Wang and Dagli [253] propose the translation of mainly SysML sequence diagrams and partly activity and block definition diagrams into colored Petri nets (CPNs). The resulting CPNs represent executable models that are subjected to static and dynamic analysis (simulation). The behavior obtained by simulation is generated in the form of message sequence Charts (MSC), which are compared to sequence diagrams. This verification is based on the visual comparison of the simulated behavior against the intended behavior. Moreover, the assessment of non-functional requirements is not considered. Carneiro et al. [39] consider SysML state machine diagrams annotated with MARTE profile [189], a UML profile for model-driven development of real-time and embedded systems. This diagram is mapped manually into timed Petri nets with energy constraints (ETPN) to estimate energy consumption and execution time for embedded real-time systems. The analysis is performed using a simulation tool for timed Petri nets. Jarraya et al. [125] consider the mapping of a synchronous version of time-annotated SysML activity diagrams into discrete-time Markov chains (DTMC). The latter model is input to the probabilistic model-checker PRISM for the assessment of functional and non-functional properties.

We focus hereafter on the works that address performance analysis of activity diagrams. In the literature, there are three major performance analysis techniques: analytical, simulative, and numerical [103]. Among various performance models, we can distinguish four classes of performance models that can be distinguished: queueing networks (QN) [26], stochastic Petri nets (SPN) [99], Markov chains (MC) [26], and stochastic process algebras (SPA) [103].

Queueing networks (QN) are applied to model and analyze resource-sharing systems. This model is generally analyzed using simulation and analytical methods. There are two classes within the family of queuing networks: deterministic and probabilistic. Among the initiatives targeting the analysis of design models (including UML/SysML) using deterministic models, Wandeler et al. [252] apply modular performance analysis based on the real-time calculus and use annotated sequence diagrams. In the context of probabilistic QN, Refs. [13, 53, 199] address performance modeling and analysis of UML 1.x design models. Cortellessa and Mirandola [53] propose extended queueing network (EQN) for UML 1.x sequence, deployment and use case diagrams. Layered queueing network (LQN) is proposed by Petriu and Shen [199] as the performance model for UML 1.3 activity and deployment diagrams. The derivation is based on graph-grammar transformations that are notoriously complex, requiring a large number of transformation rules. The time annotations are based on the UML SPT profile [176]. Balsamo and Marzolla [13] target UML 1.x use case, activity, and deployment diagrams annotated according to the UML SPT profile. These diagrams are transformed into multi-chain and multi-class QN models; these impose restrictions on the design. Specifically, activity diagrams cannot contain forks and joins, otherwise the obtained QN can only have an approximate solution [26].

Various research proposals such as [36, 132, 149, 160, 235] consider stochastic Petri net (SPN) models for performance modeling and analysis. King and Pooley [132] propose generalized stochastic Petri nets (GSPN) as performance model for combined UML 1.x collaboration and statechart diagrams. Numerical evaluations of the derived Petri net are performed in order to approximately evaluate the performance. López-Grao et al. [149] present a prototype tool for performance analysis of UML 1.4 sequence and activity diagrams based on the labeled generalized stochastic Petri nets (LGSPN). Along the same lines, Trowitzsch et al. [235] present the derivation of stochastic Petri nets (SPNs) from a restricted version of UML 2.0 state machines annotated with the SPT profile.

Alternatively, stochastic process algebras (SPA) are also extensively used for performance modeling of UML design models [17, 37, 38, 146, 202, 228, 233, 234]. Pooley [202] considers a systematic transformation of collaboration and statechart diagrams into the performance evaluation process algebra (PEPA). Canevet et al. [38] describe a PEPA-based methodology and a toolset for extracting performance measurements from UML 1.x statechart and collaboration diagrams. The state space generated by the PEPA workbench is used to derive the corresponding Continuous-Time Markov Chain (CTMC). In a subsequent work, Canevet et al. [37] present an approach for the analysis of UML 2.0 activity diagrams using PEPA. A mapping from activity to PEPA net model is provided, although it doesn't consider join nodes. Tribastone and Gilmore propose a mapping of UML activity diagrams [233] and UML sequence diagrams [234] annotated with MARTE [189] into the stochastic process algebra PEPA. Another type of process algebra is proposed by Lindemann et al. [146]: the generalized semi-Markov process (GSMP). The UML 1.x state machine and activity diagrams are addressed. Trigger events with deterministic or exponentially distributed delays are proposed for the analysis of timing in UML state diagrams and activity diagrams. Bennett and Field [17] propose the application of performance engineering to UML diagrams annotated using the SPT UML profile. System behavior scenarios are translated into the stochastic finite state processes (FSP). Stochastic FSP are analyzed using a discrete-event simulation tool. However, no algorithm is provided for the inner workings of the approach. Tabuchi et al. [228] propose a mapping of UML 2.0 activity diagrams annotated with SPT profile into interactive Markov chains (IMC) intended for performance analysis. Some features in activity diagrams are not considered, such as guards on decision nodes and probabilistic decisions. The duration of actions is expressed using a negative-exponential distribution of the delay. More recently, Gallotti et al. [87] focus on model-based analysis of service compositions by proposing the assessment of their corresponding non-functional quality attributes, namely performance and reliability. The high-level description of the service composition, given in terms of activity diagrams, is employed to derive stochastic models (DTMC, MDP, or CTMC) according to the verification purpose and the characteristics of the activity diagram. The probabilistic model-checker PRISM is used for the actual verification. However, there is neither a clear explanation of the translation steps nor a PRISM model example that illustrates the approach.

With respect to program analysis techniques for the V&V of SE design models, Garousi et al. [88] consider a model-based control flow analysis (CFA) for UML 2.0 sequence diagrams. To the best of our knowledge, this is the one and only work that can be highlighted in this research direction.

5.4 Tool Support

In this section, we focus on describing the most visible formal verification environments targeting UML models and static analyzers.

5.4.1 Formal Verification Environments

A surge of interest has been expressed in the application of model checking to the verification and validation of UML models. In this context, various tools emerged as a result of various research activities including [29, 65, 80, 135, 141, 155, 161, 212] for UML 1.x and [15, 77, 79, 93, 98, 129, 166, 258] for UML 2.x. Therein, a number of V&V framework tools are proposed such as TABU [15], HIDE [29], PRIDE [155], HUGO [212], Hugo-RT [135], and VIATRA [58]. Below, we detail some of the most relevant ones.

TABU (tool for the active behavior of UML) [15] is a tool that enables the automatic verification of reactive systems behavior modeled by state machine and activity diagrams by means of formal method techniques using the symbolic model verifier (SMV [158]) model checker. The UML version is not clearly specified but it seems to be a subset of UML 2.0. The automatic transformation performed by the tool encodes the diagrams into the SMV specification language via the XML metadata interchange (XMI) format.

Bondavalli et al. [28] express the increasing need for the integration of validation techniques and cite two projects (HIDE and GUARDS) that have been carried out with the objective to integrate a set of validation techniques into a common framework. The most relevant to our work is the HIDE (high-level integrated design environment for dependability) tool [29]. It is an approach for an integrated validation environment within a European project (*ESPRIT 27493*) based on formal verification, quantitative and timeliness analysis. Given the systems design described in UML 1.x, the overall methodology is based on two translations [27]. The first is a translation of UML structural diagrams (use case, class, object, and deployment diagrams) into timed and generalized stochastic Petri nets for dependability assessment using PANDA, a Petri net analysis tool. The second translation concerns UML statechart diagrams, which are mapped into Kripke structures for formal verification of functional properties. The resulting Kripke structure of a diagram, along with the requirements formally expressed, is used as input to the model-checker SPIN [109] to carry out the assessment of the design. Other parts of the dynamic model, mainly sequence and activity diagrams, are translated to generalized stochastic Petri nets (GSPN).

With the same goal of integrating methods for validation of design, a relatively recent research project named PRIDE [155] has been developed. It aims principally at developing a software development environment based on UML 1.4. The latter integrates a formal V&V technique supported by SPIN model checker and the quantitative dependability attributes assessment. The project concentrates essentially on dependable systems and it is an extension of an already existing environment dedicated to the modeling of hard real-time (HRT) systems using UML (HRT-UML). To use the model checker, the collection of statecharts representing a specific view of the system design is converted into a PROMELA model (the SPIN input language). The quantitative validation of system dependability attributes is based on building a dependability model, namely stochastic activity networks (SAN) [210], from a structural UML diagram. The latter provides a representation of the dependability characteristics and permits analysis of the dependability measurements of a system based on its design. Both HIDE and PRIDE are based on the same theoretical background concerning the semantic model of statechart published in [142]. However, PRIDE extends it, mainly by offering the possibility of using object state variables.

Schäfer et al. [212] present HUGO, a prototype tool for the automatic verification of UML 1.x state machines and collaboration diagrams. More precisely, the aim is to use the model-checker SPIN to verify that the interactions defined in the collaboration diagrams are actually realized by the state machines. The state machine diagrams are expressed in PROMELA and the properties represented in collaborations are expressed as a set of Büchi automata. In the same vein, Knapp et al. [135] present a prototype tool, HUGO/RT, for the automatic verification of a subset of timed state machines and time-annotated collaboration UML 1.x diagrams. It is an extension of the HUGO tool [212], which targets untimed UML state machines. Knapp et al. [135] use the model-checker UPPAAL to verify state machine diagrams (compiled to timed automata) against the properties described in the collaboration diagrams (compiled to observer-timed automaton).

5.4.2 Static Analyzers

Many innovations in modern computer programming, including object orientation and its related concepts such as type classes, inheritance, and the like are basically elaborated forms of abstraction. Accordingly, the more complexity we have in program behavior, the more the need for improved abstractions will continue to grow. However, abstractions may induce slower execution, larger memory footprint, and the execution side effects. In this respect, compiler optimizations can oftentimes avoid these disadvantages. In addition, static analyzers are borrowing core concepts and practices from compiler technology in order to "see" through the abstraction layers and infer a broad range of possible behaviors of interest, ranging from memory leaks to security violations. In the following we present a number of relevant static analyzers along with their features and potential benefits.

ASTRÉE (Analyseur Statique de logiciels Temps Réel Embarqués – Real-time Embedded Software Static Analyzer) [55] is a static program analyzer developed at the Laboratoire d'Informatique de l'École Normale Supérieure (LIENS). Its function is to prove the absence of run-time errors (RTE) in programs written in C. It achieved a number of remarkable results. In November 2003, it proved automatically the absence of any RTE in the primary flight control software of the Airbus A340 fly-by-wire system, a program containing 132,000 lines of C code. Moreover, in January 2004, it was extended to analyze the electric flight control codes then in the development and testing of the A380 series. Also, in April 2008, ASTRÉE was able to prove automatically the absence of any RTE in a C version of the automatic docking software of the European Space Agency (ESA) Jules Vernes Automated Transfer Vehicle (ATV).

Polyspace Technologies (operated now as a subsidiary of The MathWorks Inc.) offers the system code verification toolkit Polyspace [231] that can be used to verify run-time errors in applications written in C, C++, and ADA code. Before compilation and execution, it can detect and mathematically prove the absence of different classes of RTEs that may create vulnerabilities during the execution. The tool can help developers improve the code quality. Moreover, it can be used to verify the code against a set of coding rules. The product is used in various industrial domains, such as aerospace and defense, biotech industries, automotive, pharmaceutical, communications, and semiconductor industries.

Fortify Static Code Analyzer (SCA) [83] helps developers analyze source code for security vulnerabilities during the software development cycle. SCA reveals static vulnerabilities and verifies other vulnerabilities found during testing and production. With numerous rules of more than 200 vulnerability categories, this analyzer reviews the possible paths that an application may consider. In a developer-centric mode, Fortify-SCA supports a large variety of development environments and a wide range of programming languages including C/C++, .NET, Java, JSP, ASP.NET, ColdFusion, "Classic" ASP, PHP, VB6, VBScript, JavaScript, PL/SQL, T-SQL, python, COBOL. Integration in IDEs is facilitated and may produce output compliant with other dynamic executable and real-time analyzers. Rough Auditing Tool for Security (RATS)[2] is an automated code review tool initiated by Secure Software Inc., who was later acquired by Fortify Software Inc. It can perform a rough analysis of programs written in the following languages: C, C++, Perl, PHP, and Python. RATS is able to detect common security-related programming errors such as buffer overflows and race conditions.

Klocwork Truepath (KT) [134] from Kolcwork is an accurate and efficient tool for finding critical security vulnerabilities, quality defects, and architectural issues. It uses a variety of approaches to infer the run-time behavior of the application before the actual execution. The tool includes an advanced symbolic logic engine to establish the software's behavior. The analyzer is able to detect memory and resource leaks, incorrect memory de-allocation, concurrency violations, usage of uninitialized data, etc. From the code security perspective, it also verifies SQL injection, path injection, information leakage, weak encryption, buffer overflows, etc. Furthermore, KT can also reveal dead or unreachable code, unused function parameters, and local variables. The tool is used by more than 650 organizations for bug identification as well as for verifying the code's security and quality.

HP Code Advisor [102] is a static analysis tool for programs written in C and C++. It can report various programming errors found in the source code. It stores the diagnosed information in a database and with the built-in knowledge of system APIs looks deep into the code and provides meaningful feedback. HP Code Advisor can also detect a wide range of potential problems, including memory leaks, used after free, double free, array/buffer out of bounds access, illegal pointer access, un-initialized variables, unused variables, format string checks, suspicious conversion and casting, as well as out of range operations.

PMD[3] is a rule-set-based static analysis tool for Java source code. It can identify potential problems such as empty try/catch/finally/switch blocks, unused local variables, parameters and private methods, empty if/while statements, overcomplicated

---

[2] http://www.fortify.com/security-resources/rats.jsp

[3] http://pmd.sourceforge.net/

expressions, unnecessary if statements, and for loops transformable to while loops. Moreover, it can detect suboptimal code, wasteful string usage, classes with high cyclomatic complexity measurements, as well as duplicate code.

ChecKing [196] is a web application developed by Optimyth created for monitoring the quality of the software during the development process. The automated analysis includes the use of measurements obtained during the software development process (activity, requirements, defects, and changes) as well as analyzable software elements such as project documentation, source code, test scripts, build scripts.

Coverity is a software vendor that provides a static analysis tool named Prevent [56]. It can be used to perform static analysis on C, C++, and Java source code. It is based on the Stanford Checker which uses model checking to verify source correctness. One of the most notable successes of Prevent was its deployment under a U.S. Department of Homeland Security contract, who is using it to examine over 150 open-source applications for bugs. In March 2007, it was announced that its use contributed to the detection and subsequent correction of a figure of over 6000 bugs spanning across 53 projects.

The DMS Software Reengineering Toolkit [218] is a program analysis toolkit provided by Semantic Designs. It allows for the automation and customization of source code program analysis, modification, translation, or generation of software systems that are required to mix many programming languages in the context of large-scale software systems. Moreover, it has predefined language front ends for many languages (C, C++, Java, Verilog, VHDL, COBOL, etc.) allowing for quick customization.

Scitools' Understand [215] is a commercial static code analyzer that is primarily used in the field of reverse engineering, automatic documentation, and code metrics calculation for complex projects. It provides an IDE designed to help in the maintenance and understanding of old and new code. This is done by using detailed cross-references in conjunction with a variety of graphical views. Understand can parse the following languages: Ada, FORTRAN, Jovial, Pascal, K&R C, ANSI C, C++, Delphi, Java, and VHDL.

SofCheck's Inspector [222] is a static analysis tool targeting Java and Ada. It can statically determine and document the pre-conditions and post-conditions of every method or subprogram that it inspects. It can then use that information to identify logical flaws, race conditions, and redundant code.

5.5 Conclusion

The complexity and intricacy of modern system design requires effective resources for V&V. In this chapter, various approaches and relevant techniques have been presented alongside the state of the art in the verification and validation research areas targeting UML and SysML design models. The laborious nature of V&V stems from its broad scope, one that has to encompass the system's overall development life cycle. Moreover, it requires elaborate approaches as it targets the absence of logical bugs and concurrently ensures conformance to the requirements. In addition, a subsequent accreditation process is usually performed in order to officially certify that a proposed system meets the established acceptability criteria. With that in mind, we have also presented various tools for formal verification and program analysis that can fulfill different aspects of V&V pursuing high-quality system design and development.

Chapter 6
Automatic Approach for Synergistic Verification and Validation

Modeling languages, such as UML 2.x and SysML, support model-based systems engineering. They are commonly used to specify, visualize, store, document, and exchange design models. Generally, they contain all the syntactic, semantic, and presentation information regarding a given application domain. A model is a representation of the system that is used to compile the requirements in order to create executable specifications. These specifications model the system at a high level of abstraction and include all the information needed to specify the software or hardware implementation. Specific diagrams are used to capture some of the system's important aspects:

- **Requirements**, which are a description of what a system should do. They are captured by either using SysML requirement diagrams or using UML 2.0 sequence and use case diagrams.
- **Interface**, which identifies the shared boundaries of the different components of the system, whereby the information is passed. This aspect is shown using UML 2.0 class and composite structure diagrams and SysML block definition and internal block diagrams.
- **Structure**, which is shown as UML class and composite structure diagrams and SysML block definition and internal block diagrams.
- **Control**, which determines the order in which actions, states, events, and/or processes are arranged. It is captured using UML 2.x and SysML state machine, activity, and sequence diagrams.
- **Concurrency**, which is an aspect that identifies how activities, events, and processes are composed (sequence, branching, alternative, parallel composition, etc.). It is specified using UML/SysML sequence and activity diagrams.
- **Time**: It is captured by UML timing diagrams, which provide a visual representation of objects changing their states and interacting over time. UML/SysML sequence diagrams can also be used to capture the interaction between systems' entities over time using messages sending and receiving.
- **Performance**: It is the total effectiveness of the system. It relates to the timeliness aspects of how systems behave. This includes different types of quality of service characteristics, such as latency and throughput. Timing diagrams, sequence diagrams, and time-annotated activity diagrams can be used in order to

M. Debbabi et al., *Verification and Validation in Systems Engineering*,
DOI 10.1007/978-3-642-15228-3_6, © Springer-Verlag Berlin Heidelberg 2010

express performance aspects. Other performance aspects can be modeled using UML/SysML models in conjunction with specific UML profiles [176, 189].

Integrating V&V during the design phase allows one to continuously identify and correct errors, thus gain confidence in the system. With fewer errors to fix, costs at the maintenance phase are significantly reduced. Additionally, correcting errors before the actual realization of the system enables the reduction of project failure risks that occur while engineering complex systems. Furthermore, it improves the quality of systems and shortens the time to market. Once the model becomes a verified and validated executable specification, engineers can automatically generate code from the model for the purpose of prototyping and deployment. Similar to the model, the code can also be tested and verified at any point. Discovered errors can easily be corrected on the model, the code then being regenerated, all the while maintaining specification integrity between the model and its corresponding code.

In this chapter, we address the issue of model-based verification and validation of systems engineering design models expressed using UML/SysML. The main objectives are to assess the design from its structural and behavioral perspectives and to enable a qualitative as well as a quantitative appraisal of its conformance with respect to its requirements and a set of desired properties. We also elaborate a synergistic methodology and present some edifying results that justify this envisioned approach. The foundations of this approach rely on the synergistic integration of three well-established techniques: automatic formal verification, program analysis, and software engineering quantitative methods.

6.1 Synergistic Verification and Validation Methodology

The concept behind our methodology is to enable the verification and validation of more than one aspect of the system's design. A software or system design model is fully characterized by its structural and behavioral perspectives. The analysis of both views is crucial for obtaining high-quality product. Furthermore, combining quantitative and qualitative assessment techniques provides more benefits than applying only one or the other.

In the field of verification of systems and software, we propose three well-established techniques for building our V&V methodology. On the one hand, automatic formal verification techniques, namely model checking, are reported to be a successful approach to the verification of the behavior of real-life software and hardware applications. Such application domains include, among many others, digital circuits, communication protocols, and digital controllers. In addition to being fully automated formal verification techniques and capable of thoroughly exploring the state space of the system searching for potential errors, model checkers are also generally capable of generating counterexamples for failed properties. Also, their counterparts in the stochastic world, namely probabilistic model checkers, are widely applied to quantitatively analyze specifications that encompass probabilistic behavior [172].

On the other hand, static analysis, usually applied on software programs [32], is used prior to testing [21] and model checking [232]. Notably, static slicing [232] yields smaller programs, which are less expensive to verify. Furthermore, empirical methods, specifically software engineering metrics, have proved to be successful in quantitatively measuring quality attributes of object-oriented design models. Since we cannot compare what we cannot measure [66], metrics provide a means to evaluate the quality of proposed design solutions and review design decisions.

The quality of structural diagrams can be measured in terms of object-oriented metrics. Such metrics provide valuable and objective insights into the quality characteristics of the design. In addition, behavioral diagrams not only focus on the behavior of systems' elements but also show the functional architecture of the underlying system (e.g., activity diagram). Applying specific classical metrics in order to measure their quality attributes, namely the size and complexity-related metrics, may help better assess the design. In the context of behavioral verification, simulation execution of behavioral diagrams does not suffice for a comprehensive assessment of the behavior. This is due to the increasing complexity of the behavior of modern software and systems that may exhibit concurrency and stochastic executions. Model-checking techniques have the ability to track such behaviors and provide faithful assessment based on the desired specifications. Indeed, testing and simulation can only reveal the presence of errors but cannot prove their absence. Thus, our approach is based on a synergistic combination of model checking, software engineering metrics, and static analysis. The choice of these three specific techniques is deliberate, each one of them providing a means to tackle efficiently a specific issue. Together they allow a more comprehensive design assessment. More precisely, these techniques are not intended to be applied cumulatively, but rather in a synergistic manner. Indeed, this provides a significant benefit, greater than the sum of the benefits generated from each technique individually.

Figure 6.1 illustrates the synoptic of the overall proposed approach. Our V&V framework takes as input UML 2.0/SysML 1.0 design and architecture diagrams of the system under analysis along with the pre-defined requirements and desirable properties that need to be verified. The applied analysis depends on the type of the diagram under scope: structural or behavioral. While the analysis of structural diagrams is performed directly, behavioral diagrams need to be encoded into their corresponding computable model. The latter's role is to capture the meaning of the design and it allows performing an automated analysis. With respect to requirements and specifications, they are encoded, using temporal logics, into a set of properties that can be analyzed automatically. The overall results of the analysis help systems engineers get an appraisal of the design quality and take appropriate actions in order to remedy any detected deficiencies.

In order to establish the synergy, we propose to integrate static analysis techniques and metrics with model checking while verifying behavioral diagrams in order to tackle scalability issues. More precisely, program analysis techniques such as control flow and dataflow analysis are integrated before the actual model checking. They are applied on the semantic model (previously called the "computational model") in order to abstract it by focusing on the model fragments (slices) that

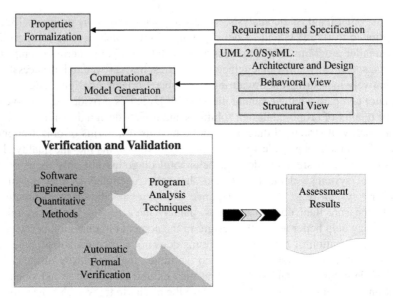

Fig. 6.1 Synergistic verification and validation proposed approach

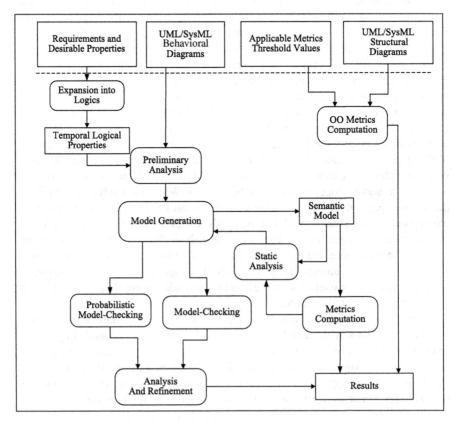

Fig. 6.2 Detailed description of our methodology

are relevant to the considered properties. The sliced model helps to narrow down the verification scope, consequently leveraging the effectiveness of the model-checking procedure. In this context, quantitative metrics are used in order to appraise the size and complexity of the semantic model prior to static analysis. This enables one to decide, prior to model checking, whether abstraction is actually needed. Figure 6.2 provides a detailed overview of our methodology.

6.2   Dedicated V&V Approach for Systems Engineering

The cornerstone of the proposed methodology is to provide an automated approach for the verification and validation of systems engineering design models by establishing a synergy between the three tiers of the considered approach, namely automatic formal verification, program analysis, and software engineering quantitative methods. Following is a presentation of each tier of our approach and its role in relation to the others.

6.2.1   Automatic Formal Verification of System Design Models

Model checking, as previously discussed, is an automatic model-based formal verification technique that targets the assessment of the behavior rather than the structure of the model according to some specified properties. Formally, model checking operates on the formal semantics describing the meaning of the model. The process of verification mainly consists in exploring the state space and checking whether a given property holds or fails. The formal semantics of the model is usually expressed in terms of extended/annotated transition system. However, the UML 2.0/SysML specifications describe informally the semantics of the diagrams and their corresponding constructs.

The automation of the V&V can be achieved by endowing the behavioral diagrams (e.g., activity, state machine) with formal semantics such as the structured operational semantics (SOS) [201]. The latter has been applied to provide specification and programming languages a formal interpretation of the corresponding meaning. Moreover, when compared to other semantics formalisms (e.g., denotational semantics), the operational semantics formalism might be more adequate for studying the behavioral aspects of a model. This characteristic is based on the natural tendency of operational semantics to describe the single-step execution capabilities of the systems. Therefore, it is helpful for explicitly describing the execution of the behavior captured by a given behavioral diagram and its corresponding state transformations within its state space.

More specifically, the first step consists in specifying an abstract syntax that represents a parsing of the graphical representation of the diagram into an abstract non-graphical mathematical notation. Thereafter, based on this syntax, the second step consists in devising a SOS-like semantics defined in terms of axioms and rules that describe local behavior. The SOS-like semantics generates a sort of transition system. The corresponding transition relation describes how the individual steps of computation take place after inductively applying the axioms and rules on a given statement [1]. Extended formalisms, such as probabilistic timed automata and Markov chains, are relevant models that enable describing semantics of behavioral diagrams that specify stochastic, probabilistic, and/or time-constrained behavior.

Concerning the properties to be verified on the model, they are generally captured in some mathematical logics, such as the linear temporal logic (LTL) [248] or the computation tree logic (CTL) [48]. To assess the SE design models, advanced temporal logics, such as timed computation tree logic (TCTL) and probabilistic computation tree logic (PCTL) [44] might be used to conveniently express properties according to the aspect to be verified (time, probability, or both). Actually, the formalization and the V&V of SysML design models are still a barely explored territory. The latter modeling language is more relevant to systems engineering and it introduces new interesting features when compared to UML such as probabilistic aspects and continuous behaviors.

6.2.2 Program Analysis of Behavioral Design Models

As mentioned before, program analysis has been successfully used in compilation, program verification, and optimization. We believe that this technique can provide significant advantages in order to achieve an efficient V&V.

Particularly, dataflow and control flow analysis, techniques which are in general applied on flow graphs representation of programs, could be used on some UML 2.0/SysML diagrams that model control flow and dataflow (e.g., activity diagram). This kind of techniques might be used in order to perform graph slicing. This, in turn, would provide a way of coping with the scalability issues (e.g., state explosion) that generally accompany the model-checking procedure. Slicing is generally performed by traversing a graph and selecting the sub-graph where the same slicing criterion holds. Since the semantic models derived from the studied behavioral diagrams are described by means of graphs (extended/annotated transition systems), it might be possible to use slicing on these semantic models. For instance, a semantic model might contain different invariants related to its nodes while some of these nodes may share the same invariant. Thus, if we consider a specific invariant as a slicing criterion, we can slice the semantic model graph accordingly. Hence, one can obtain a sub-graph where the same invariant holds.

This technique can be used in order to leverage the effectiveness of the model-checking procedure. Specifically, if some properties do not hold for a part of the model, they also do not hold for the whole model. For instance, if a safety property does not hold on at least one sub-graph, then it can be concluded that the behavior of the model is not safe, and this without requiring the verification of the remaining parts of the model. As a sub-graph has a reduced complexity when compared to the original graph, less memory space and computation time are required in the model-checking procedure. Thus, if we plan to verify whether a property holds giving a specific invariant, we only need to extract the related sub-graph.

6.2.3 Software Engineering Quantitative Techniques

In the literature, a significant number of software engineering metrics were developed in order to measure various quality attributes (e.g., size, complexity) of software systems. Many metrics were derived specifically for structural diagrams, such as the UML class and package diagrams [3, 43, 143, 167]. Software engineering metrics can also be used in the quantitative assessment of systems engineering design models. Moreover, a selection of metrics might be adopted and tailored to quantitatively assess not only the structural diagrams of the design but also its behavioral diagrams.

Similarly, in addition to applying these quantitative methods to the design itself, the same concept can be used for the semantic models derived from the behavioral diagrams. Indeed, metrics such as the cyclomatic complexity [90], the length of critical path [108], number of states, and number of transitions can be used to obtain useful quantitative measurements.

On the one hand, the length of critical path metric can provide a measurement that determines the length of the path that has to be traversed in a graph from an initial node to a destination node to achieve a given behavior with respect to a given criterion (e.g., timeliness). The critical path is different from a regular path that might traverse nodes other than the critical ones. For example, a program represented by a call graph might have as critical path the one that is needed to achieve the execution of a given subroutine in the program within minimal time delay. In the same sense, we can measure the length of critical path on the semantic models derived from behavioral diagrams given some relevant criteria related to V&V.

On the other hand, we use the cyclomatic complexity metric in order to measure the complexity of a behavioral diagram against the complexity of its corresponding semantic model. In many cases, the latter is essentially a graph that unfolds the entire dynamics of the behavioral diagram. Consequently, its complexity is usually greater than, or at least equal to, the complexity of the diagram. If this is not the case, this implies that the corresponding behavioral diagram contains some component parts (e.g., unreachable states) that are either meaningless or redundant with respect to the dynamics being modeled. This clearly shows that such quantitative methods can potentially provide the designer with important feedback information in the process of the design assessment.

6.3   Probabilistic Behavior Assessment

A range of systems inherently include probabilistic information. Probabilities can be used in order to model unpredictable and unreliable behavior exhibited by a given system. To merely satisfy the functional requirements of today's systems are insufficient; other quality standard attributes such as reliability, availability, safety, and performance have to be considered as well. In order to enable the specification of a larger spectrum of systems, SysML extends UML 2.1 activity diagrams with probabilistic features. In this context, we propose to extend our aforementioned discussed framework with probabilistic verification of SysML activity diagrams. Accordingly, we propose to integrate probabilistic model-checking techniques within the automatic formal verification module. This consists of the systematic translation of SysML activity diagrams into the input language of an appropriate probabilistic model checker. Chapters 9 and 10 detail these proposed extensions that contribute efficiently and rigorously into the V&V process.

6.4 Established Results

We have, thus far, presented and explained in this chapter the proposed approach as well as the different underlying components. We shall now discuss a number of established results emanating from the proposed approach and methodology.

With respect to the use of software engineering quantitative methods, we have considered class and package diagrams as representative diagrams of the organizational architecture of the software or the system. We applied on these diagrams a wide range of existing software engineering metrics [14, 33, 34, 43, 89, 96, 144, 150, 151] to assess the quality of the system with respect to various aspects, such as complexity, understandability, maintainability, stability, and others [3]. Among the metrics applied on UML class diagrams, we mention, for instance, coupling between object classes (CBO), depth of inheritance tree (DIT), and weighted methods per class (WMC). These metrics for object-oriented design, that aim at assessing complexity by measuring different quality attributes such as maintainability and reusability, were previously proposed by Chidamber and Kemerer [43]. We further elaborate on this topic in Chap. 7, which is dedicated to structural design assessment.

As far as the behavioral part is concerned, we have explored the case of state machine, sequence, and activity diagrams. In order to assess the dynamics of the system from the perspective of the behavioral diagrams, it is important to extract not only the syntax (graphical components and relationships) but also the corresponding semantics that are conveyed by such diagrams. For instance, a state machine shows the different states of an object related with transitions. Its dynamics is interpreted by rules encoded in the graphical representation of the diagram (states, edges, events labeling edges, etc.). These rules dictate the evolution of the state machine in its state space in response to some received events with respect to the active states. One can also derive a similar reasoning for the other behavioral diagrams. In order to perform the behavioral assessment, the diagrams' semantics have to be captured in the form of a computable model that encompasses all operational behavior and then input into the model checker. The main challenge was to find a single computable model framework that can be associated with each of the considered behavioral diagrams, namely state machine, sequence, and activity diagrams. In [3], a suitable form of a transition system is presented that can serve such a goal, called a configuration transition system (CTS). CTS states are represented by the system's configurations and the transition relation describes how a given configuration is modified after a computation step has been applied.

A configuration is defined as a snapshot in the evolution of the system at a particular point in time and from a specific view (i.e., the diagram's point of view). In other words, a configuration is specific to a particular type of behavioral diagrams. For instance, a configuration for a state machine represents a set of active states at a given moment. Consequently, the dynamics of the state machine can be captured by specifying all the possible configurations and the transitions among them. Thus, a general parameterized CTS definition may be provided and tailored according to the concrete dynamic elements of the considered behavioral diagram. The generation of the CTS for each considered behavioral diagram can be automated. In essence, the CTS can be derived by proceeding iteratively, with a breadth-first procedure, searching for all possible configurations reachable from a currently selected configuration, taken at each iteration from the newly discovered ones. This is discussed in more detail in Chap. 8.

6.5 Verification and Validation Tool

In order to put into practice our V&V approach, we have designed and implemented a software tool intended to be used in conjunction with a modeling environment from which the design model under scope can be fetched and subjected to the V&V module. The architecture of this software tool is illustrated in Fig. 6.3. The tool is a multiple document interface (MDI) application throughout which one can easily navigate among several views at once. The main interface is composed of a standard menu on the top and a vertical menu bar on the left, where one can select a specific view of a given module and load it into the MDI.

The tool interfaces with the modeling environment Artisan Real-Time Studio [7], from where the designer can load the design model and select the diagram for assessment. Once started, the tool automatically loads the assessment module associated with the selected type of diagram. For instance, if the diagram loaded is a class diagram, the metric module is then activated and the appropriate measurements are performed. A set of quantitative measurements are provided with their relevant feedback to the designer. Figure 6.4 shows a screenshot example of metrics application. For behavioral diagrams, the corresponding model-checker

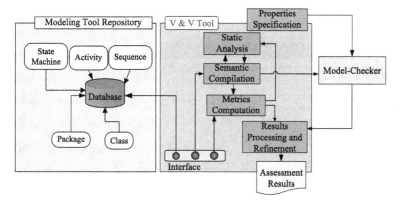

Fig. 6.3 Architecture of the verification and validation environment

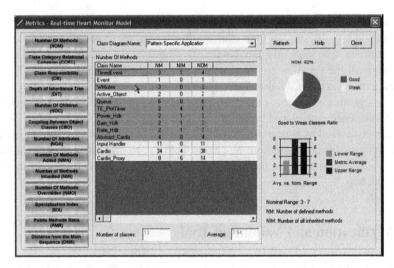

Fig. 6.4 Environment screenshot: metrics assessment

(NuSMV) code is automatically generated and generic properties, such as reachability and deadlock absence for each state of the model, are automatically verified. An assessment example using model checking is shown in Fig. 6.5. Furthermore, the tool comprises an editor with a set of pre-programmed buttons through which the user can specify custom properties. This is based on an intuitive and easy-to-learn macro-based specification language we defined. More precisely, we developed a set of macros using operators (**always, mayreach,** etc.) that are systematically

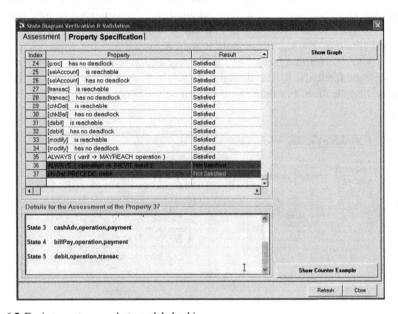

Fig. 6.5 Environment screenshot: model checking

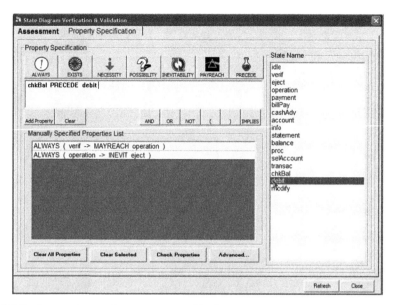

Fig. 6.6 Environment screenshot: property specification

expanded into their corresponding computation tree logic (CTL) operators. The editor interface screenshot with an example of custom properties specification is illustrated in Fig. 6.6. Finally, a specific window frame is dedicated to the presentation of the assessment results. The feedback generated by the model checker not being user-friendly nor understandable by non-experts, we built a back-end module that analyzes the provided output traces, in the case of failed properties, and renders relevant information about the counterexamples in a meaningful way, using a graphical visualization.

6.6 Conclusion

In summary, we elaborated an innovative approach that contributes to the V&V of design models expressed using the modeling languages UML and SysML. It is based on a synergy between three well-established techniques: model checking, static analysis, and empirical software engineering quantitative methods. The synergy relies on the fact that, if each one of these techniques is applied alone, the resulting outcome is only a partial assessment of the design (for instance, either structural or behavioral). In addition to qualitative analysis, our approach also enables quantitative assessment of design models. With respect to behavioral diagrams, the main challenge was to build a unified model that we call configuration transition system (CTS). CTS represents a common parametrized model that describes the semantic models of state machine, sequence, and activity diagrams. In Chap. 8, we present in detail this approach.

Chapter 7
Software Engineering Metrics in the Context of Systems Engineering

The need for reliable and high-performing software led to the emergence of software engineering. Since the birth of software engineering in 1968, new approaches and techniques were developed to govern the quality of software systems. Software metrics are used to assess the quality of software systems in terms of system attributes such as complexity, understandability, maintainability, stability. Different software metrics have been developed to measure the quality of structural and objected-oriented programming techniques.

Some of the metrics for the structural programming are the lines of code (LOC) and cyclomatic complexity (CC) [156] metrics. When the object-oriented paradigm emerged, many new metrics evolved to assess the quality of software system design and to overcome the limitations of the legacy code metrics.

7.1 Metrics Suites Overview

In order to enhance the quality in today's increasingly complex software systems' some new techniques are needed. System quality should be controlled in the early stages of design. A good software system offers components that are more robust, maintainable, reusable, etc. In the literature, many object-oriented metrics have emerged to create highly reliable software systems. Software metrics are efficient methods for assessing the quality of software design including UML class and package diagrams. By using metrics, one can get significant insights into the complexity and structure of software systems.

In the subsequent sections, we present a list of research works that have contributed to the field of software engineering techniques by proposing metric suites for UML class and package diagrams. Such metrics are extremely relevant given the current trend toward model-based software and systems engineering.

7.1.1 Chidamber and Kemerer Metrics

Chidamber and Kemerer [43] proposed a set of six metrics for object-oriented designs. This metrics suite measures the diagram's complexity by applying the

M. Debbabi et al., *Verification and Validation in Systems Engineering*,
DOI 10.1007/978-3-642-15228-3_7, © Springer-Verlag Berlin Heidelberg 2010

metrics on various quality attributes such as maintainability, reusability. From these six metrics, only the following three can be applied on UML class diagrams:

- **Coupling between object classes (CBO)**. This metric measures the level of coupling among classes. A class that is excessively coupled to other classes is detrimental to modular design and prohibits reuse and maintainability, especially when changes are required in tightly coupled classes.
- **Depth of inheritance tree (DIT)**. This metric represents the length of the inheritance tree from a class to its root class. A deep class in the tree inherits a relatively high number of methods, which in turn increases its complexity.
- **Weighted methods per class (WMC)**. It is the summation of the complexity of all the methods in the class. A simpler case for WMC is when the complexity of each method is evaluated to unity. In that case, WMC is considered as the number of methods in the class. On the other hand, high WMC value is a sign of high complexity and less reusability.

7.1.2 MOOD Metrics

Abreu et al. [34] proposed a set of metrics, named metrics for object-oriented design (MOOD), to assess the structural mechanisms of the object-oriented paradigm such as encapsulation, inheritance, and polymorphism. MOOD metrics suite can be applied on UML class diagrams as follows:

- **Method hiding factor (MHF)**. This metric is a measure of the encapsulation in the class. It is the ratio of the sum of hidden methods (private and protected) to the total number of methods defined in each class (public, private, and protected). If all the methods in the class are hidden, then the value of MHF is high and indicates that this class is not accessible and thus not reusable. An MHF value of zero signals that all the methods of the class are public, which hinders encapsulation.
- **Attribute hiding factor (AHF)**. This metric represents the average of the invisibility of attributes in the class diagram. It is the ratio of the sum of hidden attributes (private and protected) for all the classes to the sum of all defined attributes (public, private, and protected). A high AHF value indicates appropriate data hiding.
- **Method inheritance factor (MIF)** and **attribute inheritance factor (AIF)**. These two metrics represent a measure of the class inheritance degree. MIF is calculated as the ratio of all inherited methods in the class diagram to the total number of methods (defined and inherited) in the diagram. AIF is calculated as the ratio of all inherited attributes in the class diagram to the total number of attributes (defined and inherited) in the diagram. A zero value indicates no inheritance usage, which may be a flaw unless the class is a base class in the hierarchy.
- **Polymorphism factor (POF)**. This metric is a measure of overriding methods in a class diagram. It is the ratio between the number of overridden methods in a class and the maximum number of methods that can be overridden in the class.

- **Coupling factor (COF)**. This metric measures the coupling level in the class diagram. It is the ratio between the actual couplings and the maximum number of possible couplings among all the classes in the diagram. A class is coupled to another class when methods of the former access members of the latter. High values of COF indicate tight coupling, which increases the complexity and diminishes the maintainability and reusability of the class.

7.1.3 Li and Henry's Metrics

Li and Henry [144] proposed a metrics suite to measure several class diagram internal quality attributes such as coupling, complexity, and size. In the following, we present the main two metrics proposed by Li and Henry that can be applied on UML class diagrams:

- **Data abstraction coupling (DAC)**. This metric calculates the number of attributes in a class that represent other class types (composition). It measures the coupling complexity caused by the existence of abstract data types (ADT). The complexity due to coupling increases if more ADTs are defined within a class.
- **SIZE2**. This metric is defined as the number of attributes and the number of local methods defined in a class. This metric is a measure of the class diagram size.

7.1.4 Lorenz and Kidd's Metrics

Lorenz and Kidd [150] proposed a set of metrics that can be used to measure the static characteristics of a software design, such as size, inheritance, and the internal attributes of the class.

With respect to size metrics, the public instance methods (PIMs) count the public methods in a class. Moreover, the number of instance methods (NIMs) metric counts all methods (public, protected, and private) in a class. In addition, the number of instance variables (NIVs) counts the total number of variables in a class.

Furthermore, another set of metrics is proposed for measuring the class inheritance usage degree. The NMO metric gives a measure of the number of methods overridden by a subclass. The NMI is the total number of methods inherited by a subclass. Additionally, the NMA metric is the count of the methods added in a subclass.

Finally, the NMO and DIT [43] metrics are used to calculate the specialization index (SIX) of a class, which gives an indication of the class inheritance utilization.

7.1.5 Robert Martin Metrics

Robert Martin [151] proposed a set of three metrics applicable for UML package diagrams. This set of metrics measures the interdependencies among packages.

Highly interdependent packages or subsystems tend to be less flexible, thus hardly reusable and maintainable. Therefore, interdependency among packages in a system should definitely be taken into consideration.

The three metrics defined by Robert Martin: instability, abstractness, and distance from main sequence (DMS). The instability metric measures the level of instability of a package. A package is unstable if its level of dependency is higher than that of those depending on it. The abstractness metric is a measure of the package's abstraction level, which, in turn, depends on its stability. Finally, the DMS metric measures the balance between the abstraction and instability of a package. These metrics are discussed in detail in Sect. 7.3.

7.1.6 Bansiya and Davis Metrics

Bansiya and Davis [14] defined a set of five metrics to measure several object-oriented design properties, such as data hiding, coupling, cohesion, composition, and inheritance. In the following, we present only those metrics that can be applied to UML class diagrams.

The first is the data access metric (DAM) and it measures the level of data hiding in the class. DAM is the ratio of the private and protected (hidden) attributes to the total number of defined attributes in the class. The second is the direct class coupling (DCC) metric and it counts the total number of classes coupled with a given class. Finally, the measure of aggregation (MOA) metric computes the number of attributes defined in a class whose types represent other classes (composition) in the model. Bansiya and Davis metrics have been applied to a number of case studies where nominal ranges have been defined for their metrics based on the performed observations.

7.1.7 Briand et al. Metrics

Briand et al. [33] proposed a metrics suite to measure the coupling among classes in class diagrams. These metrics determine each type of coupling and the impact of each type of relationship on the class diagram quality.

In their work, Briand et al. covered almost all types of coupling occurrences in a class diagram. These types of relationships include coupling to ancestor and descendent classes, composition, class–method interactions, and import and export coupling. As a result of their work, they applied their metrics suite on two real case studies and determined that coupling is an important structural aspect to be considered when building quality models of object-oriented design. Moreover, they also concluded that import coupling has more impact on fault-proneness compared to export coupling.

7.2 Quality Attributes

UML [184] has been standardized as a modeling language for object-oriented system design. Previously, we discussed a set of object-oriented metrics proposed for measuring the quality of UML class and package diagrams.

In the following, we present the measured quality attributes. In total, a set of 15 metrics for package and class diagrams will be addressed in this book. In addition, we detail and discuss the analysis results of a class and package diagram case study. Following is a brief presentation of a number of typical quality attributes captured using the set of object-oriented metrics:

- **Stability** indicates the risk level for the occurrence of unexpected effects resulting from occasional modifications of the software.
- **Understandability** measures the degree to which the system stakeholders are able to comprehend the system specifications.
- **Maintainability** measures ease and speed with which a system design and/or implementation can be changed for perfective, adaptive, corrective, and/or preventive reasons.
- **Reusability** measures ease and speed with which a part (or more) of a system design and/or implementation can be reused.
- **Testability** represents a characteristic that suggests how easy it is to test a given application or how well are the tests able to interact with the code in order to reveal potential flaws or a combination of the two aspects.
- **Coupling** measures how strongly system parts depend on each other. Generally, a loose coupling is desirable in high-quality design. Moreover, there is a strong correlation between coupling and other system quality attributes, such as complexity, maintainability, and reusability.
- **Cohesion** refers to the degree to which system components are functionally related (internal "glue"). Generally, a strong cohesion is sought in high-quality system design.
- **Complexity** indicates the level of intricacy and compoundness. It measures the degree to which a system design is difficult to be understood and/or to be implemented.

The aforementioned quality attributes represent cornerstones in building quality software systems. In the next section, we detail the set of software engineering metrics that can be used in order to assess such system quality attributes.

7.3 Software Metrics Computation

This section details the calculation methods for the metrics previously introduced. To that effect, we present the means used to compute 15 metrics for class and package diagrams. Each metric is explained, along with its formula and the corresponding nominal range (when applicable). The selected metrics target the quality characteristics of object-oriented designs. They are used to measure quality attributes of class and package diagrams by using various criteria applied on different types of relationships (e.g., inheritance, associations, generalizations, aggregations).

7.3.1 Abstractness (A)

The abstractness [151] metric measures the package abstraction rate. A package abstraction level depends on its stability level. Calculations are performed on classes defined directly in the package and those defined in sub-packages. In UML models, this metric is calculated on all the model classes.

The abstraction metric provides a percentage between 0 and 100%, where the package contains at least one class and at least one operation in an abstract class. The following formula is used to measure the abstractness of the package diagram.

$$\text{Abstraction} = \frac{N_{ma}}{N_{mca}} \times \frac{N_{ca}}{N_c} \times 100 \qquad (7.1)$$

where N_{ma} is the number of abstract methods in all the package's classes; N_{mca} is the number of methods (abstract or not) in the package's abstract classes; N_{ca} is the number of abstract classes; N_c is the number of classes (abstract or not) of the package.

The abstractness metric [151] is indicative of how suitable package is for modification during the life cycle of the application. The more abstract a package is, the more it is extensible, resulting in a more stable package. Indeed, extensible abstract packages provide greater model flexibility. Nominal values for this metric cannot be measured, since abstractness depends on the purpose of the package.

7.3.2 Instability (I)

The instability [151] metric measures the level of instability in a package. A package is unstable if its level of dependency is higher than that of those depending. The instability of a package is the ratio of its afferent coupling to the sum of its efferent and afferent coupling. It is measured using the following formula:

$$I = \frac{\text{AC}}{\text{EC} + \text{AC}} \qquad (7.2)$$

where AfferentCoupling (AC) is the number of links (associations, dependencies, and generalizations) toward classes defined in other packages and EfferentCoupling (EC) is the number of links (associations, dependencies, and generalizations) coming from classes defined in other packages.

A package is more likely to be subject to change if the other packages that it depends on change. The instability metric does not have a nominal range since some packages may be kept in an unstable state to enable their extensibility.

7.3.3 Distance from the Main Sequence (DMS)

The distance from main sequence (DMS) [151] metric measures the appropriate balance between the abstraction and the instability of the package. Packages should be quite general in order to be consistent with the two aforementioned orthogonal criteria. Packages should also be open to modifications. However, some level of abstraction is needed as well. Therefore, a balance is required between the package abstraction and its instability. This can be measured with the following formula:

$$DMS = |Abstraction + Instability - 100| \qquad (7.3)$$

A DMS of 100% corresponds to an optimal balance between abstraction and instability. Practically, a value greater than 50% is considered to be within the nominal range of DMS.

7.3.4 Class Responsibility (CR)

The class responsibility (CR) [245] ratio is an indication of the responsibility level assigned for each class in order to correctly execute an operation in response to a message. A method is considered to be responsible if it has pre-conditions and/or post-conditions. Before taking any action, a class method should be responsible for checking whether a message is appropriate. Also, a class method should take responsibility to ensure the success of the method.

CR is a ratio of the number of methods implementing pre-condition and/or post-condition contracts to the total number of methods. CR is calculated using the following formula:

$$CR = \frac{PCC + POC}{2 \times NOM} \times 100 \qquad (7.4)$$

where PCC is the total number of methods that implement pre-condition contracts; POC is the total number of methods that implement post-condition contracts; NOM is the total number of methods.

The CR nominal range is between 20 and 75%. A value below 20% indicates irresponsible class methods. Irresponsible methods indicate that the class will react passively to the sent and received messages. Responsible methods are desirable since they diminish the number of runtime exceptions in a system. A CR value above 75%, although preferable, is seldom achieved.

7.3.5 Class Category Relational Cohesion (CCRC)

The CCRC [245] metric measures how cohesive the classes are in a class diagram design. The construction of classes in the diagram must be justified by the links that exist between the diagram classes. In the class diagram, a scarce level of relations among the classes indicates a lack of cohesiveness. Relational cohesion is the number of relationships among classes divided by the total number of classes in the diagram. The CCRC metric is calculated using the following formula:

$$CCRC = \frac{\sum_{i=1}^{N_c} NA_i + \sum_{i=1}^{N_c} NG_i}{N_c} \times 100 \qquad (7.5)$$

where

- NA is the number of association relationships for a class.
- NG is the number of generalization relationships for a class.
- N_c is the number of classes in the diagram.

A class is considered to be cohesively related to other classes when the class collaborates with other classes in order to achieve its responsibilities. A very small CCRC value indicates that some classes have little or no relationships with other classes in the design model. A CCRC nominal range is between 150 and 350%. A value greater than 350% is not desirable due to the heightened complexity it entails.

7.3.6 Depth of Inheritance Tree (DIT)

Inheritance is an important concept in object-oriented models; however, it should be mindfully used to achieve the goals of good software system design. Classes that are located deep in the inheritance tree are more complex and thus prone to difficulties of development, testing, and maintenance. To achieve a good system design, a trade-off should be considered when creating the class hierarchy. As a result, it was empirically found that a DIT metric value between 1 and 4 fulfills this goal. A value greater than 4 would overly increase the complexity of the model.

Algorithm 1 is used to measure the depth of inheritance. The recursive function "TraversTree" checks for the depth of inheritance for each class. The algorithm iterates all the classes in the diagram and records the maximum inheritance depth in *DIT Max*.

7.3.7 Number of Children (NOC)

The NOC [43] metric measures the average number of children for the classes in the class design model. It is an important metric because of the following factors:

Algorithm 1 Measuring the Depth of Inheritance (DIT) of a Class

---

```
global integer DITMax = 0
for each class c in CD do
    call TraverseTree(c)
end for
function TraverseTree(class c)
{
static integer DIT = 0
for each generalization relationship g from class c do
    get superclasses of c
    for each superclass s of class c do
        DIT = DIT + 1
        TraverseTree (s)
    end for
    if DIT GT DITMax then
        DITMax = DIT
    end if
    DIT = DIT - 1
end for
}
```

- A large number of children indicates that a larger degree of reuse is achieved.
- Too many children may indicate a misuse of subclassing, which will increase the complexity.

The NOC metric is calculated by summing up the number of children for each class in the model. This number is then divided by the total number of classes, excluding the child classes at the lowest level in the model. The NOC metric is calculated using the following formula:

$$\text{NOC} = \frac{\sum_{i=1}^{N_c} \text{NCC}_i}{N_c - \text{LLC}} \tag{7.6}$$

where NCC is the sum of children for a class; N_c is the total number of classes in the diagram; LLC is the number of classes in the lowest level of inheritance in the diagram.

A NOC value of 0 shows a lack of object orientation in the design model. A nominal range for NOC is between 1 and 4. A value within this range indicates that the goals of reusability are compliant with the goals of complexity management while promoting encapsulation. A number greater than 4 indicates a potential misuse of abstraction.

7.3.8 Coupling Between Object Classes (CBO)

The CBO metric [43] is a measure of the average degree of connectivity and inter-dependency between objects in a model. It is directly proportional to coupling and complexity and inversely proportional to modularity. Therefore, it is preferable to have a lower CBO value. This value is important due to the following reasons:

- Strong coupling inhibits the possibility of reuse.
- Strong coupling makes a class difficult to understand, correct, or change without subsequent modifications to the other classes in the model.
- Tight coupling increases the model's complexity.

CBO is calculated using the following formula:

$$\text{CBO} = \frac{\sum_{i=1}^{N_c} \text{AR}_i + \sum_{i=1}^{N_c} \text{DR}_i}{N_c} \tag{7.7}$$

where AR is the total number of association relationships for each class in the diagram; DR is the total number of dependency relationships for each class in the diagram; N_c is the number of classes in the diagram.

A CBO value of 0 indicates that a class is not related to any other classes in the model and, as such, should not be part of the system. The nominal range for CBO falls between 1 and 4 indicating that the class is loosely coupled. A CBO value above 4 may indicate that the class is tightly coupled to other classes in the model, therefore, complicating the testing and modification operations and limiting the possibilities of reuse.

7.3.9 Number of Methods (NOM)

The NOM [144] metric is the average count of methods per class. The number of methods in a class should be moderate, but not at the expense of missing or incomplete functionality. This metric is useful in identifying classes with little or no functionality thus serving mainly as data types. Moreover, a subclass that does not implement methods has little or no potential for reuse.

This metric is computed by counting the total number of methods (defined and inherited from all parents) for all the classes in the model. This number is then divided by the total number of classes in the model. Thus, NOM is calculated using the following formula:

$$\text{NOM} = \frac{\sum_{i=1}^{N_c} \text{NM}_i + \sum_{i=1}^{N_c} \text{NIM}_i}{N_c} \tag{7.8}$$

where NM is the number of methods for a class; NIM is the total number of inherited methods by a class; N_c is the number of classes in the diagram.

The NOM metric nominal range lies between 3 and 7 and indicates that the class has a reasonable number of methods. A NOM value greater than 7 indicates the need for decomposing the class into smaller classes. Alternatively, a value greater than 7 may indicate that the class does not have a coherent purpose. A value less than 3 indicates that a class is merely a data construct rather than a fully fledged class.

7.3.10 Number of Attributes (NOA)

The NOA [150] metric measures the average number of attributes for a class in the model. This metric is useful in identifying the following important issues:

- A relatively large number of attributes in a class may indicate the presence of coincidental cohesion. Therefore, the class needs to be decomposed into smaller parts in order to manage the complexity of the model.
- A class with no attributes means that a thorough analysis must be done on the semantics of the class. It could also indicate that it is a utility class rather than a regular class.

The NOA metric is the ratio of the value obtained by counting the total number of attributes (defined and inherited from all ancestors) for each class in the model to the total number of classes in the model. It is calculated using the following formula:

$$\text{NOA} = \frac{\sum_{i=1}^{N_c} \text{NA}_i + \sum_{i=1}^{N_c} \text{NIA}_i}{N_c} \tag{7.9}$$

where NA is the total number of attributes for a class in the diagram; NIA is the total number of inherited attributes for a class in the diagram; N_c is the number of classes in the diagram.

A nominal range for NOA falls between 2 and 5. A value within this range indicates that a class has a reasonable number of attributes, whereas a value greater than 5 may indicate that the class does not have a coherent purpose and requires further object-oriented decomposition. A value of 0 for a particular class may designate that it represents a utility class.

7.3.11 Number of Methods Added (NMA)

The NMA [150] metric plays a significant role in the assessment of the class specialization. A class with too many added methods indicates an overspecialization when compared to the functionality of its ancestors. Consequently, inheritance would be rendered less effective due to the major differences between the subclass and its ancestors. It is the ratio of all the added methods in the diagram to the total number of classes in the diagram. It is computed using the following formula:

$$\text{NMA} = \frac{\sum_{i=1}^{N_c} \text{AM}_i}{N_c} \tag{7.10}$$

where MA is the total number of added methods for a class and, N_c is the number of classes in the diagram.

This metric has a nominal range between 0 and 4. A value greater than 4 indicates that a class contains major changes when compared to its ancestors. A class with an NMA value above 4 hinders the inheritance usefulness.

7.3.12 Number of Methods Overridden (NMO)

The NMO metric [150] also plays a significant role in the assessment of the class specialization. A class with too many redefined methods implies that little or no functionality is reused, which may indicate misuse of inheritance. It counts the number of redefined methods in the class and is calculated as follows:

$$NMO = \frac{\sum_{i=1}^{N_c} RM_i}{N_c} \qquad (7.11)$$

where RM is the total number of redefined methods in a class and, N_c is the number of classes in the diagram.

A class that inherits methods must use them with a minimum of modifications. A class with a high number of redefined methods is hardly making use of the inheritance concept. This metric has a nominal range between 0 and 5.

7.3.13 Number of Methods Inherited (NMI)

To maintain the usefulness of inheritance in a class, the number of inherited methods that are not redefined (overridden) should be relatively greater than the redefined ones. The NMI [150] metric is the ratio of the total number of non-redefined methods to the total number of inherited methods in a class. The following formula measures the value of NMI:

$$NMI = \frac{NOHO}{HOP} \times 100 \qquad (7.12)$$

where NOHO is the number of non-redefined methods in a class and, HOP is the number of inherited methods in a class.

The ratio of inherited methods should be high. This metric contrasts with the previously presented NMO metric. A low number of inherited methods indicates a lack of specialization. An ideal value of 100% is hardly achievable due to the fact that some behaviors need to be modified in order to satisfy some new requirements.

7.3.14 Specialization Index (SIX)

Excessive method overriding is undesirable due to the increase in the model complexity and maintenance and the diminished reusability it incurs. Additionally, overridden methods may be found at deeper levels in the inheritance hierarchy. To that effect, the NMO metric is multiplied by the DIT metric and divided by the total number of methods in the class in order to measure its specialization index. Thus, the SIX metric is computed using the following formula:

$$SIX = \frac{NMO \times DIT}{NM} \times 100 \qquad (7.13)$$

where NMO is the number of overloaded methods; DIT is the depth of inheritance value; and NM is the total number of methods in a class.

The deeper in the inheritance hierarchy a class is, the more difficult it would be to efficiently and meaningfully use method overriding. This is due to the fact that it would be more difficult to understand the relationship between the class and its ancestors. In this manner, overridden methods in lower levels of the hierarchy are more easily developed and maintained. A value falling between 0 and 120% is considered in the nominal range. For a root class, the specialization indicator is 0.

7.3.15 Public Methods Ratio (PMR)

The PMR [145] metric measures the access control restrictiveness of a class and indicates how many methods in a class are accessible from other classes. The usefulness of this metric is based on the following considerations:

- Too many public methods preclude the goal of encapsulation, which is a desirable property of an object-oriented design.
- The absence of public methods indicates an isolated entity in the design.

This PMR metric is the ratio of public methods (defined and inherited) to the total number of methods (defined and inherited) in the class. It is calculated using the following formula:

$$PMR = \frac{PM + PIM}{DM + IM} \qquad (7.14)$$

where PM is the total number of public defined methods in a class; PIM is the total number of public inherited methods in a class; DM is the total number of defined methods in a class; and IM is the total number of inherited methods in a class.

A PMR metric nominal range falls between 5 and 50% and indicates that the class has a reasonable number of public methods. A value below 5% is only acceptable for abstract classes; otherwise the class functionality will be concealed. Conversely, a value above 50% indicates a lack of encapsulation. As a rule, only methods that export some functionality should be visible to other classes.

7.4 Case Study

We selected a case study example depicting a real-time heart monitoring system. The diagram consists of three packages. The first one contains the window's components that display the monitoring results. The second package contains the platform-specific heart monitoring tools, whereas the third package contains the heart monitoring components.

This diagram is a good example due to the various types of relationships among the classes. In the following paragraphs, we will present the assessment results. When applying these metrics on the diagram in Fig. 7.1, the analysis results indicate that some classes in the model have a high complexity, thus having a weak reusability potential.

Table 7.1 shows the metrics related to package diagrams. The DMS metric measures the balance between the abstraction and instability levels in the package. As shown in the table, the three packages in the diagram fall within the nominal range of DMS.

Since the abstraction and instability metrics do not have nominal ranges due to the difference in the design perspectives, the DMS is a compromise between their values. Abstraction and instability metrics do not have nominal ranges due to the fact that packages should depend on other packages in order to employ composition. However, they must also be easily modifiable. The zero abstractness value for the three packages shows that these packages are not easily extendable and modifiable. Also, the metric in the second column shows a relatively high instability value, indicating that the three packages are subject to change if other packages change.

Table 7.2 presents the analysis results of the class diagram inheritance-related metrics. The DIT metric shows a proper use of inheritance. Moreover, the use of inheritance in this diagram does not have a negative impact on its complexity level. Furthermore, our tool results show that the diagram has a shallow inheritance tree which indicates a good level of understandability and testability.

With respect to the NOC metric, the analysis shows that only four classes in the diagram have a good NOC value. In a class diagram, the number of children is an indication of the class reusability in the diagram.

The analysis results also show that five classes in the diagram have a weak NOM value. On the other hand, the class diagram has an overall NOM that lies within the nominal range. The problem of unsuitable NOM values may be addressed by decomposing the existing classes to smaller new classes that would include the

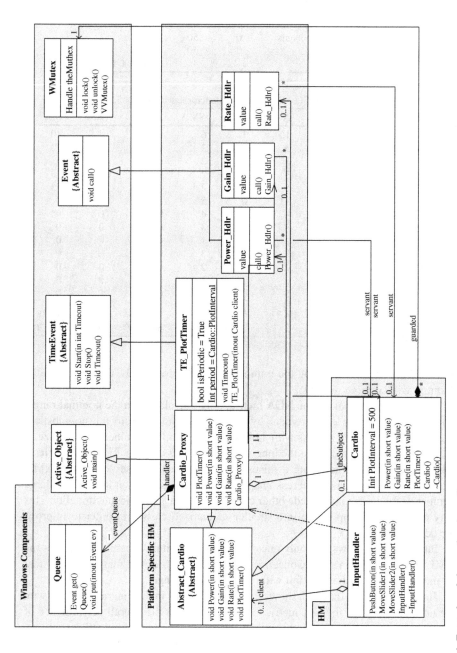

Fig. 7.1 Examples of class and package diagrams

Table 7.1 Package diagram metrics

Package name	A	I	DMS
Platform-specific HM	0	49	51
HM	0	49	51
Windows components	0	50	50
Average	0	50	50
Nominal range	–	–	50–100%

Table 7.2 Class diagram inheritance-related metrics

Class name	DIT	NOC	NOM	NOA	NMA	NMI	NMO	SIX
Cardio	1	0	10	1	6	0	4	40
Rate_Hdlr	1	0	3	1	2	0	1	33
Gain_Hdlr	1	0	3	1	2	0	1	33
Power_Hdlr	1	0	3	1	2	0	1	33
TE_PlotTimer	1	0	5	2	2	67	3	43
Cardio_Proxy	1	0	11	0	5	33	4	0
Abstract_Cardio	0	2	4	0	4	0	0	0
WMutex	0	0	3	1	3	0	0	0
Event	0	3	1	0	1	0	0	0
TimedEvent	0	1	3	0	3	0	0	0
Active_Object	0	1	2	0	2	0	0	0
Queue	0	0	3	0	3	0	0	0
Input_Handler	0	0	5	0	5	0	0	0
Average	0.46	0.88	4.31	0.54	3.08	25	1.08	18.38
Nominal range	1–4	1–4	3–7	2–5	0–4	50–100%	0–5	0–120%

number of methods exceeding the nominal range. Consequently, the classes in the diagram will be more reusable.

Table 7.2 shows that for the NOA metric, only one class is in the nominal range. This calls for further enhancement by adding new attributes to the non-abstract classes in the diagram. A class with a high number of attributes increases its size.

The NMA metric measures the inheritance usefulness degree. Three classes have a high NMA value, indicating a misuse of inheritance. Classes with high NMA may be difficult to reuse, whereas classes with no specialization and having large number of methods may impede other classes from reusing their functionality. This may require a decomposition into smaller specialized classes in order to improve the design.

Table 7.2 also shows that only one class in the inheritance hierarchy satisfies the NMI metric nominal range. Concerning the NMO metric, the analysis shows that all the classes in the diagram fall within the nominal range.

The last metric in Table 7.2 shows that all the classes in the diagram comply with the nominal range of the SIX metric. The latter reflects the overall performance of the class diagram from the perspective of inheritance in object-oriented design.

The CBO metric measures the level of coupling between classes, where a high coupling would result in an increase in the complexity. Table 7.3 shows seven classes outside the CBO nominal range while six classes fall within it. This shows

Table 7.3 Class diagram general metrics

Class name	CR	CCRC	CBO	PMR
Cardio	0	200	1	100
Rate_Hdlr	0	200	1	100
Gain_Hdlr	0	200	1	100
Power_Hdlr	0	200	1	100
TE_PlotTimer	0	100	0	100
Cardio_Proxy	0	700	5	100
Abstract_Cardio	0	100	1	100
WMutex	0	0	0	100
Event	0	0	0	100
TimedEvent	0	0	0	100
Active_Object	0	0	0	100
Queue	0	0	0	100
Input_Handler	0	200	2	100
Average	0	146	0.92	100
Nominal range	20–75%	150–350%	1–4	5–50%

an increased complexity and suggests further modification by reducing the number of relationships between the classes.

The CCRC metric measures the cohesion of classes within the diagram. This metric reflects the diagram's architectural strength. Table 7.3 shows a good CCRC level for only five classes, whereas the remaining eight classes have a weak CCRC level. In addition, we can see that the average CCRC is outside of the nominal range, indicating a cohesion problem between the classes.

The CR metric results in Table 7.3 show that none of the classes in the diagram are implementing pre-conditions and/or post-conditions. CR is measured in the cases where a class method should be responsible to check whether a message is correct before taking any action. In the current example, the CR value can be enhanced by adding pre/post-conditions to those methods that need to check the validity of messages prior to or after the execution of an action. In the design of a class diagram, the use of pre/post-conditions should be carefully considered. Therefore, this metric is useful, especially for checking systems with real-time messaging.

Finally, for the PMR metric, Table 7.3 shows that all methods in the class diagram are accessible, which inhibits encapsulation in the diagram. This requires some adjustment of the access control level for all the classes in the diagram.

7.5 Conclusion

Software engineering metrics can provide very valuable insights into many quality attributes relevant in software and system design. Moreover, metrics can be useful for assessing already existing designs when exploring possible avenues of improvement.

In this chapter we presented a set of relevant metric suites for software and systems engineering design models captured by UML class and package diagrams. Their usefulness was demonstrated by means of a case study, wherein a set of 15 metrics was used in order to assess the quality of an object-oriented system design. The case study demonstrated how different object-oriented techniques, such as inheritance or association, can affect various quality attributes, such as reusability and complexity. Furthermore, we showed how the evaluated quality attributes can serve as pointers for design enhancement.

Chapter 8
Verification and Validation of UML Behavioral Diagrams

It is generally accepted that any system that has an associated dynamics can be abstracted to one that evolves within a discrete state space. Such a system is able to evolve through its state space assuming different configurations, where a configuration can be understood as the set of states to which the system abides at any particular moment. Hence, all the possible configurations summed up by the dynamics of the system, and the transitions thereof, can be coalesced into a configuration transition system (CTS). In this setting, we present the usefulness of this concept when modeling the dynamics of behavioral design models expressed in modeling languages such as UML.

In the context of verifying design models expressed as UML 1.x activity diagrams, Eshuis and Weiringa [80] explore an idea similar to CTS. However, the CTS concept has a more general nature and can be conveniently adapted to be used for a broad range of behavioral diagrams, including state machine activity and sequence diagrams. In essence the CTS is basically a form of automaton. It is characterized by a set of configurations that include a (usually singleton) set of initial configurations and a transition relation that encodes the dynamic evolution of the CTS from one configuration to another. Moreover, in accordance with the required level of abstraction, the CTS's flexible configuration structure may include more or less of the dynamic elements of the behavioral diagram. Thus, it offers an abstraction scalability that permits efficient dynamic analysis by adjusting the scope to the desired parameters of interest.

8.1 Configuration Transition System

Given an instance of a behavioral diagram, one can generate the corresponding CTS provided that the elements of the diagram are both established and understood and there exists (and is defined) a step relation enabling one to systematically compute the next configuration(s) of the diagram from any given configuration.

When the variables of interest, within the dynamic domain of a behavioral diagram, can be abstracted to boolean state variables, each of the enclosed

M. Debbabi et al., *Verification and Validation in Systems Engineering*,
DOI 10.1007/978-3-642-15228-3_8, © Springer-Verlag Berlin Heidelberg 2010

configurations within the CTS can be represented by the set of states that are active[1] simultaneously. Furthermore, the transition relation of the CTS links configuration pairs by a label comprising all those variable values (e.g., events, guards) that are required to trigger the change from the current configuration to the next one. Note that, in order to achieve tractability, the configuration space must be bounded. In other words, we have to assume a finite countable limit for every variable within the dynamic domain of the diagram. Hereafter, we further detail the CTS concept.

Definition 8.1 (Dynamic domain) The set of heterogeneous attributes that characterize the evolution of a behavioral diagram D represents its dynamic domain and it is denoted as D_Δ.

A configuration can be understood as a snapshot in the evolution of a set of dynamic elements of a system at a particular point in time and from a specific view.

Definition 8.2 (Configuration) For an established variable ordering, a configuration c is a particular binding of a set of values to the set of variables in the dynamic domain D_Δ of a behavioral diagram.

Given a diagram D and its corresponding dynamic domain D_Δ, if for every attribute $a_{1,...,n} \in D_\Delta$, we can find a corresponding positive integer $i_{1,...,n}$, so that for each projection of the dynamic domain $\pi_{a_k}(D_\Delta), k \in 1, \ldots, n$ we have $\max |\pi_{a_k}(D_\Delta)| < 2^{i_k}$, then a configuration c belonging to the CTS of D needs at most $I = \sum i_k$ bits, while the number of possible CTS configurations is at most 2^I. Notwithstanding, the actual number of configurations is usually much smaller and is restricted to the number of configurations reachable from the initial set of configurations. Moreover, the state attributes are in most the cases confined to boolean values.

Definition 8.3 (Configuration Transition System) A CTS is a tuple $(C, \Lambda, \rightarrow)$, where C is a set of configurations taken from the same view, Λ is a set of labels, and $\rightarrow \subseteq C \times \Lambda \times C$ is a ternary relation, called a transition relation. If $c_1, c_2 \in C$ and $l \in \Lambda$, the common representation of the transition relation is $c_1 \xrightarrow{l} c_2$.

Since the dynamics of a particular diagram is captured by the corresponding CTS, it is then considered as the underlying semantic model. Consequently, the CTS can be used to systematically generate the model-checker input.

Moreover, the CTS structure can also provide useful feedback to the designer. Thus, after the generated CTS may be graphically visualized using a suitable graph editor such as daVinci [238], the latter can be used in order to provide an overall visual appraisal of the diagram's complexity with respect to the number of nodes

---

[1] Though usually a *true* boolean value denotes the active status of a state, the *false* boolean value might similarly be used, as long as the convention is used consistently.

and edges. It can also be used as a quick feedback when applying corrective measures, giving some insights about the resulting increase or decrease of the diagram's behavioral complexity.

8.2 Model Checking of Configuration Transition Systems

The following paragraphs detail the back-end processing required for the model-checking procedure of the CTS model. The chosen model checker is NuSMV [47], an improved version of the original SMV [158].

The encoding of a transition system in the NuSMV input language basically involves a grouping in at least the three following main syntactic declarative divisions.[2]

First, we need a syntactic block, wherein the state variables are defined along with their type and range. Second, we have to specify an initialization block, wherein the state variables are given their corresponding initial values or a range of possible initial values. Third, we have to describe the dynamics of the transition system in a so-called next clause block, wherein the logic governing the evolution of the state variables is specified. Based on this, the state variables can be updated in every next step taking into account the logical valuation done at the current step.

The CTS can be used to systematically generate its corresponding encoding into the model-checker input language by constructing the three declarative divisions mentioned above. As presented in the foregoing section, the CTS dynamics is given in the form of pairwise configuration transition relations. Hence, any given CTS transition links a source configuration to a destination configuration. Consequently, it might be conceivable to encode each configuration as a distinct entity in the NuSMV model. However, one can note that, in a given CTS, the number of configurations may be significantly higher than the number of states that are members of different configurations. Also, the properties to be verified ought to be expressed on states and not on configurations. It follows that, in order to encode the CTS representation into the model-checker language in a compact and meaningful way, we need to use, as dynamic entities, the configuration states rather than the configurations themselves. This will be reflected accordingly in all three declarative blocks.

Thus, after the establishment of the dynamic entities, one can proceed with the compilation of the three code blocks. The first one consists of enumerating the labels associated with each dynamic entity, along with its type and range. The second one is compiled by using the initial configuration of the CTS in order to specify the initial values. The third one, more laborious in nature, consists in analyzing the CTS transitions in order to determine its state-based evolution from its configuration-based one.

---

[2] If appropriate, one might use various other convenient constructs while encoding a transition system in NuSMV as well as various levels of hierarchy, where a main module is referring to several other sub-modules, due to the modular aspect that some particular transition systems might exhibit. However, this has no semantic impact with respect to the considered declarative divisions.

More precisely, for every state s in any given destination configuration that is part of one or more transition relations of the CTS, we need to

1. specify the conditions that are required for the activation of s, for each destination configuration, and
2. specify that, in the absence of such conditions, s would be deactivated.

The aforementioned activation conditions can be expressed for every destination configuration as boolean predicates. These predicates are in the form of conjunctions over the active status belonging to each state in the corresponding source configuration, along with the test term for the transition trigger, if such is the case. However, there may be more general cases where the source configuration elements might contain both multiple value and boolean state variables. In this situation, the activation condition predicates would also include value test terms for the corresponding multivalued variables. Consequently, for each state[3] variable in the configurations of the CTS model, we have to specify what we would henceforth denote as transition candidates. Specifically, a candidate for each state s represents the disjunctive combination over the activation conditions of all the destination configurations that have s as a member.

In mathematical terms, under the convention that the *true* boolean value represents for each state its "active" status and given the structures:

- S, the set of all states in the CTS configurations;
- C, the set of all configurations in the CTS;
- Λ, the set of all trigger event labels in the CTS;
- $\rightarrow \subseteq (src : C \times lbl : \Lambda \times dst : C)$, the transition relation;
- $e \in \Lambda$, trigger event label;

we can determine the following:

$$\forall t \in \rightarrow .c = \pi_{dst}(t).A_c = \bigwedge(\pi_{src}(t) \wedge e \equiv \pi_{lbl}(t));$$
$$\forall s \in S.\forall c \in \{C | \exists t \in \rightarrow .s \in C = \pi_{dst}(t)\}.A_s = \bigvee A_c;$$

where

- A_c is the set of CTS configuration activation conditions;
- A_s is the activation condition set of the states in the CTS configurations.

Given that A_s contains the transition candidates for each state, we can use it in order to compile the corresponding evolution logic in the *next* clause block for each state in the CTS configurations. Thus, the dynamics of the CTS is encoded at state level. This stems from specifying that each state is activated at the next step whenever the transition candidate for the state is satisfied (*true*) in the current step and, conversely, deactivated if not.

---

[3] In the presented context, a state should be understood as any boolean or multivalued variable that is part of one or more CTS configurations.

8.3 Property Specification Using CTL

The verification process by means of model checker requires the precise specification of properties for the potential benefits of this technique to unfold. The NuSMV model checker primarily uses CTL [61] temporal logic for this purpose. This logic has interesting features and great expressivity. CTL properties can be used to express general safety and liveness as well as more advanced properties like conditional reachability, deadlock freedom, sequencing, precedence. In the following paragraphs, we briefly introduce the CTL logic and its operators.

CTL is used for reasoning about computation trees that are unfolded from state transition graphs. CTL properties refer to the computation tree derived from the transition graph. The paths of a computation tree represent every possible computation of its corresponding model. Moreover, CTL is classified as a branching time logic since it has operators describing properties on the branching structure of the computation tree.

CTL properties are built using atomic propositions, propositional logic, boolean connectives, and temporal operators. The atomic propositions correspond to the variables in the model. Each temporal operator consists of two components: a path quantifier and an adjacent temporal modality.

The temporal operators are interpreted in the context of an implicit current state. In general, it is possible to have many execution paths forming at the current state. The path quantifier indicates whether the modality defines a property that should hold for all the possible paths (universal path quantifier A) or only for some of them (existential path quantifier E).

Figure 8.1 depicts a computation tree along with a number of basic CTL properties that hold at various points in the computation tree.

Figure 8.2 presents the syntax of CTL formulas and Table 8.1 explains the meaning underlying the temporal modalities.

Though the syntax of CTL allows the specification of a broad range of properties, it is a known fact that, except for very simple cases, the task of accurately capturing a given specification in CTL can be quite tricky and cumbersome. In order to alleviate this issue, one can use some intuitive macros that can be automatically expanded to their corresponding CTL equivalents, thus allowing for a convenient

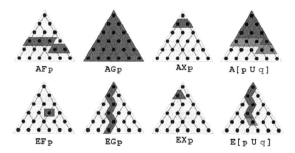

Fig. 8.1 Basic computation trees and their corresponding CTL properties (source [6])

$$\phi ::= p \qquad \text{(Atomic propositions)}$$
$$| \quad !\phi \mid \phi \wedge \phi \mid \phi \vee \phi \mid \phi \rightarrow \phi \qquad \text{(Boolean Connectives)}$$
$$| \quad AG\ \phi \mid EG\ \phi \mid AF\ \phi \mid EF\ \phi \qquad \text{(Temporal Operators)}$$
$$| \quad AX\ \phi \mid EX\ \phi \mid A[\ \phi\ U\ \phi] \mid E[\ \phi\ U\ \phi] \quad \text{(Temporal Operators)}$$

Fig. 8.2 CTL syntax

Table 8.1 CTL modalities

G p	Globally, p is satisfied for the entire subsequent path
F p	Future (Eventually), p is satisfied somewhere on the subsequent path
X p	neXt, p is satisfied at the next state
p U q	Until, p has to hold until the point that q holds and q must eventually hold

way of expressing the specification with minimal, or even with no prior knowledge of temporal logic.

Examples of useful CTL macros include

- ALWAYS
- NEVER
- MAYREACH
- INEVIT
- POSSIB
- NECESS
- PRECEDE

Later, we provide a number of case studies wherein the use of CTL macros will be demonstrated for specifying the design properties to be verified using model checking.

8.4 Program Analysis of Configuration Transition Systems

In the following, we discuss the use of program analysis techniques (data and control flow) on our semantic model, namely the CTS. These techniques can potentially improve the effectiveness of the model-checking procedure by narrowing the scope of the verification to what we might call semantic projections of the transition system.

The goal is to identify and extract those parts of the CTS that exhibit properties that can be used in order to simplify the transition system that is supplied to the model checker. The aspects that we are interested in are the data and control flow. The former is applied by basically searching for the presence of invariants (e.g., specific variable values or relations) whereas the latter can be used in order to detect control flow dependencies among various parts of the transition system. Consequently, the CTS may be sliced into smaller independent subgraphs that can be individually subjected to the model-checking procedure.

Though it might be possible to specify some properties that could span across more than one subgraph of the original CTS, the slicing can safely be done under the following conditions:

1. The properties to be verified fall into liveness[4] or safety category[5];
2. No property specification should involve sequences or execution traces that require the presence of the initial state more than once.

It must be noted that the second constraint does not represent a major hindrance for the verification potential. In this respect, the presence of invariants assures that either revisiting the initial state or entering it for the first time is equivalent with respect to the dynamics of the transition system.

It must, however, be mentioned that, even though some of the configuration subgraphs derived might be rather simple, it is nevertheless required for the model-checking procedure that one specifies all the elements of the original model for each transition system input to the model checker. This must be done in order to preserve the original elements[6] of the transition system, all the while ensuring that the underlying dynamics is captured by the configuration subgraph in question.

Moreover, due to the fact that the dynamics may be severely restricted in some cases, one has to take this fact into account when interpreting the model-checking results. Thus, even though it might be the case that a liveness property fails for a transition system corresponding to a particular subgraph, the property should not be immediately declared as failed for the original model. The property in question passes as long as there is at least one subgraph whose transition system satisfies it. Conversely, whenever a safety property fails for a particular subgraph, then it is declared as failed for the original model as well. Notwithstanding, this task can be automated and virtually transparent.

In order to illustrate more effectively how data and control flow analysis can be applied on the CTS model, we provide an edifying example in Sect. 8.5, wherein we detail the verification and validation procedure of the state machine diagram. The application of program analysis techniques are described in Sect. 8.5.3.

8.5 V&V of UML State Machine Diagram

In this chapter, we describe the verification and validation procedure of the state machine diagram by means of model checking. A state machine is a specification that thoroughly describes all the possible behaviors of some discrete dynamic

---

[4] Liveness properties capture a system behavior that will eventually occur (e.g., eventually something "good" will happen).

[5] A safety property is usually capturing a behavior that must always occur (e.g., at any point, nothing "bad" happens).

[6] Certain elements of the transition system may be needed when specifying various properties.

model. The state machine diagram representation contains hierarchically organized states that are related by transitions labeled with events and guards.

The state machine evolves in response to events that trigger the corresponding transitions provided that the source state is active, that the transition has the highest priority, and that the guard on the transition is *true*. If transitions conflict, priorities are assigned to decide which transition will fire. Higher priority is assigned to transitions whose source states are nested deeper in the containment hierarchy.

8.5.1 Semantic Model Derivation

The hierarchical structure of the state machine diagram can be represented as a tree, where the root is the top state, the basic states are the leaves, and all the other nodes are composite states. The tree structure can be used to identify the least common ancestor (LCA) of a transition's source and target states. This is useful in identifying, after firing a transition, the states that will be deactivated and those that will be activated. An appropriate labeling (encoding) of the states is required in order to capture the hierarchical containment relation among them, that is, we have "is ancestor of"/"is descendant of" relations within the set of states. Moreover, each state down the hierarchy is labeled in the same manner as the table of contents of a book (e.g., 1., 1.1., 1.2., 1.2.1.).

The labeling procedure consists of assigning Dewey positions and is presented in Algorithm 2, where the operator $+_c$ denotes string concatenation (with implicit operand-type conversion). To that effect, the labeling of the states is achieved by executing Algorithm 2 on the top state with label "1.", and thus recursively labeling all states. The information encoded in the label of each state can be used to evaluate the relation among the states: For any two states s and z of a state machine where s_l and z_l represent their respective labels, (s "is ancestor of" z) holds if s_l is a proper prefix of z_l (e.g., $s_l =$ "1.1.", $z_l =$ "1.1.2."). Conversely (s "is descendant of" z) holds if z_l is a proper prefix of s_l.

The state labeling is used in order to find the LCA state of any pair of states under the top state[7] by identifying the common prefix. The latter represents the label of the LCA state and can be more formally expressed in the following way:

For any pair of states (s, z), $s_l \neq$ "1." $\neq z_l$, $\exists ! l p \neq \varepsilon$ such that lp is the greatest (longest) proper prefix of both s_l and z_l. Consequently, $\exists ! lcaState =$ LCA(s, z) such that $lcaState_l = lp$.

While for any pair of states under the top, there is a unique LCA, it is also possible to have states that do not share "is ancestor of"/"is descendant of" relations (e.g., $s_l =$ "1.1.1.", $z_l =$ "1.2.1.").

A configuration is the set of states of the state machine where the *true* value is bound to active states and the *false* value to inactive ones. To avoid redundancy,

---

[7] The LCA of any two states is the closest state in the containment hierarchy that is an ancestor of both of them.

Algorithm 2 Hierarchical State Labeling

$labelState$(State s, Label l)
$s_l \leftarrow l$
for all substate k in s **do**
    $labelState(k, l +_c indexof(k) +_c ".")$;
end for

---

for every configuration one only needs to specify the states that are active. However, to support a mechanism whereby all the configurations of a state machine can be generated, we keep in each configuration two additional lists, one containing the value of all the guards for that particular configuration and the other containing a so-called join pattern list of configurations. The join pattern list terminology is borrowed from [84] and it is used to record various synchronization points that may be reached in the evolution of the state machine from one configuration to another.

In the following, we explain the procedure used for the generation of the CTS, presented by Algorithm 3. The CTS is obtained by a breadth-first search iterative procedure. The main idea consists of exploring, for each iteration, all the new configurations reachable from the current configuration, identified as *CurrentConf*. Moreover, three main lists are maintained. One, denoted by *FoundConfList*, records the so far identified and explored configurations. The second one is holding the newly found, but unexplored, configurations and is denoted by *CTSConfList*. Finally, the third list is used to record the identified transitions from one configuration to another and is denoted by *CTSTransList*. Additionally, we have a container list, denoted by *CTScontainer* that holds all the state and guard elements of the state machine, along with an initially empty join pattern list placeholder.

The iterative procedure starts with *CTSConfList* containing only the initial configuration of the state machine, denoted by *initialConf*. In each iteration, a configuration is popped from *CTSConfList* and represents the value of *CurrentConf* for the current iteration. From *CurrentConf*, the three subsumed lists (*crtStateList*, *crtGList*, and *crtJoinPatList*) are extracted. In order to be able to properly evaluate the value of the guards before firing the transitions, the *crtGList* is inspected to check if it contains an unspecified (*any*) guard value. If it does, then two new configurations are added to *CTSConfList*, wherein the unspecified guard value is assigned the *true* and *false* values, respectively, and the next iteration immediately starts. Otherwise, if *FoundConfList* does not contain *CurrentConf* then the latter is added to *FoundConfList*.

Based on a list of possible incoming events referred to as *EventList*, we pick each element one by one and dispatch it, each time restoring the state machine to the current configuration by assigning the latter to the *CTScontainer*. The dispatching operation is a generic procedure that is responsible for the event processing and uses the state containment hierarchy labeling in order to properly move the state machine from the current configuration to the next. Thus, the corresponding enabled transitions labeled with the dispatched event are triggered respecting their priorities and also, should a previously unidentified configuration be discovered, it is added to *CTSConfList*.

Algorithm 3 Generation of the State Machine CTS

FoundConfList = ∅
CTSConfList = { initialConf }
CTSTransList = ∅
CTScontainer = {DiagramStateList,guardValueList,∅}
while CTSConfList *is not* empty **do**
    CurrentConf = pop(CTSConfList)
    crtStateList = get(CurrentConf,0)
    crtGList = get(CurrentConf,1)
    crtJoinPatList = get(CurrentConf,2)
    if crtGList *contains Value* "any" **then**
        splitIndex = getPosition(crtGList, "any")
        crtGList[splitIndex] = true
        CTSConfList = CTSConfList ∪ { crtStateList, crtGList, crtJoinPatList }
        crtGList[splitIndex] = false
        CTSConfList = CTSConfList ∪ { crtStateList, crtGList, crtJoinPatList }
      continue
    end if
    if FoundConfList *not contains* CurrentConf **then**
        FoundConfList = FoundConfList ∪ CurrentConf
    end if
    for each event *e* in EventList **do**
        setConf(CTScontainer, CurrentConf)
        dispatch(CTScontainer, *e*)
        nextConf = getConf(CTScontainer)
        if nextConf *not equals* CurrentConf **then**
            CTSConfList = CTSConfList ∪ nextConf
            crtTrans = {CurrentConf, *e*, nextConf}
            if CTSTransList *not contains* crtTrans **then**
                CTSTransList = CTSTransList ∪ {crtTrans}
            end if
        end if
    end for
end while

Whenever the next found configuration is different from the current one, a new transition between *CurrentConf* and the next found configuration is formed and if not already present, it is added to *CTSTransList*. After adding all the new possible successor (next) configurations of the current configuration to the *CTSConfList*, the next iteration starts. The procedure stops when no elements can be found in *CTSConfList*. Thus, by applying the above algorithm, we obtain the CTS corresponding to a given state machine.

8.5.2 Case Study

In the following, we present a case study related to a UML 2.0-based design describing an automated teller machine (ATM). We perform V&V of this design with respect to predefined properties and requirements.

The ATM interacts with a potential customer (user) via a specific interface and communicates with the bank over an appropriate communication link. A user that requests a service from the ATM has to insert an ATM card and enter a personal identification number (PIN). Both pieces of information (the card number and the PIN) need to be sent to the bank for validation. If the credentials of the customer are not valid, the card will be ejected. Otherwise, the customer will be able to carry out one or more transactions (e.g., cash advance or bill payment). The card will be retained in the ATM machine during the customer's interaction until the customer wishes for no further service. Figure 8.3 shows the UML 2.0 state machine diagram of the ATM system.

The model is based on a hypothetical behavior and is meant only as an example. Moreover, it intentionally contains a number of flaws in the design in order to outline the usefulness of the approach in discovering problems in the behavioral model. The diagram has several states that we will present in accordance to the diagram containment hierarchy.

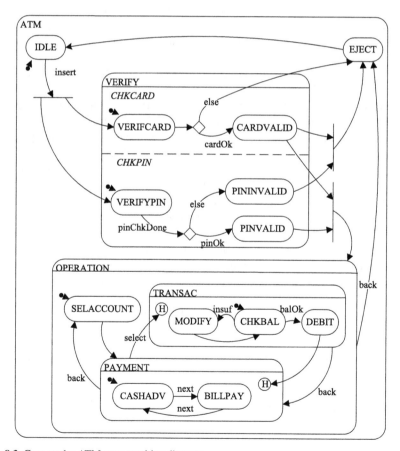

Fig. 8.3 Case study: ATM state machine diagram

The top container state ATM encloses four substates: IDLE, VERIFY, EJECT, and OPERATION. The IDLE state, wherein the system waits for a potential ATM user, is the default initial substate of the top state. The VERIFY state represents the verification of the card's validness and authorization. The EJECT state depicts the phase of termination of the user's transaction. The OPERATION state is a composite state that includes the states that capture several functions related to banking operations. These are the SELACCOUNT, PAYMENT, and TRANSAC.

The SELACCOUNT state is where an account, belonging to card owner, has to be selected. When the state SELACCOUNT is active, and the user selects an account, the next transition is enabled and the state PAYMENT is entered. The PAYMENT state has two substates, respectively, for cash advancing and bill payment. It represents a two-item menu, controlled by the event next. Finally, the TRANSAC state captures the transaction phase and includes three substates: CHKBAL for checking the balance, MODIFY for modifying the amount, if necessary, and DEBIT for debiting the account.

Each one of the PAYMENT and TRANSAC states contains a shallow history pseudostate. If a transition targeting a shallow history pseudostate is fired, the most recently active substate in the composite state containing the history connector is activated.

When applying formal analysis to assess the state machine diagram, the steps are as follows. We first convert the diagram to its corresponding semantic model (CTS) as depicted in Fig. 8.4. Each element is represented by a set (possibly singleton) of states and variable values of the state machine diagram. Thereafter, we automatically specify deadlock and reachability properties for every state. Furthermore, we also provide user-defined properties in both macro- and CTL notations.

After completing the model-checking procedure, the results obtained pinpoint some interesting design flaws in the ATM state machine design.

The model checker determined that the OPERATION state exhibits deadlock, meaning that once entered, it is never left. This is because in UML state machine diagrams, whenever there are conflicting transitions with the same trigger, higher priority is given in the case where the source state is deeper in the containment hierarchy.

Moreover, the transitions that have no event are fired as soon as the state machine reaches a stable configuration containing the corresponding source state. This is precisely the case with the transition from SELACCOUNT to PAYMENT. But, no configuration allows the operation state to be exited. This can also be seen by looking at the corresponding CTS where, we can notice that once a configuration that contains the OPERATION state is reached, there is no transition to a configuration that does not contain the OPERATION state.

In addition to the automatically generated properties, there are some relevant user-defined properties, described in both macro- and CTL notations.

The first property (property (8.1)) asserts that it is always true that if the VERIFY state is reached then, from that point on, the OPERATION state should be reachable:

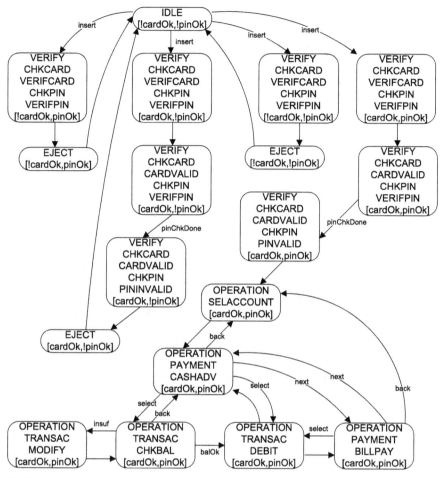

Fig. 8.4 CTS of the ATM state machine

ALWAYS VERIFY → MAYREACH OPERATION

$$CTL : AG((VERIFY \rightarrow (E[!(IDLE) U OPERATION]))) \qquad (8.1)$$

The next property (property (8.2)) asserts that it is always true that, after reaching the OPERATION state, it is inevitable to reach and EJECT state at a later point:

ALWAYS OPERATION → INEVIT EJECT

$$CTL : AG((OPERATION \rightarrow (A[!(IDLE) U EJECT]))) \qquad (8.2)$$

```
IDLE [!cardOk,!pinOk];
VERIFY,CHKCARD,VERIFCARD,CHKPIN,VERIFPIN [cardOk,pinOk];
VERIFY,CHKCARD,CARDVALID,CHKPIN,VERIFPIN [cardOk,pinOk];
VERIFY,CHKCARD,CARDVALID,CHKPIN,PINVALID [cardOk,pinOk];
OPERATION,SELACCOUNT [cardOk,pinOk];
OPERATION,PAYMENT,CASHADV [cardOk,pinOk];
OPERATION,TRANSAC,DEBIT [cardOk,pinOk].
```

Fig. 8.5 State machine counterexample

The last property (property (8.3)) states that the state CHKBAL must precede the state DEBIT:

$$CHKBAL \; PRECEDE \; DEBIT$$
$$CTL : (!E[!(CHKBAL) \; U \; DEBIT]))) \tag{8.3}$$

Property (8.1) turned out to be satisfied when running the model checker. This was expected. However, properties (8.2) and (8.3) failed. In this respect, from the automatic specifications, we noticed that state operation is never left once entered (it exhibits deadlock) and does not have state eject as a substate. The failure of property (8.3) was accompanied by a trace provided by the model checker, depicted in Fig. 8.5. Though the model checker can provide a counterexample for any of the failed properties, we present the counterexample for property (8.3) as it captures a critical and unintended behavior.

The foregoing counterexample is represented by a series of configurations (semi-colon separated). Moreover, whenever two or more states are present in a given configuration, a comma separates them in the notation. Additionally, for each configuration, the variable values are enclosed in square brackets. In this case, the failure is due to the presence of a transition from the PAYMENT state to the shallow history connector of the TRANSAC state. This allows for the immediate activation of the DEBIT state upon reentering the TRANSAC state by its history connector.

The counterexample can help the designer to infer the necessary changes to fix the identified design flaw. The first modification consists in adding a trigger, such as select, to the transition from the SELACCOUNT state to the PAYMENT state. This will eliminate the deadlock state and property (8.2). The second modification corrects the problem related to property (8.3). It consists in removing the history connector of the TRANSAC state and changing the incoming transition from this target directly to the TRANSAC state. Figure 8.6 depicts the corrected ATM state machine diagram. After re-executing the V&V process on the corrected diagram, all the specifications, both automatic and user-defined properties, were satisfied.

8.5.3 Application of Program Analysis

In the following, we show the use of program analysis on the configuration transition system of the state machine case study presented in Sect. 8.5.2. In the corresponding

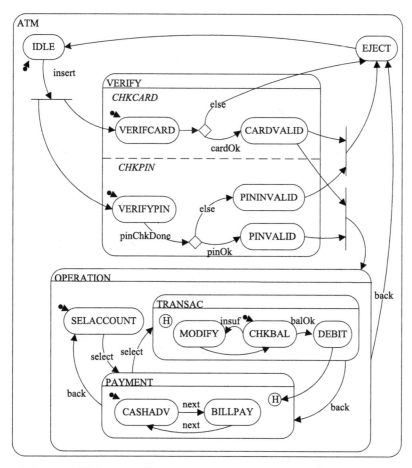

Fig. 8.6 Corrected ATM state machine

CTS, presented in Fig. 8.4, every configuration contains various values for the
variables cardOk and pinOk. Whenever we have an exclamation mark preceding
a variable in a particular configuration, this means that the variable is *false* in that
configuration.

There are several subgraphs where certain invariants hold. Figure 8.7 presents
these subgraphs, each of them having invariants that can be abstracted. In Fig. 8.7a,
we notice the invariant !cardOk. Similarly, Fig. 8.7b shows another subgraph where
the invariant !pinOk holds. In the subgraph of Fig. 8.7c, both !cardOk and !pinOk
invariants hold. Additionally, Fig. 8.8 depicts a subgraph that is independent from
the control flow perspective. To that effect, once the control is transferred to this
subgraph, it is never transferred outside of it.

The subgraphs identified in the previous paragraph represent the basis that
enables us to slice (decompose) the initial model into several independent parts that
can then be analyzed separately. Obviously, the subgraphs have reduced complexity

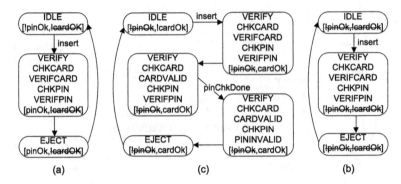

Fig. 8.7 Dataflow subgraphs

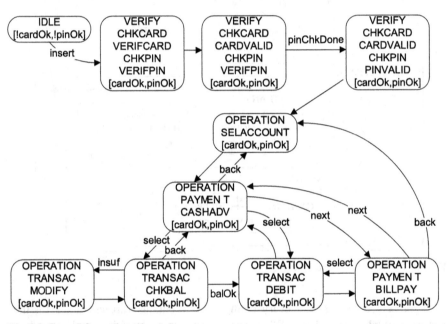

Fig. 8.8 Control flow subgraph

when compared to the original model. Accordingly, for each of them, the corresponding transition system subjected to model checking requires fewer resources in terms of memory space and computation time. The benefits of the slicing procedure are emphasized in the statistics below. Since the model checker is using binary decision diagrams (BDDs) for storing the generated state space in a highly compact manner, this serves as an eloquent comparison parameter (see Table 8.2 for the corresponding statistics). We can note that, while for verifying the initial CTS graph the model checker allocated between 70,000 and 80,000 BDD nodes (depending on the variable ordering), the number of allocated BDD nodes for the sliced subgraphs is significantly reduced. Indeed, for the graphs in Fig. 8.7a and b,

Table 8.2 Statistics related to model checking memory foot print

Graph	Memory footprint (BDD nodes)
Figure 8.4	70,000–80,000
Figure 8.7a	≈ 4000
Figure 8.7b	≈ 4000
Figure 8.7c	≈ 8000
Figure 8.8	28,000–33,000

the number of BDD nodes is around 4000, whereas the graph in Fig. 8.7c required around 8000 BDD nodes and the graph in Fig. 8.8 required about 28,000–33,000 nodes.

8.6 V&V of UML Sequence Diagram

Sequence diagrams are used in order to describe the communication required to fulfill an interaction. A sequence diagram, as defined by UML 2.0, is a diagram composed of a set of lifelines, which correspond to objects interacting in a temporal order. The abstraction of the most general interaction unit is called *InteractionFragment* [181] and it represents the basic piece of interaction.

8.6.1 Semantic Model Derivation

In a given sequence diagram, every interaction fragment can be conceptually considered as an interaction [181]. Moreover, combined fragment (i.e., *CombinedFragment*) [181] is a specialization of *InteractionFragment* that has an interaction operator corresponding to one of the following constructs: *Seq*, *Alt*, *Opt*, *Par*, or *Loop*. These constructs are examples of *CombinedFragment*. The interaction between lifelines is represented by message exchange. More specifically, it represents a communication (e.g., raising a signal, invoking an operation, or creating or destroying an instance of an object).

Generally, the sequence diagram can be used to capture attributes such as latency and precedence. By extracting all possible execution paths of a given sequence diagram, one can construct a corresponding transition system.

To proceed with the generation of the corresponding CTS, we have to first encode the messages in a particular syntax. By convention, we can assume that each message label starts with the sender actor and terminates with the receiving one. Consequently, each exchanged message *Msg* is written in the following format: S_Msg_R, where the sender of *Msg* is denoted as S and the receiver as R. In this case, a configuration is a set of messages sent in parallel (separated by a comma in the notation). Messages that are not enclosed in any *CombinedFragment*, but rather in *Seq*, each represents a singleton configuration. States are messages sent in parallel and the transitions are based on the sequencing operator. Thus, the transitions are derived from the sequencing events between the messages in the sequence diagram.

8.6.2 Sequence Diagram Case Study

The sequence diagram presented below depicts a possible execution scenario of the interaction between three actors of a banking system: The user, the ATM, and the bank. Though there are other possible execution scenarios, we will only focus on the one shown in Fig. 8.9.

The diagram comprises three main *CombinedFragment*: two are related to the authentication process and one to a banking transaction operation. The first *CombinedFragment* (*Par*) captures the validation of the card and a request for the PIN. The second *CombinedFragment* is an alternative choice (*Alt*) that captures the validation of the PIN. A subsequent *CombinedFragment* (*Alt*) depicts a possible interaction of using the cash advance service in the case where the credentials are valid.

In order to assess this diagram, we convert it to its corresponding semantic model, which is the CTS depicted in Fig. 8.10. Since deadlock and reachability properties are generic specification, we only present some of the relevant properties, such as service availability and safety. We describe each of them in two different notations: macro and CTL.

The first property (property (8.4)) is a kind of service availability specification. It asserts that it is always the case that, if the user inserts his card, then it should be possible to have an execution path where the ATM advances cash:

$$\text{ALWAYS U\_insertCard\_A} \ \rightarrow \ \text{MAYREACH A\_pickCash\_U}$$
$$CTL: \text{AG(U\_insertCard\_A} \ \rightarrow \ \text{E[!(end) U A\_pickCash\_U])} \quad (8.4)$$

The second property (property (8.5)) is a safety property. It asserts that it is always the case that should the credentials not be valid, then there should be no possibility for the user to request a banking operation:

$$\text{ALWAYS (!CardOk or !PINOk)} \rightarrow \text{MAYREACH (A\_waitAccount\_U)}$$
$$CTL: \text{AG((!Cardok \textit{or} !PINOk)} \rightarrow !(\text{E[!(end) U A\_waitAccount\_U])}) \quad (8.5)$$

The third property (property (8.6)) is related to an ergonomic specification stating that, whenever the specified amount exceeds the level of available funds, it should be possible for the user to request a new cash advance operation if the user wishes to correct the amount:

$$\text{ALWAYS A\_insufFunds\_U} \ \rightarrow \ \text{POSSIB U\_CashAdvance\_A}$$
$$CTL: \text{AG(A\_insufFunds\_U} \ \rightarrow \ \text{EX(U\_CashAdvance\_A))} \quad (8.6)$$

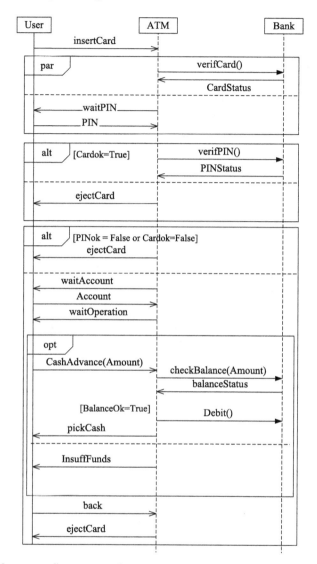

Fig. 8.9 ATM sequence diagram example

When subjecting the sequence diagram to V&V, only properties (8.4) and (8.5) are satisfied, while property (8.6) fails. The model checker was able to produce a counterexample for the failed property. The interpreted result of the corresponding trace is the CTS path depicted in Fig. 8.11.

The identified path contains a series of messages (separated by semicolons) that are exchanged between the actors. Hence, when analyzing the counterexample, one can note that it is not possible to reach state U_cashAdv_A from state A_insuf_U. Thus, we can conclude that the sequence diagram does not comply with all the specified requirements.

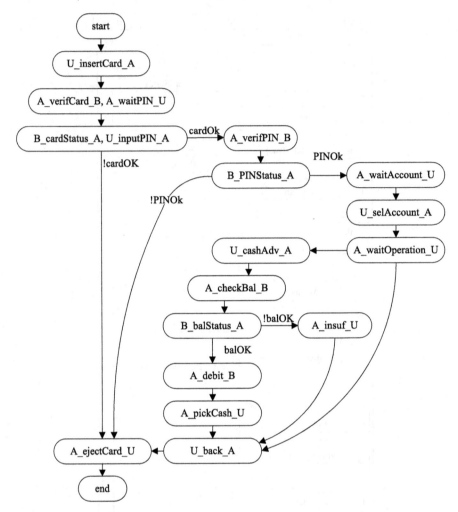

Fig. 8.10 The CTS of the ATM sequence diagram example

```
start; U_insertCard_A; A_verifCard_B, A_waitPIN_U;
B_cardStatus_A, U_inputPIN_A; A_verifPIN_B; B_PINStatus_A;
A_waitAccount_U; U_selAccount_A; A_waitOperation_U;
U_cashAdv_A; A_checkBal_B; B_balStatus_A;
A_insuf_U; U_back_A;
```

Fig. 8.11 Sequence diagram counterexample for property (8.6)

8.7 V&V of UML Activity Diagram

The UML activity diagram basically inherits the structured development concept of flowchart, being essentially its object-oriented equivalent. As such, it can be used for business process modeling, for modeling various usage scenarios, or for capturing the detailed logic of a complex operation. It must be noted that the activity and state machine diagrams are related to some extent. However, while a state machine diagram focuses on the state of a given object as it is undergoing a process (or on a particular process that captures the object state), an activity diagram focuses on the flow of activities of a particular process or operation involving one or more interacting objects. Specifically, the activity diagram shows the nature of the relations established among the activities involved in carrying out a process or operation, typically including relations such as sequencing, conditional dependency, synchronization.

8.7.1 Semantic Model Derivation

The semantic model derivation for the activity diagram inherits an idea stemming from the work of Eshuis and Weiringa [80] and consists of encoding the activity diagram dynamics by generating its reachable configurations.

In a similar manner to the one presented in the case of the state machine, the activity diagram is converted to its corresponding CTS. Accordingly, each configuration is represented by the set of actions that are concurrently active (*true* value is bound to active actions). Likewise, in order to generate all the reachable configurations of the activity diagram, there is in every configuration the two additional lists: one that corresponds to the values of all the guards for that configuration and the second being the join pattern list for that configuration. The join pattern is also required because the activity diagram allows for forking and joining activity flows as well as cross-synchronization among different activity flows. Thus, as in the case of the state machine, the join pattern list is used in order to record various synchronization points that may be reached while generating the configurations of the activity diagram. Consequently, the procedure used for the CTS generation in the case of activity diagram is a variation of the state machine CTS generation algorithm presented in Sect. 8.5.1, the main difference being that, instead of generating the CTS configurations by using a list of possible incoming events, we track each activity flow associated with each concurrent action that is a member of every new identified configuration. The procedure is presented in Algorithm 4, where the modification consists in picking each state in *crtStateList* and computing all the possible next configurations reachable by any control transfer to a successor state in the same activity flow.

8.7.2 Activity Diagram Case Study

The selected case study for the activity diagram presents a compound usage operation of the UML 2.0 ATM design, whose state machine diagram was previously

---

Algorithm 4 Generation of the Activity CTS (reusing part of Algorithm 3)

FoundConfList = { }
CTSConfList = { initialConf }
CTSTransList = ∅
CTScontainer = {DiagramStateList,guardValueList,∅}
while CTSConfList *is not* empty **do**
    CurrentConf = pop(CTSConfList)
    crtStateList = get(CurrentConf,0)
    crtGList = get(CurrentConf,1)
    crtJoinPatList = get(CurrentConf,2)
    if crtGList *contains Value* "any" **then**
        splitIndex = getPosition(crtGList, "any")
        crtGList[splitIndex] = true
        CTSConfList = CTSConfList ∪ { crtStateList, crtGList, crtJoinPatList }
        crtGList[splitIndex] = false
        CTSConfList = CTSConfList ∪ { crtStateList, crtGList, crtJoinPatList }
      continue
    end if
    if FoundConfList *not contains* CurrentConf **then**
        FoundConfList = FoundConfList ∪ CurrentConf
    end if
    for each state *s* in crtStateList **do**
        setConf(CTScontainer, CurrentConf)
        execute(*s*)
        nextConf = getConf(CTScontainer)
        if nextConf *not equals* CurrentConf **then**
            CTSConfList = CTSConfList ∪ nextConf
            crtTrans = {CurrentConf, nextConf}
            if CTSTransList *not contains* crtTrans **then**
                CTSTransList = CTSTransList ∪ {crtTrans}
            end if
        end if
    end for
end while

---

presented in Sect. 8.5.2. Likewise, the usage operation scenario is a hypothetical one and reflects a typical cash withdrawal operation that a potential customer (user) might perform. In the following paragraphs, we detail the intended operation, captured by the activity diagram, along with some relevant properties. Figure 8.12 shows the UML 2.0 activity diagram of the ATM cash withdrawal operation.

The operation begins with the Insert Card activity. Thereafter, two execution flows are forked, corresponding, respectively, to the Read Card and Enter Pin actions. The activity flow starting with Read Card continues to the Authorize Card action, while the one starting with Enter Pin continues to the Authorize Pin action. Both Authorize Card and Authorize Pin actions are followed by corresponding test branching points. In the case where both the user card and PIN check out, the two activity flows are joined together and the Initiate transaction action is started. This is followed, in order, by the Select amount, Check Balance actions, and a decision node. If the latter guard is satisfied, then

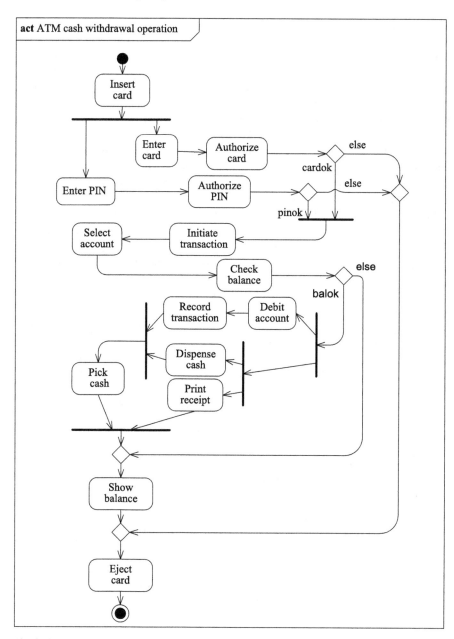

Fig. 8.12 ATM activity diagram example

two new activity flows fork. The first activity flow begins with the Debit account action and continues on with the Record Transaction action. The second one forks anew to Dispense Cash and Print Receipt actions. The three activity flows that are executing at this point are cross-synchronizing in the following manner: the Record Transaction activity flow is joined together along with the Dispense Cash activity flow into a single activity flow that subsequently continues with the execution of the Pick Cash action. The latter is then joined with the remaining one that was executing the Print Receipt action. Finally, the control is transferred to Show Balance and then to Eject Card, the latter finishing the whole operation. For cases where the authorization test branching points are not satisfied because the card and/or the PIN number do not check out, the control is transferred to the Eject Card action.

In order to outline the benefits of the model-checking procedure, the presented case study intentionally contains a number of flaws that are going to be identified during the verification procedure. Furthermore, to subject the activity diagram to the model checker, the following steps are required. First, the diagram is converted to its corresponding CTS depicted in Fig. 8.13, which represents its semantic model. Therein, each element is represented by a set (possibly singleton) of activity nodes. Second, we automatically specify deadlock and reachability properties for every action node in the diagram. Third, user-defined specifications intended to capture the desired behavior are presented in both macro- and CTL notations.

The first property (property (8.7)) asserts that, executing the InsertCard action implies that it is inevitable to reach at a later point the EjectCard action:

$$\text{Insert\_Card} \; \rightarrow \; \text{INEVIT Eject\_Card}$$
$$CTL: \text{Insert\_Card} \; \rightarrow \; \text{A[!(end) U Eject\_Card]} \qquad (8.7)$$

Next property (property (8.8)) asserts that it is always the case that whenever the system is executing the InsertCard action, this implies that AuthCard action precedes the EjectCard action:

$$\text{ALWAYS Insert\_Card} \; \rightarrow \; \text{Auth\_Card PRECEDE Eject\_Card}$$
$$CTL: \text{AG((Insert\_Card} \; \rightarrow \; \text{(!E[!(Auth\_Card) U Eject\_Card])))} \; (8.8)$$

Another property (property (8.9)) asserts that it is always the case that executing the Init_Transac action implies that the PickCash action may be reachable at a later point:

$$\text{ALWAYS Init\_Transac} \; \rightarrow \; \text{MAYREACH Pick\_Cash}$$
$$CTL: \text{AG((Init\_Transac} \; \rightarrow \; \text{(E[!(end) U Pick\_Cash])))} \qquad (8.9)$$

The fourth property (property (8.10)) is asserting that the DebitAccount action should precede the DispenseCash action:

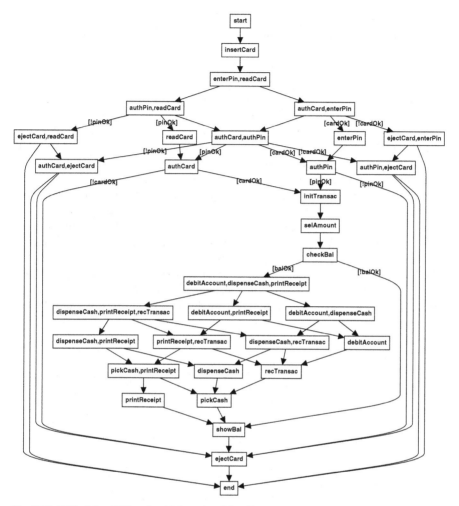

Fig. 8.13 CTS of the ATM cash withdrawal activity diagram

$$Debit\_Account\ PRECEDE\ Dispense\_Cash$$
$$CTL: (!E[!(Debit\_Account)\ U\ Dispense\_Cash]))) \qquad (8.10)$$

The fifth property (property (8.11)) asserts that the EjectCard action should never be followed by other actions:

$$NEVER\ (Eject\_Card\ \&\ POSSIB\ !end)$$
$$CTL: !EF(Eject\_Card\ \&\ EX\ !end) \qquad (8.11)$$

After running the model checker, the obtained results indicate that no unreachable or deadlock states were detected in the model. With respect to the manual specifications, properties 8.7 and 8.9 are satisfied. However, properties 8.8, 8.10, and 8.11 are violated. The counterexamples for properties 8.8 and 8.10 are presented, respectively, in Figs. 8.14 and 8.15.

Property (8.11) failed since there are reachable configurations that contain the Eject_Card action together with another action, such as Read_Card.

The cash withdrawal operation activity requires a number of modifications in order to have all the specified properties pass. Figure 8.16 presents the corrected version of the activity diagram. Several corrections were performed on the flawed activity diagram. The authorization test branching points are cascaded in sequence rather than concurrently after joining the activity flows forked for reading the card and entering the PIN. Moreover, the Dispense_Cash and Record_Transaction actions are swapped to enforce their execution after the Debit_Account action. Running again the V&V procedure on the corrected activity diagram, all properties were satisfied.

In Chaps. 9 and 10, we further describe an appropriate verification procedure involving probabilistic model-checking techniques for assessing design models expressed as SysML activity diagrams annotated with probability artifacts and time constraints.

```
Insert_Card;
Enter_Pin,Read_Card;
Authorize_Card,Enter_Pin;
Eject_Card,Enter_Pin;
```

Fig. 8.14 Activity diagram counterexample for property (8.8)

```
Insert_Card;
Enter_Pin,Read_Card;
Authorize_Pin,Read_Card;
Authorize_Card,Authorize_Pin;
Authorize_Pin;
Init_Transac;
Sel_Amount;
Check_Bal;
Debit_Account,Dispense_Cash,Print_Receipt;
Debit_Account,Print_Receipt;
```

Fig. 8.15 Activity diagram counterexample for property (8.10)

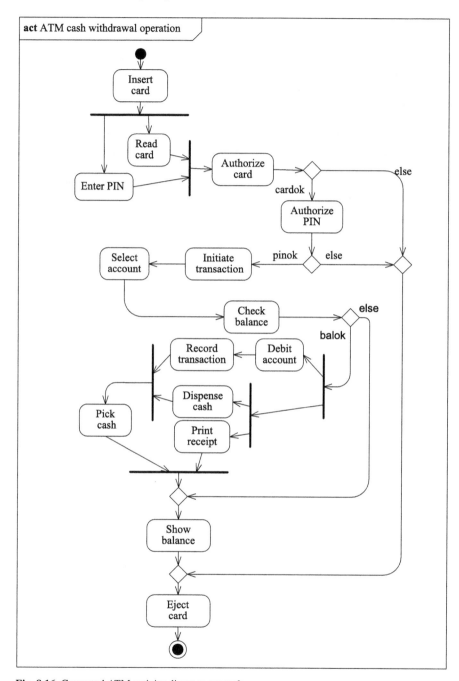

Fig. 8.16 Corrected ATM activity diagram example

8.8 Conclusion

In this chapter, we presented an automatic approach for the V&V of behavioral design models expressed in the UML modeling language. The approach presented employs the concept of configuration transition system (CTS) which can be tailored in order to construct corresponding semantic models for UML behavioral diagrams, such as state machine, activity, and sequence. Each resulting semantic model can be used as input to a model checker (e.g., NuSMV) in order to perform an automatic verification of various properties specified in temporal logic (e.g., CTL). The assessment results can serve as a basis for validating or debugging design models. With respect to the latter, a valuable feedback is found in the counterexamples generated for the failed properties during model checking.

Chapter 9
Probabilistic Model Checking of SysML Activity Diagrams

Incorporated modeling and analysis of both functional and non-functional aspects of today's systems behavior represents a challenging issue in the field of formal methods.

In this chapter, we look at integrating such an analysis on SE design models, focusing on probabilistic behavior. Indeed, SysML 1.0 [187] extends UML activity diagrams with probabilistic features. Thus, we propose to translate SysML activity diagrams into the input language of the probabilistic model-checker PRISM [204]. In Sect. 9.1, we explain our approach for the verification of SysML activity diagrams. In Sect. 9.2, we present the algorithm implementing the translation of SysML activity diagrams into PRISM input language. Section 9.3 is dedicated to the description of the property specification language, namely PCTL*. Finally, Sect. 9.4 illustrates the application of our approach on a SysML activity diagram case study.

9.1 Probabilistic Verification Approach

Our objective is to provide a technique by which we can analyze SysML activity diagrams from functional and non-functional points of view in order to discover subtle errors in the design. This allows one to reason with regard to the correction of the design from these standpoints, before the actual implementation. In these settings, probabilistic model checking allows the performance of both qualitative and quantitative analyses of the model. It can be used to compute expectation on systems performance by quantifying the likelihood of a given property being violated or satisfied in the system model. In order to carry out this analysis, we design and implement a translation algorithm that maps SysML activity diagrams into the input language of the selected probabilistic model checker. Thus, an adequate performance model that correctly captures the meaning of these diagrams has to be derived. More precisely, the selection of a suitable performance model depends on the understanding of the behavior captured by the diagram as well as its underpinning characteristics. It also has to be supported by an available probabilistic model checker.

M. Debbabi et al., *Verification and Validation in Systems Engineering*,
DOI 10.1007/978-3-642-15228-3_9, © Springer-Verlag Berlin Heidelberg 2010

The global state of an activity diagram can be characterized using the location of the control tokens. A specific state can be described by the position of the token at a certain point in time. The modification in the global state occurs when some tokens are enabled to move from one node to another. This can be encoded using a transition relation that describes the evolution of the system within its state space. Therefore, the semantics of a given activity diagram can be described using a transition system (automata) defined by the set of all the states reachable during the system's evolution and the transition relation thereof. SysML activity diagrams allow modeling probabilistic behavior, using probabilistic decision nodes. The outgoing edges of these nodes, quantified with probability values, specify probabilistic branching transitions within the transition system. The probability label denotes the likelihood of a given transition's occurrence. In the case of a deterministic transition, the probability is equal to 1. Furthermore, the behavior of activity diagrams presents non-determinism that is inherently due to parallel behavior and multiple instances execution. More precisely, fork nodes specify unrestricted parallelism, which can be described using non-determinism in order to model interleaving of flows' executions. This corresponds, in the transition system, to a set of branching transitions emanating from the same state, which allows the description of asynchronous behavior. In terms of probability labels, all transitions occurring due to non-determinism are labeled with probability equal to 1.

In order to select the suitable model checker, we need to first define the appropriate probabilistic model for capturing the behavior depicted by SysML activity diagrams. To this end, we need a model that expresses both non-determinism and probabilistic behavior. Thus, Markov decision process (MDP) might be a suitable model for SysML activity diagrams. Markov decision processes describe both probabilistic and non-deterministic behaviors. They are used in various areas, such as robotics [9], automated control [100], and economics [111]. A formal definition of MDP is given in the following [209]:

Definition 9.1 A Markov decision process is a tuple $M=(S, s_0, Act, Steps)$, where

- S is a finite set of states;
- $s_0 \in S$ is the initial state;
- Act is a set of actions;
- $Steps: S \rightarrow 2^{Act \times Dist(S)}$ is the probabilistic transition function that assigns to each state s a set of pairs $(a, \mu) \in Act \times Dist(S)$, where $Dist(S)$ is the set of all probability distributions over S, i.e., the set of functions $\mu: S \rightarrow [0, 1]$ such that $\sum_{s \in S} \mu(s) = 1$.

We write $s \xrightarrow{a} \mu$ if, and only if, $s \in S$, $a \in Act$, and $(a, \mu) \in Steps(s)$, and we refer to it as a step or a transition of s. The distribution μ is called an a-successor of s. For a specific action $\alpha \in Act$ and a state s, there is a single α-successor distribution μ for s. In each state s, there is a non-deterministic choice between elements of $Steps(s)$ (i.e., between the actions). Once an action–distribution pair (a, μ) is selected, the action is performed and the next state, for example, s', is determined probabilistically according to the distribution μ, i.e., with a probability equal to $\mu(s')$. In the case of μ of the form $\mu^1_{s'}$ (meaning the unique distribution on s', i.e., $\mu(s') = 1$), we denote the transition as $s \xrightarrow{a} s'$ rather than $s \xrightarrow{a} \mu^1_{s'}$.

Among the existing probabilistic model checkers, we have selected PRISM model checker. The latter is a free and open-source model checker that supports MDPs analysis and whose input language is both flexible and user-friendly. Moreover, PRISM is widely used in many application domains on various real-life case studies and is recognized for its efficiency in terms of data structure and numerical methods. In summary, to apply probabilistic model checking on SysML activity diagrams, these diagrams will need to be mapped into their corresponding MDPs using PRISM input language. With respect to properties, they must be expressed using probabilistic computation tree logic (PCTL*), which is commonly used in conjunction with discrete-time Markov chains (DTMC) and MDP [20]. Figure 9.1 illustrates the synopsis of the proposed approach.

In the next section, we present the algorithm that we devise for the systematic mapping of SysML activity diagrams into the corresponding PRISM MDP code.

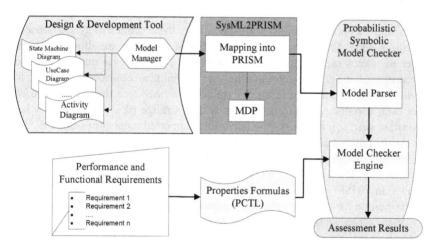

Fig. 9.1 Probabilistic model checking of SysML activity diagrams

9.2 Translation into PRISM

To translate SysML activity diagrams into PRISM code, we assume a single initial node and a single activity final node. Nevertheless, this is not a restriction, since we can replace a set of initial nodes by one initial node connected to a fork node and a set of activity final nodes by a merge node connected to a single activity final node.

Definition 9.2 A SysML activity diagram is a tuple $A = (N, N_0, type, next, label)$ where

- N is the set of activity nodes of types action, initial, final, flow final, fork, join, decision, and merge;
- N_0 is the initial node;
- $type: N \rightarrow \{action, initial, final, flowfinal, fork, join, decision, merge\}$ that associates with each node its corresponding type;
- $next: N \rightarrow \mathcal{P}(N)$ a function that returns for a given node the set (possibly singleton) of nodes that are directly connected to it via its outgoing edges;
- $label: N \times N \rightarrow Act \times]0, 1]$ a function that returns the pair of labels (g,p), namely the guard and the probability on the edge connecting two given nodes.

We rely on a fine-grained iterative translation of SysML activity diagrams into MDP. Indeed, the locus of control is tracked on both action and control nodes. Thus, each of these nodes is represented by a variable in the corresponding PRISM model. The join node represents a special case since the corresponding control passing rule is not straightforward [188] compared to the other control node rules. More precisely, a join node has to wait for a locus of control on each incoming edge in order to be traversed. Therefore, we need to keep a variable for each pin of a given join node. We also define a boolean formula corresponding to the condition of synchronization at each join node. Moreover, multiple instances of execution are allowed, thus the number of tokens in a given node is represented by an integer number denoting active instances at a certain point in time. At this point, we consider that in realistic systems a certain number of instances are active at the same time. Therefore, we model each variable as being an integer within a range $[0, \ldots, max\_inst]$ where the constant max_inst represents the maximum supported number of instances. This value can be tailored according to the application's needs.

Aside from the variables, the commands encode the behavior dynamics captured by the diagram. Thus, each possible progress of the locus of control corresponds to a command in PRISM code. The predicate guard of a given command corresponds to the precondition for triggering the control passing whereas the updates represent its effect on the global state. A given predicate guard expresses the ability of the source nodes to pass the control and also the destination nodes to accept it. A given update expresses the effect that control passing has on the number of active instances of the source and destination nodes. For instance, the fork node F1 in Fig. 9.5 passes the control to each of its outgoing edges on condition that it possesses at least one locus of control and that the destination nodes are able to receive the token (did not reach their maximum number of instances). The modification in the control configuration has to be reflected in the updates of the command, where the fork node looses one locus of control and the number of active instances of the destination nodes increases. The corresponding PRISM command can be written as follows:

```
[F1]          F1>0 & Autofocus<max_inst & DetLight<max_inst &
                         D3<max_inst & !End  →
                 F1'=F1-1 & Autofocus'=Autofocus-1 &
                    DetLight'=DetLight-1 & D3'=D3-1;
```

This dependency of the predicates and updates on the nodes at source and at destination of the control passing inspired us to develop the systematic mapping procedure. In fact, the principle underlying our algorithm is that the predicates and updates for the source and destination nodes are generated separately so that, when composed together, they provide the whole final command. The commands are generated according to the type of the source node and the number of outgoing edges. For instance, in the case where the source node is a non-probabilistic decision node, the algorithm generates as many commands as outgoing edges. Concerning the probabilistic decision node, a only single command is needed, where the updates are the sum of all the probabilistic occurrences associated with different probabilistic choices. For a fork node, a single command enables all the outgoing target nodes. Finally, a single command suffices for nodes with a unique outgoing edge, such as action, join, merge, and initial.

The algorithm translating SysML activity diagrams into the input language of PRISM is presented in Figs. 9.2, 9.3, and 9.4. The algorithm visits the activity nodes using a depth-first search procedure and generates on-the-fly the PRISM commands. The main procedure $T(A,N)$ is illustrated in Fig. 9.2 and is continued in Fig. 9.3. Initially, the main procedure $T(A,\{N_0\})$ is called where A is the data structure representing the activity diagram and N_0 is the initial node. It is then called recursively, where N represents the set (possibly singleton) of the next nodes to be explored. The algorithm uses a function $C(n, g, u, n', p)$ illustrated in Fig. 9.4 where n is the current node representing the action name of the command, g and u are expressions, and n' is the destination node of n. The function C serves the generation of different expressions related to the destination node n', returning the final resulting command to be appended into the output of the main algorithm.

We make use of the usual *Stack* data structure with fundamental operations such as *pop*, *push*, and *empty*. We define user-defined types such as

- *PrismCmd* : a record type containing the fields *act*, *grd*, and *upd* corresponding respectively to the action, the guard and the update of the command of type *PrismCmd*.
- *Node* : a type defined to handle activity nodes.
- *PRISMVarId* : a type defined to handle PRISM variables identifiers.

The variable *nodes* is of type *Stack* and serves to temporarily store the nodes that are to be explored by the algorithm. At each iteration, a current node *cNode* is popped from the stack *nodes* and its destination nodes in the activity diagram are stored in the list of nodes *nNode*. These destination nodes will be pushed in the stack in the next recursive call of the main algorithm. If the current node is already visited

```
nodes as Stack;
cNode as Node;
nNode as list_of_ Node;
vNode as list_of_ Node;
cmd as PrismCmd;
varfinal, var as PRISMVarId;
cmdtp as PrismCmd;
procedure T(A,N)
        / * Stores all newly discovered nodes in the stack */
    for all n in N do
        nodes.push(n);
    end for
    while not nodes.empty() do
        cNode := nodes.pop();
        if cNode not in vNode then
            vNode := vNode.add(cNode);
            if type(cNode)= final then
                cmdtp := C(cNode, eq(varfinal,1), raz(vars), null, 1.0);
            else
                nNode := next(cNode);
        / * Return the PRISM variable associated with the cNode */
            var :=  prismElement(cNode);
            if type(cNode)= initial then
                cmdtp := C(cNode, eq(var,1), dec(var), nNode, 1.0)
            end if
            if type(cNode) in {action, merge} then
        / * Generate the final PRISM command for the edge cNode-nNode */
                cmdtp := C(cNode, grt(var,0), dec(var), nNode, 1.0);
            end if
            if type(cNode)= join then
                cmdtp := C(cNode, var, raz(pinsOf(var)), nNode, 1.0);
            end if
            if type(cNode)= fork then
                cmdtp1 := C(cNode, grt(var,0), dec(var), nNode[0], 1.0);
                cmdtp := C(cNode, cmdtp1.grd, cmdtp1.upd, nNode[1], 1.0));
            end if
```

Fig. 9.2 Translation algorithm of SysML activity diagrams into MDP – part 1

by the algorithm it is stored in the set of nodes *vNode*. In accordance with the current node's type, the parameters to be passed to the function C are computed. We denote by *varfinal* the PRISM variable identifier of the final node and *vars* represents the set of all PRISM variables of the current activity diagram. Finally, *max* is a constant value specifying the maximum value of all PRISM variables (of type integer). The algorithm terminates when the stack is empty and all instances of the main algorithm have stopped running. All the PRISM commands generated by the algorithm T are appended into a list of commands *cmd* (using the utility function *append*), which allows us to build the performance model.

We make use of the following utility functions:

- The functions *type*, *next*, and *label* are related to the accessing of the activity diagram structure and components.

> **if** *type(cNode)= decision* **then**
> $g := \Pi(label(cNode, nNode[0]), 1)$;
> $upd := and(dec(var), set(g, \text{true}))$;
> $cmdtp1 := C(cNode, grt(var,0), upd, nNode[0], 1.0)$;
> $g := \Pi(label(cNode, nNode[1]), 1)$;
> $upd := and(dec(var), set(g, \text{true}))$;
> $cmdtp2 := C(cNode, grt(var,0), upd, nNode[1], 1.0)$;
> /*Append both generated commands together before final appending */
>   *append(cmdtp, cmdtp1)*;
>   *append(cmdtp, cmdtp2)*;
> **end if**
> **if** *type(cNode)= pdecision* **then**
> $g := \Pi(label(cNode, nNode[0]), 1)$;
> $p := \Pi(label(cNode, nNode[0]), 2)$;
> $upd := and(dec(var), set(g, \text{true}))$;
> $cmdtp1 := C(cNode, grt(var,0), upd, nNode[0], p)$;
> $g := \Pi(label(cNode, nNode[1]), 1)$;
> $q := \Pi(label(cNode, nNode[1]), 2)$;
> $upd := and(dec(var), set(g, \text{true}))$;
> $cmdtp2 := C(cNode, grt(var,0), upd, nNode[1], q)$;
> /* Merge commands into one final command with a probabilistic choice */
> $cmdtp := merge(cmdtp1, cmdtp2)$;
> **end if**
> **end if**
> /* Append the newly generated command into the set of final commands */
>   *append(cmd, cmdtp)*;
> $T(A, nNode)$;
>   **end if**
>   **end while**
> **end procedure**

Fig. 9.3 Translation algorithm of SysML activity diagrams into MDP – part 2

- The function PRISMELEMENT takes a node as parameter and returns the PRISM element (either a variable of type integer or a formula) associated with the node.
- The function PINPRISMELEMENT takes two nodes as parameters, where the second is a *join* node and returns the PRISM variable related to the specific pin.
- Various functions are used in order to build the expressions needed in the guard or the updates of the commands. The function *raz* returns the expression that is the conjunction of the expression of resetting the variables taken as parameter to their default values. The function $grt(x,y)$ returns the expression $x > y$, while function $less(x,y)$ returns the expression $x < y$. The function $dec(x)$ returns the expression $x' = x - 1$. The function $inc(x)$ returns the expression $x' = x + 1$. The function $not(x)$ returns the expression $!x$. The function $and(x,y)$ returns the expression $x \& y$. The function $eq(x,y)$ returns the expression $x = y$. The function $set(x,y)$ returns the expression $x' = y$.
- The Π is the conventional projection that takes two parameters, a pair (x, y) and an *index* (1 or 2), and returns x, if $index = 1$, and y if $index = 2$.
- The function *pinsOf* takes as input the PRISM formula corresponding to a join node and extracts the corresponding pins variables into a list of PRISM variables.

```
function C(n, g, u, n′, p)
    var :=  prismElement(n′);
    if type(n′)=flowfinal then
        /* Generate the final PRISM command */
        cmdtp := command(n,g,u,p);
    end if
    if type(n′)=final then
        u′ := inc(var);
        cmdtp := command(n, g, and(u,u′), p);
    end if
    if type(n′)=join then
        /* Return the PRISM variable related to a specific pin of the join */
        varpin :=pinPrismElement(n,n′);
        varn :=prismElement(n);
        g1 := not(varn);
        g2 :=less(varpin,max);
        g′ := and(g1,g2);
        u′ :=inc(varpin,1);
        cmdtp = command(n,and(g,g′),and(u,u′),p);
    end if
    if type(n′) in {action,merge,fork,decision,pdecision} then
        g′ := less(var,max);
        u′ := inc(var,1);
        cmdtp = command(n,and(g,g′),and(u,u′),p);
    end if
    return cmdtp;
end function
```

Fig. 9.4 Function generating PRISM commands

- The function *command* takes as input, in this order, the action name a, the guard g, the update u, the probability of the update p and returns the expression $[a]\, g\ \rightarrow\ p : u$.
- The function *merge* merges two sub-commands, taken as parameters, into one command consisting of a set of probabilistic updates. More precisely, it takes two parameters $cmdtp1\ =\ [a]\, g1\ \rightarrow\ p : u1$ and $cmdtp1\ =\ [a]\, g2\ \rightarrow\ q : u2$, then generates the command $[a]\, g1\ \&\ g2\ \rightarrow\ p : u1\ +\ q : u2$.

9.3 PCTL* Property Specification

In order to apply probabilistic model checking on the MDP model resulting from the translation algorithm, we need to express the properties in an appropriate temporal logic. For MDP models, we can use either LTL [248], PCTL [44], or PCTL* [248]. The probabilistic computation tree logic (PCTL) [44] is an extension of CTL [48], mainly with the added probability operator $\mathcal{P}$. PCTL* subsumes PCTL and LTL [248]. It is based on PCTL, where arbitrary combinations of path formulas and only propositional state formulas are allowed [10].

PCTL* syntax according to [10] is as follows:

$$\phi \ ::= \ true \mid a \mid \neg \phi \mid \phi \wedge \phi \mid \mathcal{P}_{\bowtie p}[\psi]$$
$$\psi \ ::= \ \phi \mid \psi_1 \, \mathcal{U}^t \, \psi_2 \mid \psi_1 \, \mathcal{U} \, \psi_2 \mid \mathcal{X}\psi \mid \psi_1 \wedge \psi_2 \mid \neg \psi$$

where a is an atomic proposition, $t \in \mathbb{N}$, $p \in [0, 1] \subset \mathbb{R}$, and $\bowtie \in \{ >, \geq, <, \leq \}$.

PRISM extends the latter syntax in order to quantify probability values with the operator $\mathcal{P} =?$. For the case of MDP, all non-determinism has to be resolved. Thus, properties quantifying the probability actually reason about the minimum or maximum probability, over all possible resolutions of non-determinism, that a certain type of behavior is observed. Measuring the minimum/maximum probabilities provides the worst/best-case scenarios.

9.4   Case Study

In order to explain our approach, we present a SysML activity diagram of a hypothetical model of a digital photo-camera device. The diagram captures the functionality of taking a picture as illustrated in Fig. 9.5. The corresponding dynamics are rich enough to allow the verification of several interesting properties that capture important functional aspects and performance characteristics. We deliberately modeled some flaws into the design in order to demonstrate the applicability as well as the benefits of our approach. The process captured by the digital photo-camera activity diagram starts by turning on the camera (TurnOn). Subsequently, three parallel execution flows are spawned. The first one begins by (AutoFocus) followed by a decision checking the status of the memory (memFull guard). In the case where the memory is full, the camera cannot be used and it is turned off. The second parallel flow is dedicated to the detection of the ambient lighting conditions (DetLight) and it determines whether the flash is needed in order to take a picture. The third flow allows charging the flash (ChargeFlash) if it is not already charged. The action (TakePicture) executes in two possible conditions: either it is sunny ($sunny = true$) and the memory is not full ($memFull = false$) or the flash (Flash) is needed because of the lack of luminosity ($sunny = false$). Thereafter, the picture is stored in the memory of the camera (WriteMem) and the activity diagram ends after turning off the camera (TurnOff).

By applying our algorithm on the SysML activity diagram case study, we end up with the MDP described using PRISM language as shown in Fig. 9.6 and continued in Fig. 9.7. After supplying the model to PRISM, the latter constructs the reachable state space in the form of a state list and a transition probability matrix.

At the beginning, one can search for the presence of deadlock states in the model. This is expressed using property (9.1). It is also possible to quantify the worst/best-case probability of such a scenario happening using properties (9.2) and (9.3):

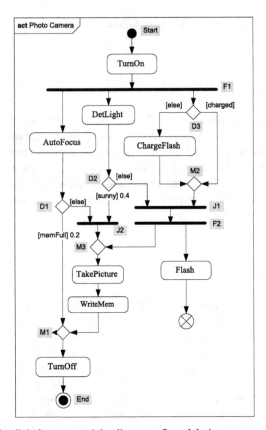

Fig. 9.5 Case study: digital camera activity diagram – flawed design

$$\text{``init''} \;\Rightarrow\; P>0\,[\,F\,\text{``deadlock''}\,] \tag{9.1}$$

$$Pmax =?\,[\,F\,\text{``deadlock''}\,] \tag{9.2}$$

$$Pmin =?\,[\,F\,\text{``deadlock''}\,] \tag{9.3}$$

The labels `"init"` and `"deadlock"` in property (9.1) are built-in labels that are true for, respectively, initial and deadlocked states. Property (9.1) states that, from an initial state, the probability of eventually reaching a deadlocked state is greater than 0. This returns *true*, which means that the property is satisfied in some states of the model. However, after further investigation, we found that there is only one deadlocked state due to the activity final node in the activity diagram. This deadlock can be accepted since, according to the desired execution, at the activity final node, the activity terminates and there are no outgoing transitions.

It is also important in the case of activity diagram to verify that we can eventually reach the activity final node once the activity diagram has started. Such a property

```
mdp
const int max_inst = 1;
formula J1 = J1_pin1>0 & J1_pin2>0 ;
formula J2 = J2_pin1>0 & J2_pin2>0 ;

module mainmod
memful : bool init false;
sunny : bool init false;
charged : bool init false;
Start : bool init true; TurnOn : [0 .. max_inst] init 0; F1 : [0 .. max_inst] init 0;
Autofocus : [0 .. max_inst] init 0; DetLight : [0 .. max_inst] init 0;
D3 : [0 .. max_inst] init 0; ChargeFlash : [0 .. max_inst] init 0;
D1 : [0 .. max_inst] init 0; D2 : [0 .. max_inst] init 0; F2 : [0 .. max_inst] init 0;
J1_pin1 : [0 .. max_inst] init 0; J1_pin2 : [0 .. max_inst] init 0;
J2_pin1 : [0 .. max_inst] init 0; J2_pin2 : [0 .. max_inst] init 0;
M1 : [0 .. max_inst] init 0; M2 : [0 .. max_inst] init 0; M3 : [0 .. max_inst] init 0;
TakePicture : [0 .. max_inst] init 0; WriteMem : [0 .. max_inst] init 0;
Flash : [0 .. max_inst] init 0; TurnOff : [0 .. max_inst] init 0; End : bool init false;

[Start] Start & TurnOn<max_inst & !End  →  Start'=false & TurnOn'=TurnOn +1;

[TurnOn] TurnOn>0 & F1<max_inst & !End  →  TurnOn'=TurnOn − 1 & F1'=F1 +1;

[F1] F1>0 & Autofocus<max_inst & DetLight<max_inst & D3<max_inst & !End  →
   F1'= F1 − 1 & Autofocus'=Autofocus + 1 & DetLight'=DetLight + 1 & D3'=D3 + 1;

[Autofocus] Autofocus>0 & D1<max_inst& !End  →
   Autofocus'=Autofocus − 1 & D1'=D1 + 1;

[DetLight] DetLight>0 & D2<max_inst& !End  →
   DetLight'= DetLight − 1 & D2' = D2 + 1 ;

[D3] D3>0 & ChargeFlash <max_inst& !End  →
   ChargeFlash'= ChargeFlash + 1 & D3'=D3 − 1& (charged'=false);

[D3] D3>0 & M2<max_inst& !End  →
    M2' = M2 + 1 & D3'= D3 − 1& (charged'=true);

[D1] D1>0      & M1<max_inst & J2_pin1<max_inst & !J2 & !End  →
   0.2 : (M1'=M1 + 1) & (D1'=D1 − 1)& (memful' = true) +
   0.8 : (J2_pin1'=J2_pin1 + 1) & (D1'=D1 − 1)& (memful' = false);

[D2] D2>0 & J2_pin2<max_inst & J1_pin1<max_inst & !J1 & !J2 & !End  →
   0.6 : (J1_pin1'=J1_pin1 + 1) & (D2'=D2 − 1) & (sunny'=false) +
   0.4 : (J2_pin2'=J2_pin2 + 1) & (D2'=D2 − 1) & (sunny'=true);

[ChargeFlash] ChargeFlash>0 & M2<max_inst& !End  →
   M2'= M2 + 1  & ChargeFlash'=ChargeFlash − 1;
```

Fig. 9.6 PRISM code for the digital camera case study – part 1

```
[M2] M2>0     & J1_pin2<max_inst & !J1 & !End  →
M2'= M2 − 1 & J1_pin2'=J1_pin2 + 1;

[M1]  M1>0 &TurnOff <max_inst     & !End →
TurnOff'=TurnOff + 1 & M1'= M1  − 1;

[J2] J2  &TakePicture <max_inst & !End  →
 TakePicture'=TakePicture + 1 & J2_pin1'=0 & J2_pin2'=0 ;

[J1]  J1 & F2<max_inst & !End  →
F2'=F2 + 1 & J1_pin1'=0 & J1_pin2'=0 ;

[F2] F2>0     & Flash<max_inst & TakePicture <max_inst & !End  →
 F2'=F2 − 1 & Flash'= Flash + 1 & TakePicture'=TakePicture + 1;

[TakePicture] TakePicture >0 & WriteMem<max_inst & !End  →
TakePicture' = TakePicture − 1 & WriteMem'= WriteMem  +1;

[WriteMem] WriteMem >0 & M1<max_inst & !End  →
 WriteMem'= WriteMem − 1 & M1'=M1 +1;

[TurnOff] TurnOff >0 & !End  →
TurnOff'=TurnOff − 1 & End'=true;

[End] End     →
 TurnOn'=0 & F1'=0 & Autofocus'=0 & DetLight'=0 & D3'=0 & ChargeFlash'=0 & D1'=0
& D2'=0 & J1_pin1'=0 & J1_pin2'=0 & F2'=0 & J2_pin1'=0 & J2_pin2'=0 & M1'=0 &
 M2'=0 & M3'=0 & TakePicture'=0 & WriteMem'=0 & Flash'=0 & TurnOff'=0&
 (memful' = false) & (sunny'=false) & (charged'=false);

endmodule
```

Fig. 9.7 PRISM code for the digital camera case study – part 2

is stated in property (9.4). Properties (9.5) and (9.6) are used in order to quantify the probability of such a scenario happening:

$$\text{TurnOn} \geq 1 \ \Rightarrow \ \text{P>0 [F End]} \tag{9.4}$$

$$\text{Pmax} =? \ [\ \text{F End }] \tag{9.5}$$

$$\text{Pmin} =? \ [\ \text{F End }] \tag{9.6}$$

Property (9.4) returns *true* and properties (9.5) and (9.6) both return the probability value 1. This represents satisfactory results, the final activity being always reachable.

The first functional requirement states that the TakePicture action should not be activated if the memory is full (memfull=true) or if the Autofocus action is still ongoing. Thus, we would like to evaluate the actual probability for this scenario to happen. Since we are relying on MDP model, we need to compute the minimum (9.7) and the maximum (9.8) probability measures of reaching a state where either the memory is full or the focus action is ongoing while taking a picture:

$$\text{Pmin} =? [\ \text{true U (memfull} \mid \text{Autofocus} \geq 1)\& \text{TakePicture} \geq 1\ ]\ (9.7)$$

$$\text{Pmax} =? [\ \text{true U (memfull} \mid \text{Autofocus} \geq 1)\& \text{TakePicture} \geq 1\ ]\ (9.8)$$

The expected likelihood for this scenario should be null (impossibility). However, the model checker determines a non-zero probability value for the maximum measurement (Pmax = 0.6) and a null probability for the minimum. This shows that there is a path leading to an undesirable state, thus pointing out to a flaw in the design. On the activity diagram, this is caused by a control flow path that leads to the TakePicture action and this being done independently of the evaluation of the memfull guard and of the termination of the action AutoFocus. In order to correct this misbehavior, the designer must alter the diagram so that the control flow reaching the action AutoFocus and subsequently evaluating the guard memfull to false has to synchronize with all the possible paths leading to TakePicture. This might be done using a fork node that splits two threads, each having to synchronize with a possible flow before activating TakePicture. Thus, we block the activation of TakePicture action unless AutoFocus eventually ends and memory space is available in the digital camera. Figure 9.8 illustrates the corrected SysML activity diagram.

As the main function of the digital photo camera device is to take pictures, we would like to measure the probability of taking a picture in normal conditions. The corresponding properties are specified as follows:

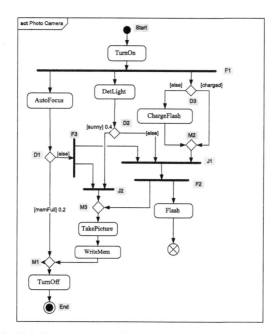

Fig. 9.8 Case study: digital camera activity diagram – corrected design

$$Pmin =? [true \text{ U TakePicture} \geq 1] \tag{9.9}$$

$$Pmax =? [true \text{ U TakePicture} \geq 1] \tag{9.10}$$

The measures provided by the model checker are, respectively, Pmin $= 0.8$ and Pmax $= 0.92$. These values have to be compared with the desired level of reliability of the system.

We applied probabilistic model checking on the corrected design in order to compare both the flawed and corrected SysML activity diagrams. The comparison is summarized in Table 9.1. The correction of the design has removed the flaw revealed by property (9.8), the probability value became 0. However, we lost in terms of reliability in the best-case scenario, since the maximum probability calculated for property (9.10) has dropped to 0.8 instead of 0.92.

Table 9.1 Comparative assessment of flawed and corrected design models

Properties	Flawed design	Corrected design
(9.1)	true	true
(9.2)	1	1
(9.3)	1	1
(9.4)	true	true
(9.5)	1	1
(9.6)	1	1
(9.7)	0.0	0.0
(9.8)	0.6	0.0
(9.9)	0.8	0.8
(9.10)	0.92	0.8

9.5 Conclusion

This chapter presented a translation algorithm that was designed and implemented in order to enable probabilistic model checking of SysML activity diagrams. The algorithm maps these diagrams into their corresponding Markov decision process (MDP) models. The code is written in the input language of the selected probabilistic model checker, i.e., PRISM. Moreover, a case study was presented in order to show the practical benefits of using the presented approach. Finally, MDP allowed the interpretation and analysis of SysML activity diagrams for systems that exhibit asynchronous behavior. In Chap. 10, we present a methodology for analyzing SysML activity diagrams with a specific consideration for time constraints on activity action nodes.

Chapter 10
Performance Analysis of Time-Constrained SysML Activity Diagrams

Many modern systems are now being developed by aggregating other subsystems and components that may have different expected, though not exactly determined, characteristics and features. As such, these kinds of systems may exhibit features such as concurrency and probabilistic behavior. In this context, appropriate models are needed in order to effectively capture the system behavior. Among SysML behavioral diagrams, activity diagrams [23] represent a highly interesting and expressive behavioral model, due to both its suitability for functional flow modeling and its similarity to the extended functional flow block diagrams (EFF-BDs) [24] commonly used by systems engineers. The SysML specification [187] has redefined and widely extended activity diagrams using the profiling mechanism of UML. The main extensions concern the support of continuous and probabilistic systems modeling.

10.1 Time Annotation

In this section, we examine time constraints and probability specifications in SysML activity diagrams. SysML activity diagrams are meant to describe control flow and dataflow dependencies among the functions and/or processes defined by the system. Activity modeling is used for coordinating behaviors in the system being modeled. Particularly, these behaviors may require a time duration to execute and terminate. Thus, we need to specify such constraints in order to be able to verify time-related properties for quantitative analysis, especially in the real-time system domains such as industrial manufacturing control, robotics, and various embedded systems. Such systems need to be engineered under strict functional performance requirements. However, annotation of time constraints on top of SysML activity diagrams is not clearly defined in the standard [187]. The only existing extension containing performance and time aspects can be found in the UML profile for schedulability, performance, and time (SPT) [179] adopted for UML 1.4. Unfortunately, SysML did not import this profile and adopting it would require to upgrade it accordingly. In fact, the SysML specification [187] gives a mere recommendation to use the simple time model defined in [186] that might be used in order to annotate activity

M. Debbabi et al., *Verification and Validation in Systems Engineering*,
DOI 10.1007/978-3-642-15228-3_10, © Springer-Verlag Berlin Heidelberg 2010

diagrams. The *SimpleTime* [186] is a UML 2.x sub-package related to the *CommonBehavior* package. It allows time specification constraints, such as interval of time and duration on the sequence diagram. However, its usage for activity diagrams is not clearly specified. Another proposed alternative to specify time constraints is to use timing diagrams, even though they are not part of the SysML specification. Consequently, we propose an appropriate and straightforward time annotation, similar to the simple time model. The proposed notation allows us to specify duration variability with respect to action termination, which provides a flexible means of estimating execution durations.

The execution time of a behavior depends on various parameters such as resource availability and rates of incoming dataflows. This may result in a variation of the total time needed for behavior completion. Consequently, if an action terminates within a bounded time interval, then a probability distribution for terminating the action can be established with respect to the corresponding execution time interval. Thus, we propose a suitable discrete-time annotation on top of action nodes in the SysML activity diagram that specifies the estimation of the time duration of an action execution. We consider a time reference maintained by a global clock C. When an activity diagram starts, C is reset to zero. Since we consider a discrete-time model, the clock readings are included in the set of positive integers denoted by *Int*. We define the *activation time* as the duration of time wherein an action node is active. Moreover, since we consider that a transition taken on an activity edge is timeless, time annotations are specified only for action nodes in the form of a time interval $I = [a, b]$, where $a, b \in Int$ are evaluated relatively to the start of the activation time of the corresponding action. Time value a represents the earliest time for the execution completion and time value b is the latest. However, some actions may need a fixed time value to complete execution, i.e., $a = b$. In such a case, a time value is used. Furthermore, the time annotation can be omitted if the activation time of an action is negligible compared to other actions. Finally, the selection of an appropriate unit of time from the sequencing and performance perspectives has to be relevant to the intent of the system designer.

Note that it is preferable to select a convenient time unit by scaling down, if possible, the actual values by the same factor. Such abstraction may add benefits to the performance of the both model-checking and the semantic model generation procedures. Usually, the smallest value of time durations can be considered as the time unit. The impact of widely separated timescales and the benefits of abstraction are discussed later. As depicted in Fig. 10.1, the action TurnOn requires exactly 2 units of time to terminate; Action AutoFocus terminates within the interval [1,2]; The action TakePicture execution time is negligible.

The features defined in SysML activity diagrams for modeling probabilistic systems are mainly probabilities assigned on the transitions emanating from probabilistic decision nodes and obeying a specific probability distribution. Accordingly, the assigned values should sum up to unity. The probability on a given edge expresses the likelihood that a value stemming from a decision node will traverse the corresponding edge. Figure 10.1 illustrates how the probability value is specified on the outgoing edges of the decision nodes testing their corresponding guards. For instance, the decision node testing the guard charged has the following semantic

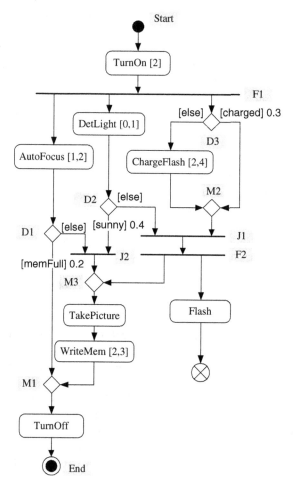

Fig. 10.1 Digital camera activity diagram-flawed design

interpretation: there is a likelihood of 0.3 that the outcome of the decision node will be (charged=true) and the corresponding edge traversed.

10.2 Derivation of the Semantic Model

We introduced in Chap. 8 the concept of configuration transition system (CTS) that can be used to model the dynamics of various behavioral diagrams. In essence, the CTS is a form of automaton characterized by a set of configurations that include a (usually singleton) set of initial configurations and also a transition relation that encodes the dynamic evolution of the CTS from one configuration to another. However, the CTS model assumes a background computation of some sort that is responsible for the change in the set of dynamic parameters, a computation which is abstracted to a possible transition from one configuration to another. While this abstraction can be suitable in many cases, it might need more refinement in cases where features such as the duration of the computation and/or the likelihood of a decision must be taken into account in relation to the dynamic elements of the model. Thus, it becomes apparent that an enriched model is required in order to capture the aforementioned features. Since the most important elements of interest in the dynamics corresponding to various behavioral diagrams are usually represented by state variables or action blocks, we will consider these artifacts as dynamic elements.

When modeling a system with an aggregation or network of automata, communication can be used in order to achieve synchronization. Also, time quantization techniques can be employed in order to capture the time-related system dynamics modeled by the communicating automata into a compact computable model suitable for automatic verification purposes. Accordingly, the approach consists in mapping the SysML activity diagram into a corresponding network of discrete-time Markov chains (DTMCs) representing a discrete-time transition systems with discrete probability distributions.

The main motivation behind the selection of a network of DTMCs as the semantic interpretation for SysML activity diagram is based on the reasoning that activity diagrams can be used in order to specify the coordination of behaviors that the system exhibits. According to the specification, the actions belonging to a given activity diagram may possibly be performed by different parts of the modeled system. These parts, and the relationship among them, are specified by using the block definition diagram and internal block diagram. In order to highlight in the activity diagram the part (block) of the system that is assigned the responsibility of performing a given behavior/action, the designer may use the swimlane construct. In this setting, the actions that are placed along the same swimlane are performed in the same corresponding block of the system. From the internal block diagram perspective, which describes the internal structure of a system in terms of its parts, ports, and connectors, the diagram may show the allocation of activity invocation to the parts of the system. Furthermore, a swimlane generally corresponds to a concurrent thread in the activity diagram. Thus, one can decompose the activity diagram into a set of threads (possibly singleton). In essence, the threads are collaborating, and they may synchronize at certain points in order to proceed with the remaining operations. Moreover, when modeling time-dependent behavior, the same passage of time, or more precisely the same time flow rate, must be allowed for all the interacting threads.

10.3 Model-Checking Time-Constrained Activity Diagrams

Our verification approach relies on model checking, which has been successfully applied in hardware systems verification. Moreover, it is an appropriate choice to assess behavioral aspects since it is automatic, is comprehensive, and has solid mathematical foundations. The principal function of model checking is to enable systematic verification by examining whether a given model satisfies a specified property. The result is either a positive answer (the system satisfies the specification) or a negative one (the system violates the specification). However, this represents only a qualitative assessment. On the other hand, probabilistic model checking allows performing a quantitative analysis of the model. It is needed in order to quantify the likelihood of a given property being either violated or satisfied by the modeled system.

Basically, the semantic interpretation of SysML activity diagrams can be encoded into the input language of a probabilistic model checker such as the probabilistic symbolic model checker (PRISM). It was first developed at the University of Birmingham [239] and then moved on to the University of Oxford [240]. It has been widely applied to analyze systems from many application domains, including communication, multimedia, and security protocols. In addition to PRISM's wide application, many of its features also motivated our choice. Essentially, in order to have a compact model, PRISM makes use of efficient data structures such as multi-terminal binary decision diagram (MTBDD), sparse matrices, as well as a hybrid of these two. Moreover, the applied numerical methods are reported to be time and memory wise. A comprehensive comparative study of probabilistic model checkers can be found in [193]. We employ PRISM model checker capabilities to determine the actual probability value for a given behavior occurrence and also to test the satisfaction of a number of probabilistic properties related to time-bounded reachability. These properties depend on the functional requirements and performance specifications of the system. Figure 10.2 illustrates a synopsis of the proposed approach.

Thus, we propose an algorithm that systematically encodes SysML activity diagrams into their corresponding DTMC model expressed using PRISM language.

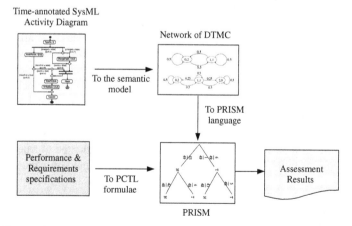

Fig. 10.2 Proposed approach

10.3.1 Discrete-Time Markov Chain

The DTMC represents a discrete-time transition system with discrete probability distributions that can efficiently capture the intended behavior of the activity diagram. Furthermore, it is lightweight compared to the other probabilistic models supported by PRISM.[1]

The trade-off involved in selecting a discrete-time model consists of either having a more fine-grained representation (at the expense of higher costs in terms of verification feasibility) or a less fine-grained one that can in turn significantly boost the verification performance, thus allowing for more elaborated models to be verified.

A concise definition of the DTMC model [208] is as follows:

Definition 10.1 A discrete-time Markov chain (DTMC) is a tuple $\mathcal{D} = (S, \bar{s}, \mathbf{P})$, where S is a finite set of states, $\bar{s} \in S$ is the initial state, and $\mathbf{P} : S \times S \to [0, 1]$ is a transition probability matrix, such that $\sum_{s' \in S} \mathcal{P}(s, s') = 1$ for all $s \in S$, where $\mathcal{P}(s, s')$ is the probability of making a transition from a state s to a state s'.

10.3.2 PRISM Input Language

PRISM language uses a state-based language that relies on the concept of reactive modules that was defined by Alur and Henzinger [5]. Reactive modules are basically similar to a set of interacting transition systems, where transitions can be labeled by probabilities. These transition systems may be represented within the same model by a number of different modules that may interact together and, depending on the model, evolve either in a synchronous or interleaved manner. The fundamental elements of a PRISM model are modules, variables, and commands. A module can be thought of as a process that runs concurrently with other modules and may interact with them. The set of variables defines the global state of the system. Internally, PRISM parses the system description and translates the set of modules into a single system module in a compositional manner. Consequently, the probabilistic model corresponding to the system description file represents the parallel composition of its modules. PRISM supports three parallel composition styles that are similar to the process algebra mechanism (i.e., on common actions): full parallel composition with synchronization on common actions, asynchronous parallel composition with no synchronization at all, and a restricted parallel composition with synchronization limited to only a specific set of actions. Finally, a PRISM command is an action in the model that is composed of an action name, a guard expression, and a set of update expressions. The action name, placed between square brackets, is used for synchronization purposes. If a command's guard is evaluated to true, the set of updates occur depending on a probabilistic distribution defined over the updates.

---

[1] Relating to the other probabilistic models supported by PRISM, CTMC can be viewed as DTMC with an infinitesimally small time step whereas MDP is extending DTMC with non-determinism [140].

10.3.3 Mapping SysML Activity Diagrams into DTMC

There are two possible choices of encoding activity diagram semantics into PRISM language: either to represent the semantics of the whole diagram as a single module or to decompose the diagram into processes and encode each one as a module. In the latter case, the whole activity diagram behavior is specified using the result of the parallel composition of the generated PRISM modules. The second choice appears more interesting since it is more intuitive to specify the behavior of the parts composing the activity diagram with their possible interactions than to work out the full behavior of an activity that could be quite complex. Also, we delegate the composition of the whole DTMC to PRISM, along with other tedious tasks including the computation and normalization of the compound probability distributions (in case of concurrent probabilistic decision nodes) and the behavior resulting from the overlapping of time intervals. In the context of our approach, we instruct PRISM to compose the modules synchronously.

In order to achieve an efficient and intuitive decomposition of the activity diagram, we propose to decompose activity diagrams into a set of threads (possibly singleton). The rationale behind this is based on the following: activity diagrams are composed of a set of flows. Some flows are composed sequentially, while others are composed concurrently. This composition is achieved using activity control nodes. We define a thread as being a sequence of actions that traverse neither fork nodes nor join nodes because these nodes are used to generate concurrent activity flows. Each identified thread is encoded as a module in the system description, where each module is of itself a DTMC. The interaction between these modules is determined by the activity control nodes, which are basically at the beginning and at the end of the threads. The parallel composition of all the modules (DTMCs) results in a network of DTMCs, which is in itself a DTMC.

Algorithm 5 defines the mapping of a given time-annotated SysML activity diagram into its PRISM DTMC model. The first step consists of extracting the control flow relations from the structure of the diagram. Then, the diagram is decomposed into a number of threads, according to Algorithm 6. Prior to the code generation, the interaction and coordination between threads have to be considered in order to encode the modules' interactions. The corresponding auxiliary function is denoted as `getCoordinationPts`. The other functions are self-explanatory, their names being inferred from their objectives.

10.3.4 Threads Identification

Prior to threads identification, various control nodes in the activity diagram have to be assigned unique labels so as to encode them appropriately. We assume a single initial node in a given activity diagram labeled with `Start`. A prerequisite of the thread identification procedure is the set, denoted as `CFR` and, composed of control flow relations among the nodes of the activity diagram. The `CFR` is a set of tuples representing the activity edges, where each tuple is composed of the source node,

---

Algorithm 5 SysML Activity Diagram to PRISM DTMC: *parseAD*(**A**)

Init CFR as List;
      /∗ Control Flow Relations ∗/
Init Threads, SSP, Commands as Map;
Init variables, guards, formulas as List;
CFR = generateCFR(A);
      /∗ Extract control flow relations ∗/
Threads = getThreads(CFR);
      /∗ Explores CFR and extract the threads ∗/
SSP = getCoordinationPts(CFR,Threads);
      /∗ Generates a map of synchronization points between threads ∗/
for all item in Threads **do**
    key = item.ThreadId;
    newModule = createModule(key);
      /∗ Create a module for each thread ∗/
    variables = getLocalVariables(item,SSP,key);
    newModule.addDeclaration(variables,key);
    PRISMCode.addGlobalVariables(variables);
    formulas = setFormulas(SSP,variables,key);
    PRISMCode.addFormulas(formulas);
    guards=setGuards(variables,formulas,key);
    Commands.put(key,guards);
    updateCommands(Commands,item,key);
    newModule.addCommands(Commands);
    PRISMCode.add(newModule);
      /∗ Add the module to the main PRISM code ∗/
end for

---

the target node, the guard (if any), and the probability value (if any). The generation of the CFR can be achieved by using an auxiliary function generateCFR. The thread identification procedure is a breadth-first search of the control flow relations CFR as detailed in Algorithm 6.

In Algorithm 6, the map data structure Threads stores the output of the algorithm, the stack StackNodes contains unexplored nodes, and the list Visited comprises the visited nodes. The auxiliary function getAllCFR(pos,node) returns the list of control flows containing the node in the position pos (possible pos values are "source" or "target"). The auxiliary function getNode(y,pos) returns the node in the control flow y that has the position pos. During the node exploration, a new thread is allocated for each outgoing flow when a fork or a join node is encountered. In the same sequencing flow, the same thread identifier is used. Note that for the merge node, this depends on whether or not the same thread is allocated for the incoming flows. In the first case, the same thread identifier is allocated for the outgoing flow; otherwise, a new one is created. For the sake of simplicity, the algorithm shows only the case of allocating a new thread identifier for the outgoing flow of merge nodes. However, it must be noted that to allocate a new thread identifier each time in all the cases will only impact the complexity of the code and not the complexity of the model's dynamics.

Algorithm 6 Thread Identification: getThreads(CFR)

Init Threads as Map;
Init StackNodes as Stack;
    /* StackNodes is a stack of unexplored nodes */
Init Visited, tempListCFR as List;
ThreadID = 1;
tempListCFR := getAllCFR('source','Start');
Threads.put(ThreadID,tempListCFR);
Visited.add(Start);
StackNodes.push(getNode(tempListCFR,'target'));
while not StackNodes.empty() and not CFR.empty() **do**
    CurrentNode = StackNodes.pop();
    if Visited.contains() or CurrentNode instOf Final **then**
        continue;
    end if
    if currentNode instOf Action or Decision **then**
        tempListCFR = getAllCFR('source',CurrentNode);
        for all y in tempListCFR **do**
            key = getCFR('target',CurrentNode).getThreadID();
            Threads[key].add(y);
            StackNodes.push(getNode(y,'target'));
            CFR.delete(y);
        end for
    end if
    if currentNode instOf Fork or Join or Merge **then**
        tempListCFR = getAllCFR('source',CurrentNode);
        for all y in tempListCFR **do**
            Threads.put(ThreadID++,y);
            StackNodes.push(getNode(y,'target'));
            CFR.delete(y);
        end for
    end if
    Visited.add(CurrentNode);
end whilereturn Threads

The synchronization mechanism among the modules allows for two or more concurrent activity flows or execution threads to "experience" the same passage of time with respect to time constraints that may be specified for each of them. Consequently, each thread has its own clock variable that is used to track the passage of time in the current state of the thread.

The dynamics of the synchronously composed DTMC models ensure that all the clock variables are updated (advanced or reset) synchronously. Thus, the clock variable of each thread is either advanced as a result of a self-transition or reset whenever the current state is left. Furthermore, whenever the clock variable of a thread falls within the time constraint interval of the current state, the control can either remain in the current state or be transferred to another state reached by a transition from the current state according to a probability distribution. The choice for such a distribution may depend on the actual system being modeled.

The derived PRISM modules forming the DTMC network modeling the activity diagram are composed synchronously in a CSP-like manner (i.e., synchronization over common actions). This allows the proper updating of the clock variables corresponding to action execution in the different threads. Each module is composed of two main parts: one containing the declaration of its state variables and another encoding the dynamics thereof by means of commands guarded by predicates that may span over the state variables that may also belong to any of the modules.

Furthermore, each command is labeled with the same action `step` and also has a set of updates of its state variables. Specifically, every module can read the value of all the variables but can only change the value of the variables declared within its scope. In each module, the state variables correspond to action nodes, guards of the decision nodes, and clocks corresponding to the identified thread in the activity diagram. If required, each module can also contain additional boolean state variables that might be needed for thread merging or synchronization. The dynamic evolution of each module is determined by selecting a matching command whose boolean predicate evaluates to *true*. Consequently, based on the current value of the variables, each module updates its own variables upon the execution of a matching command.

Since the modules are always synchronizing on the action `step`, this means that no module can evolve independently of the others. More precisely, at each synchronizing step, every module is equally given the possibility to update its variables. Moreover, in order to allow the system to progress, each module contains a command whose guarding predicate is the negated disjunction of all the others in the same module. The updates of the guarding predicate are trivially keeping the same values of the state variables. Similarly, in order to ensure the proper termination of the activity behavior, each command predicate contains the negation of the state designated as the activity final node.

10.4 Performance Analysis Case Study

In order to explain our approach, we present a case study of a hypothetical model of a digital photo-camera device. The system model is composed of a SysML activity diagram containing time constraints. It captures the functionality of taking a picture as depicted in Fig. 10.1. For the sake of clarity and understanding, the model consists of only one activity diagram. Presenting a more complicated model might affect the presentation of the approach, since the resulting code and reachability graph would be too large to be followed by the reader. However, as it will be subsequently shown, a simple model does not preclude a highly dynamic behavior. Moreover, the corresponding dynamics are rich enough to allow for the verification of several interesting properties that capture important functional aspects and performance characteristics. We intentionally modeled some flaws into the design in order to demonstrate the applicability of our approach.

In order to proceed with the assessment of the activity diagram, the main step consists in the generation of the DTMC model that captures the behavior of the system. Moreover, the specification properties that have to be checked are supplied in PCTL logic according to the syntax required by the model checker. The model generated for the digital photo-camera activity diagram is shown in Fig. 10.3 and continued in Fig. 10.4, where each module represents a thread in the activity diagram. Table 10.1 depicts the thread allocation according to the control flow relations' set of the flawed activity diagram in Fig. 10.1. After supplying the model and

```
probabilistic
formula t1_fin = TurnOn & t1_ck >= t1_tb;
formula t1_idle = ! ( End | Start | TurnOn);
const t1_tb = 2;
module t1
Start : bool init true; TurnOn : bool; t1_ck : [0..t1_tb];
    [step] ! End & Start                    →    Start'=false & TurnOn'=true;
    [step] ! End & TurnOn & t1_ck < t1_tb   →    t1_ck'= t1_ck +1;
    [step] ! End & t1_fin                    →    TurnOn'=false & t1_ck'=0;
    [step] t1_idle                           →    true;
endmodule

formula sync_t2_t3 = t2_j & t3_j; formula sync_t3_t4 = t3_j_2 & t4_j;
formula t2_idle = ! (End | t1_fin | Autofocus | sync_t2_t3 | t2_m );
const t2_lb = 1; const t2_ub = 2;
module t2
Autofocus : bool; memfull : bool; t2_j : bool; t2_m : bool; t2_ck : [0..t2_ub];
    [step] ! End & t1_fin                      →    Autofocus'=true;
    [step] ! End & Autofocus & t2_ck < t2_lb   →    t2_ck'= t2_ck +1;
    [step] ! End & Autofocus & t2_ck >= t2_lb & t2_ck<t2_ub  →  0.5 : (t2_ck'= t2_ck + 1) +
                                                0.5*0.2 : (Autofocus'=false) & (memfull'= true) &
                                                          (t2_m'=true) & (t2_ck'=0) +
                                                0.5*0.8 : (Autofocus'=false) & (t2_j'=true) &
                                                          (t2_ck'=0);
    [step] ! End & Autofocus & t2_ck = t2_ub   →    0.2 : (Autofocus'=false) & (memfull'= true) &
                                                          (t2_m'=true) & (t2_ck'=0) +
                                                0.8 : (Autofocus'=false) & (t2_j'=true) &
                                                          (t2_ck'=0);
    [step] ! End & sync_t2_t3                   →    t2_j'=false;
    [step] ! End & t2_m                         →    t2_m'=false;
    [step] t2_idle                             →    true;
endmodule

formula t3_idle = ! (End | t1_fin | DetLight | sync_t2_t3 | sync_t3_t4 );
const t3_lb = 0; const t3_ub = 1;
module t3
DetLight : bool; sunny : bool; t3_j : bool; t3_j_2 : bool; t3_ck : [0..t3_ub];
    [step] ! End & t1_fin                      →    DetLight'=true;
    [step] ! End & DetLight & t3_ck < t3_lb    →    t3_ck'= t3_ck +1;
    [step] ! End & DetLight & t3_ck >= t3_lb & t3_ck<t3_ub  →  0.5 : (t3_ck'= t3_ck +1) +
                                                0.5*0.4 : (DetLight'=false) & (sunny'=true) &
                                                          (t3_j'=true) & (t3_ck'=0) +
                                                0.5*0.6 : (DetLight'=false) & (t3_j_2'=true)&
                                                          (t3_ck'=0) ;
    [step] ! End & DetLight & t3_ck = t3_ub    →    0.4 : (DetLight'=false) & (sunny'=true) &
                                                          (t3_j'=true) & (t3_ck'=0) +
                                                0.6 : (DetLight'=false) & (t3_j_2'=true) &
                                                          (t3_ck'=0);
    [step] ! End & sync_t2_t3                   →    t3_j'=false;
    [step] ! End & sync_t3_t4                   →    t3_j_2'=false;
    [step] t3_idle                             →    true;
endmodule
```

Fig. 10.3 PRISM code for the digital camera activity diagram example – part 1

```
formula t4_idle = ! (End | t1_fin | ChargeFlash | sync_t3_t4 ); const t4_lb = 2; const t4_ub = 4;
module t4
ChargeFlash : bool; charged : bool; t4_j : bool; t4_ck : [0..t4_ub];
    [step] ! End & t1_fin                      →       0.7 : (ChargeFlash'=true) +
                                                         0.3 : (charged'=true) & (t4_j'=true);
    [step] ! End & ChargeFlash & t4_ck < t4_lb       →        t4_ck' = t4_ck + 1;
    [step] ! End & ChargeFlash & t4_ck >= t4_lb & t4_ck<t4_ub →      0.5 : (t4_ck' = t4_ck + 1) +
                                                0.5 : (ChargeFlash'=false) & (t4_j'=true) & (t4_ck'=0)
    [step] ! End & ChargeFlash & t4_ck=t4_ub         →         ChargeFlash'=false & t4_j'=true & (t4_ck'=0);
    [step] ! End & sync_t3_t4              →    t4_j'=false;
    [step]     t4_idle                    →    true;
endmodule

formula t5_idle = ! ( End | sync_t2_t3 | sync_t3_t4 | TakePicture | WriteMem | t5_m);
const t5_lb = 2; const t5_ub = 3;
module t5
TakePicture : bool; WriteMem : bool; t5_m : bool; t5_ck : [0..t5_ub];
    [step] ! End & sync_t2_t3              →       TakePicture'=true;
    [step] ! End & sync_t3_t4              →       TakePicture'=true;
    [step] ! End & TakePicture            →       TakePicture'=false & WriteMem'=true;
    [step] ! End & WriteMem & t5_ck<t5_lb         →       t5_ck' = t5_ck + 1;
    [step] ! End & WriteMem & t5_ck >= t5_lb & t5_ck<t5_ub  →      0.5 : (t5_ck' = t5_ck + 1) +
                                                0.5 : WriteMem'=false & t5_m'=true & (t5_ck'=0);
    [step] ! End & WriteMem & t5_ck=t5_ub         →       WriteMem'=false & t5_m'=true & (t5_ck'=0);
    [step] ! End & t5_m                   →    t5_m'=false;
    [step]     t5_idle                    →    true;
endmodule

formula t6_idle = ! (End | sync_t3_t4 |  Flash );
module t6
Flash : bool;
    [step] ! End & sync_t3_t4              →       Flash'=true;
    [step] ! End & Flash                  →       Flash'=false;
    [step]     t6_idle                    →    true;
endmodule

formula t7_idle = ! ( End | t2_m | t5_m | TurnOff);
module t7
TurnOff : bool; End : bool;
    [step] ! End & t2_m                   →       TurnOff'=true;
    [step] ! End & t5_m                   →       TurnOff'=true;
    [step] ! End & TurnOff                →       TurnOff'=false & End'=true;
    [step]     t7_idle                    →    true;
endmodule
```

Fig. 10.4 PRISM code for the digital camera activity diagram example – part 2

Table 10.1 Thread allocation for the flawed design

Threads	Control flow relations set
ID1	(start,TurnOn); (TurnOn,F1)
ID2	(F1,Autofocus); (Autofocus,D1); (D1,M1); (D1,J2)
ID3	(F1,DetLight); (DetLight,D2); (D2,J2); (D2,J1)
ID4	(F1,D3); (D3,ChargeFlash); (D3,M2); (ChargeFlash,M2); (M2,J1)
ID5	(J2,M3); (F2,M3); (M3,TakePicture); (TakePicture,WriteMem); (WriteMem,M1)
ID6	(F2,Flash)
ID7	(M1,TurnOff); (TurnOff,End)

the specification properties to the model checker, the latter constructs the state space
in the forms of a state list and a transition probability matrix. Numerical analysis
obtained from the model allows properties verification.

In order to represent in a user-friendly way the dynamics of the model, we generate a reachability graph containing both the information on the states and their
transition relations (as illustrated in Fig. 10.5). The latter shows a highly dynamic
behavior resulting from the concurrency of the threads in the activity diagram in
conjunction with the overlapping completion intervals of various activity nodes.

In the following, we present the results obtained by verifying a number of interesting properties expressed in the syntax of the temporal logic defined by PRISM
and based on PCTL.

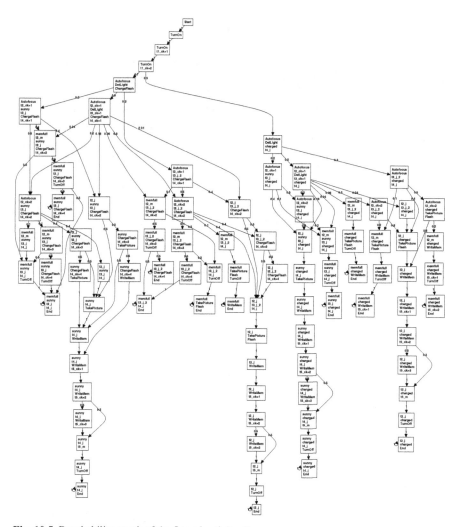

Fig. 10.5 Reachability graph of the flawed activity diagram

The first property (10.1) illustrates a general functional requirement, namely that the TakePicture action should not be activated if either the memory is full memfull=true or the Autofocus action is still ongoing. It instructs the model checker to determine the probability value for this scenario happening:

$$P =? [\ true\ U\ (memfull\ |\ Autofocus)$$
$$\&\ TakePicture\ ] \qquad (10.1)$$

The expected likelihood in a good design should be null (impossibility). However, the model checker determines a non-zero probability value, thus pointing out a flaw in the design. In order to determine more precisely the reason of the misbehavior, the property can be restated separately for memfull and Autofocus. Since the value of this probability is greater than 0, this means that there is a path leading to a state in the reachability graph that leads to either the TakePicture action being activated while the memory is full or before deactivating Autofocus. This can be determined to be caused by the existence of a control flow path in the activity diagram leading to the TakePicture action without testing the memfull guard. In order to correct this misbehavior, the designer must alter this control flow path such that either it tests the memfull guard or it synchronizes with the other control flow path testing it.

The next property (10.2) states that the probability of taking a picture after turning on the camera should be 0.75 or greater and it is expressed as follows:

$$TurnOn \Rightarrow P\ >=\ 0.75\ [\ true\ U\ TakePicture\ ] \qquad (10.2)$$

When analyzing this property over the DTMC corresponding to the activity diagram, it turns out to be satisfied. This tells us that the model meets the minimum required level of reliability on that basic functionality, i.e., taking a picture.

Property (10.3) builds on the previous one and is used to check if the probability of taking a picture using the flash after turning on the camera is at least 0.6.

$$TurnOn \Rightarrow P\ >=\ 0.6\ [\ true\ U\ TakePicture\ \&$$
$$Flash\ ] \qquad (10.3)$$

The model checker determines that property (10.3) fails for the specified probability value. One can instruct PRISM to determine whether there is a probability value for which the property would pass by restating the property as in (10.4). Consequently, the value obtained is 0.56:

$$P =? [\ true\ U\ TakePicture\ \&\ Flash\ \{TurnOn\}\ ] \qquad (10.4)$$

The last property (10.5) further refines the previous one and it is intended to assess one of the critical performance characteristic of the digital camera in a worst case scenario. It is a probabilistic-timed reachability property that measures the probability of reaching a scenario in the model within a certain time bound.

Specifically, it evaluates the probability of reaching the `TakePicture` action within a time bound in poor lighting conditions, starting from the beginning of the `TurnOn` action with the flash discharged:

$$P =? [!\texttt{sunny} \& !\texttt{charged U<=10 TakePicture}$$
$$\& \texttt{Flash \{TurnOn \& t1\_ck=0\}]} \qquad (10.5)$$

The result of the verification of property (10.5) shows a rather poor performance of the model in a worst-case scenario.

To have a better appraisal of the impact of the design changes in the diagram, we also performed the verification of the corrected diagram (Fig. 9.8 with added time constraints annotation). Table 10.2 summarizes the assessment results with respect to the performance evaluation for both the flawed and corrected designs.

We can notice that we have a trade-off between performance and reliability. Indeed, on the one hand property (10.1) has a null value for the corrected design, as required. On the other hand, property (10.5) shows performance degradation in the case of the corrected design. However, property (10.4) results show that the corrected design exceeds the minimum level of reliability and thus meets the requirement stated by property (10.3).

With respect to the size of the performance model reachability graph, we can notice in Table 10.3 that, in terms of number of states and transitions, the two models have almost the same complexity.

Table 10.2 Comparative table of the assessment results for the flawed and corrected designs

Properties	Flawed design	Corrected design
(10.1)	0.1245	0
(10.2)	True	True
(10.3)	False	True
(10.4)	0.5685	0.7999
(10.5)	0.3885	0.252

Table 10.3 Comparative table of the performance model reachability graph complexity

	Flawed design	Corrected design
Number of states	92	93
Number of trans.	139	140

10.5 Scalability

This section discusses the scalability of our approach based on numerical results. Our objective is to study the performance of our approach when applied on more complex activity diagrams. It is worthy of notice that the behavioral complexity of an activity diagram is not related to the number of its action nodes but rather to the intricate dynamics it may capture. Accordingly, the main factors that have a direct impact on the behavioral complexity are the concurrency aspect and the probabilistic duration of actions. We study below the impact of concurrency and timed behavior on important parameters related to the performance of our approach, such as the size of the DTMC model, the size of the MTBDD, the time needed by PRISM to construct the model, and the time and memory consumption of the model-checking procedure.

From the activity diagram's perspective, adding concurrency means adding parallel flows of actions emanating from fork nodes. From PRISM's code perspective, with respect to our approach, adding new concurrent flows means adding one or more modules corresponding to concurrent threads. We chose to add a new concurrent thread that emanates from the fork node F1 in Fig. 10.1. Accordingly, we replicated the module t4 and made some necessary adjustments, such as changes to the idle formula, the names of the local variables, and the joining condition formulae.

With respect to timed behavior, by varying the constants corresponding to the time interval bounds in PRISM code, we can adjust the time interval scales and their overlapping. The constants are t1_tb, t2_lb, t2_ub, t3_lb, t3_ub, t4_lb, t4_ub, t5_lb, and t5_ub as presented in the first column of Table 10.4.

In order to study the impact of these two factors on our approach, we performed several experiments consisting in applying variants of the previously discussed parameters and recording the following information:

- The time required to build the model
- The number of DTMC states
- The number of DTMC transitions
- The number of MTBDD nodes
- The size of the matrix (number of rows and columns)

Concerning model checking, we verified the same properties on the different models obtained in the previously mentioned experiments. We recorded the following model-checking-related information:

- The total time
- The maximum memory consumption, i.e., the memory footprint

Table 10.4 Time intervals bounds values per experiment

	T.1	T.2	T.3	T.4	T.5
t1_tb	2	2	20	20	20
t2_lb	1	1	1	1	10
t2_ub	2	2	2	2	20
t3_lb	0	10	100	1000	0
t3_ub	1	20	150	1020	10
t4_lb	2	15	75	1000	20
t4_ub	4	40	80	1200	40
t5_lb	2	2	20	2000	20
t5_ub	3	3	30	3000	30

In Table 10.4 we report the different time-related experiments, namely T.1, T.2, T.3, T.4, and T.5, and the different values that we assigned to each time constant. The time values for the experiment T.1 represent the original constants in the case study. The next three experiments, namely T.2, T.3, and T.4, are meant to show widely separated timescales between the time duration for the Autofocus action and the duration of the other actions. We consider around 10 units of time difference in T.2, 100 units of time in T.3, and 1000 units of time difference in T.4. These experiments are done to study the impact of widely dissimilar timescales that preclude scaling down the interval-bound constants with the same factor. Experiment T.5 shows the benefit of abstraction (i.e., scaling down the time constants by the same factor) on the overall procedure. For T.5, the corresponding values of the constants represent exactly 10 times the constants of T.1. With respect to concurrency, we have chosen three experiments, namely C.0, C.1, and C.2, where we add, respectively, 0, 1, and 2 new modules to the original model.

As a notation convention, we use T.1+C.1 to indicate that both T.1 and C.1 are applied together. This means that we set the time values of T.1 and we add one new concurrent module to the existing modules in the PRISM code of Figs. 10.3 and 10.4.

The experiments were performed using a Pentium 4 Intel machine with the following characteristics: CPU 2.80 GHZ, with 1.00 GB of RAM. We set the PRISM tool to use the "Hybrid" engine and the Jacobi method. Note that, hardware resources allowing, it is possible to configure PRISM to use a larger amount of memory for MTBDDs, thus allowing larger models to be assessed.

Tables 10.5, 10.6, and 10.7 present the information related to the model construction. Tables 10.8, 10.9, and 10.10 show the time and memory consumption for the model-checking procedure.

In the following, we discuss the numerical results corresponding to the aforementioned series of experiments. Figure 10.6 illustrates the effect of widely separated timescales on the MTBDD size. One can notice that the size of the MTBDD increases only to some extent for the experiment T.1+C.0, T.2+C.0, and T.3+C.0. However, it increases significantly for experiment T.4+C.0, where the difference between the smallest and all the other time values is of about three orders of magnitude. In this setting, it can be safe to consider the smallest value as negligible in duration compared to the other values. The chart in Fig. 10.7 shows the effect of two important factors that impact the MTBDD size. The first one relates to the

Table 10.5 Experimental results: varying time constants with no added concurrency (C.0)

	T.1	T.2	T.3	T.4	T.5
Time (s)	0.578	0.828	1.687	77.813	2.0
DTMC					
Number of states	92	233	487	18294	877
Number of transitions	139	439	741	26652	1588
MTBDD					
Number of nodes	1573	2501	2954	27049	7002
Rows/cols	29r/29c	36r/36c	46r/46c	56r/56c	44r/44c

Table 10.6 Experimental results: varying time constants and adding one new concurrent module (C.1)

	T.1	T.2	T.3	T.4	T.5
Time (s)	1.656	2.687	5.297	249.625	4.609
DTMC					
Number of states	222	833	967	49214	2459
Number of transitions	375	1949	1499	87192	5204
MTBDD					
Number of nodes	2910	7474	7068	118909	15630
Rows/cols	35r/35c	45r/45c	56r/56c	70r/70c	53r/53c

Table 10.7 Experimental results: varying time constants and adding two new concurrent modules (C.2)

	T.1	T.2	T.3	T.5
Time (s)	18.75	13.281	25.078	19.453
DTMC				
Number of states	566	2735	1957	7243
Number of transitions	1105	8059	3123	19300
MTBDD				
Number of nodes	4553	15612	11449	27621
Rows/cols	41r/41c	54r/54c	66r/66c	62r/62c

Table 10.8 Model-checking performance results – part 1

	T.1+C.0		T.2+C.0		T.3+C.0		T.4+C.0		T.5+C.0	
	Time	Mem	Time	Mem	Time	Mem	Time	Mem	Time	Mem
Properties	(s)	(KB)	(s)	(KB)	(s)	(KB)	(s)	(KB)	(s)	(KB)
(10.1)	0.094	23.6	0.0	0.0	0.0	0.0	0.016	0.0	0.375	96.9
(10.2)	0.109	22.9	0.438	19.4	1.953	28.6	54.125	398.7	1.547	111.8
(10.3)	0.062	20.4	0.297	46.7	1.906	69.9	36.5	891.8	0.953	92.7
(10.4)	0.078	20.4	0.296	46.7	1.828	69.9	42.797	891.8	0.719	92.7
(10.5)	0.046	21.9	0.125	48.1	0.25	66.3	11.281	834.6	0.156	94.4
Total time	0.389		1.156		5.937		144.719		3.75	
Max memory		23.6		48.1		69.9		891.8		111.8

Table 10.9 Model-checking performance results – part 2

	T.1+C.1		T.2+C.1		T.3+C.1		T.4+C.1		T.5+C.1	
	Time	Mem	Time	Mem	Time	Mem	Time	Mem	Time	Mem
Properties	(s)	(KB)	(s)	(KB)	(s)	(KB)	(s)	(KB)	(s)	(KB)
(10.1)	0.109	46.3	0	0	0	0	0.094	0	1.016	217.9
(10.2)	0.375	45.8	2.141	38.7	5.219	46.3	–	–	2.765	249.5
(10.3)	0.187	41.7	1.406	134.5	4.141	171.2	–	–	2.093	211.1
(10.4)	0.188	41.7	1.484	134.5	4.125	171.2	136.265	2710.8	2.157	211.1
(10.5)	0.094	41.1	0.687	137.9	0.547	133.5	35.312	2562.2	0.797	198.7
Total time	0.953		5.718		14.032		–		8.828	
Max memory		46.3		137.9		171.2		–		249.5

Table 10.10 Model-checking performance results – part 3

Properties	T.1+C.2		T.2+C.2		T.3+C.2		T.5+C.2	
	Time (s)	Mem (KB)	Time (s)	Mem (KB)	Time (s)	Mem (KB)	Time (s)	Mem (KB)
(10.1)	0.375	79.5	0.016	0	0	0	2.25	429.4
(10.2)	1.641	79.4	8.156	85.3	10.532	75.2	10.171	471.7
(10.3)	0.859	73.5	6.516	289.3	9.89	291.8	7.358	420.1
(10.4)	0.968	73.5	5.891	289.3	9.297	291.8	5.563	420.1
(10.5)	0.656	73.6	3.859	353.9	1.938	249.2	2.594	449.0
Total time	4.499		24.438		31.657		27.936	
Max memory		79.5		353.9		291.8		471.7

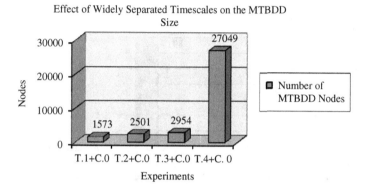

Fig. 10.6 Effect of widely separated timescales on MTBDD size

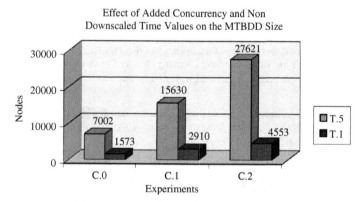

Fig. 10.7 Effect of added concurrency and non-downscaled time values on the MTBDD size

added concurrency. As expected, the increased concurrency results in a more complex model. The second factor relates to the omitting of downscaling time values.

One can notice that larger time values also lead to increased complexity. Elevated time values for all the time bounds allow scaling them down with the same factor.

This abstraction is of benefit to the model-checking procedure since it decreases the size of the model while preserving the underlying dynamics. This type of abstraction is also presented in other research initiatives related to probabilistic model checking [74].

Figures 10.8, 10.9, and 10.10 illustrate the effect on model-checking performance of the widely separated timescales and the added concurrency in the absence of downscaling abstraction. For the presented experiments, the maximum amount of time used by the model-checking procedure is 144.72 s whereas the maximum amount of memory is around 891.8 KB.

In spite of the complexity of the new activity diagrams considered in these experiments, the values on time and memory consumption are within a reasonable range.

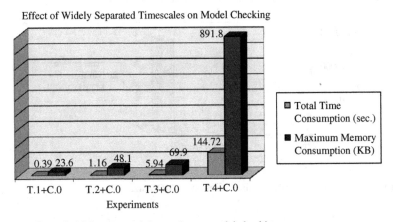

Fig. 10.8 Effect of widely separated timescales on model checking

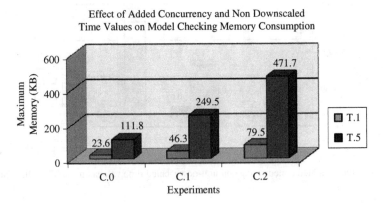

Fig. 10.9 Effect of added concurrency and non-downscaled time values on model-checking: memory consumption

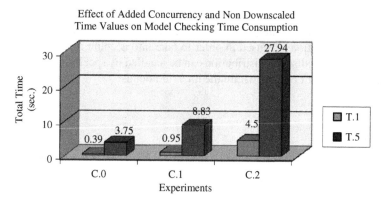

Fig. 10.10 Effect of added concurrency and non-downscaled time values on model-checking: time consumption

Also, the assessment can be further optimized by applying the recommendations previously stated, namely

- Considering as negligible timed actions, if it is safe to do so within the tolerated margins of error, when their corresponding time values are at a difference greater than two orders of magnitude compared to the others
- Scaling down (abstracting), if possible, by the same factor the time constants
- Reconsidering unnecessary concurrency in the design

10.6 Conclusion

In this chapter, we presented a novel automatic approach for the assessment of SysML 1.0 activity diagrams from the functional and performance perspectives. The relevance of assessing SysML 1.0 activity diagrams is related to their importance and their wide usage in many domains including business process and functional flows modeling, to name but a few. The approach is covering the core features, namely the control flows, the structured activities, and the probabilistic decisions. We have also used time annotations on top of the action nodes based on the simple time model. In addition, this annotation technique provides the means to specify action duration with a probabilistic estimation. Moreover, the properties to be assessed are formally expressed in PCTL temporal logic.

With respect to the scalability, we showed a number of experiments that demonstrate positive results from the perspective of the DTMC model size and the required resources in terms of time and memory. The presented assessment approach allows for refinement by performing appropriate time-related abstractions. In addition, in the case of larger designs that are usually exhibiting a high level of modularity, one can perform a block-level assessment, where the concurrency aspect is expected to be lower. In regard to the probabilistic estimation of actions termination, a uniform delay distribution was used in order to take into account resource contention. However, any other discrete distribution can be handled by specifying discrete probabilities for each unit of time within the interval bounds.

Chapter 11
Semantic Foundations of SysML Activity Diagrams

In this chapter, we propose to study the semantic foundations of SysML activity diagrams. A formalization of the semantics will allow us to build a sound and rigorous framework for the V&V of design models expressed using these diagrams. To this end, we design a dedicated formal language, called activity calculus (AC), used in order to mathematically express and analyze the behaviors captured by SysML activity diagrams. In the following, the syntactic and semantic definitions of the AC language are presented in Sect. 11.1. Therein, a summary of the informal mapping of the diagram constructs into AC terms with an illustrative example is also provided. In order to illustrate the usefulness of such a formal semantics, a case study is presented in Sect. 11.2 consisting of a SysML activity diagram for a hypothetical design of a banking operation on an automated teller machine (ATM). We apply the semantic rules on the case study in order to show how this may uncover subtle errors in the design. Finally, Sect. 11.3 defines the underlying Markov decision process that describes SysML activity diagram semantics.

11.1 Activity Calculus

The activity calculus is built with the goal in mind to provide a dedicated calculus that captures the rich expressiveness of activity diagrams and formally models the behavioral aspects using operational semantics framework. It is mainly inspired by the concept of process algebras, which represent a family of approaches used for modeling concurrent and distributed systems.

Apart from ascribing a rigorous meaning to the informally specified diagrams, formal semantics provides us with an effective technique to uncover design errors that could be missed by intuitive inspection. Furthermore, it allows the application of model transformations and model checking. Practically, the manipulation of the graphical notations as it is defined in the standard does not provide the flexibility offered by a formal language. There is a real need to describe this behavior in a mathematical and a rigorous way. Thus, our formal framework allows the automation of the validation using existing techniques such as probabilistic model

M. Debbabi et al., *Verification and Validation in Systems Engineering*,
DOI 10.1007/978-3-642-15228-3_11, © Springer-Verlag Berlin Heidelberg 2010

checking. Moreover, it allows reasoning about potential relations between activity diagrams from the behavioral perspective and deriving related mathematical proofs.

To the best of our knowledge, this is the first calculus of its kind that is dedicated to capture the essence of SysML activity diagrams. While reviewing the state of the art, we cannot find proposals along the same line as our activity calculus. With respect to UML 2.x activity diagrams, most of the research initiatives use existing formalisms such as CSP in [216], the interactive Markov chain (IMC) in [228], and variants of Petri nets formalism in [224–226]. Although these formalisms have well-established semantic domains, they impose some serious limitations to the expressiveness of activity diagrams (e.g., disallow multiple instance of actions). The majority of reviewed initiatives express the activity diagrams as data structure tuple. Very few proposals provide a dedicated algebraic-like notation [82, 234], where only Tabuchi et al. [228] aim at defining a semantic framework. The main supported features that make our calculus distinguishable is its ability to express various control flows with mixed and nested forks and joins that are allowed by UML specification. Furthermore, AC allows multiple instances and includes both guarded and probabilistic decision. Finally, AC allows us to define an operational semantics for SysML activity diagrams that are intuitive and original based on tokens propagation. In the following, we explain in detail the syntax and semantics of our activity calculus.

11.1.1 Syntax

From the structural perspective, an activity diagram can be viewed as a directed graph with two types of nodes (action and control nodes) connected using directed edges. Alternatively, from the dynamic perspective, the activity diagram behavior amounts to a specifically ordered execution of its actions. This order depends on the propagation of the control locus (token) that starts from the initial node. When an action receives a token, it becomes active and starts executing. When its execution terminates, it delivers the token to its outgoing edges. Moreover, multiple instances of the same action may execute concurrently if more than one control token is received. During the execution, the activity diagram structure remains unchanged; however, the location of the control tokens changes. Thus, the behavior (the meaning) depicted by the activity diagram can be described using a set of progress rules that dictates the tokens movement through the diagram. In order to specify the presence of control tokens, we use the word marking (borrowed from the Petri net formalism).

We assume that each activity node in the diagram (except initial) is assigned a unique label. Let $\mathcal{L}$ be a collection of labels ranged over by l, l_0, l_1, ... and N any node (except initial) in the activity diagram. We write $l : N$ to denote an l-labeled activity node N. Labels serve different purposes. Mainly, a label l is used for uniquely referring to an l-labeled activity node in order to model a flow connection

$$
\begin{aligned}
\mathcal{A} &::= \epsilon & \mathcal{B} &::= \overline{\mathcal{A}} \\
&\mid \iota \rightarrowtail \mathcal{N} & &\mid \iota \rightarrowtail \mathcal{M} \\
& & &\mid \overline{\iota} \rightarrowtail \mathcal{N} \\
\mathcal{N} &::= \epsilon & \mathcal{M} &::= \overline{\mathcal{N}} \\
&\mid l : \otimes & &\mid l : Merge(\mathcal{M}) \\
&\mid l : \odot & &\mid l : x.Join(\mathcal{M}) \\
&\mid l : Merge(\mathcal{N}) & &\mid l : Fork(\mathcal{M}, \mathcal{M}) \\
&\mid l : x.Join(\mathcal{N}) & &\mid l : Decision_p(\langle g \rangle \mathcal{M}, \langle \neg g \rangle \mathcal{M}) \\
&\mid l : Fork(\mathcal{N}, \mathcal{N}) & &\mid l : Decision(\langle g \rangle \mathcal{M}, \langle \neg g \rangle \mathcal{M}) \\
&\mid l : Decision_p(\langle g \rangle \mathcal{N}, \langle \neg g \rangle \mathcal{N}) & &\mid \overline{l : a}^n \rightarrowtail \mathcal{M} \\
&\mid l : Decision(\langle g \rangle \mathcal{N}, \langle \neg g \rangle \mathcal{N}) & &\mid \overline{\mathcal{M}}^n \\
&\mid l : a \rightarrowtail \mathcal{N} & & \\
&\mid l & &
\end{aligned}
$$

Fig. 11.1 Unmarked syntax (*left*) and marked syntax (*right*) of activity calculus

to the already defined node. Particularly, labels are useful for connecting multiple incoming flows toward merge and join nodes. The syntax of the AC language is defined using the Backus-Naur-Form (BNF) notation in Fig. 11.1. The AC terms are generated using this syntax. We can distinguish two main syntactic categories: unmarked terms and marked terms. An unmarked AC term, typically given by $\mathcal{A}$, corresponds to the diagram without tokens. A marked AC term, typically given by $\mathcal{B}$, corresponds to an activity diagram with tokens. The difference between these two categories is the added "overbar" symbol for the marked terms (or sub-terms) denoting the presence and the location of a token. A marked term is typically used to denote an activity diagram while its execution is in progress. The idea of decorating the syntax was inspired by the work on Petri net algebra in [19]. However, we extended this concept in order to handle multiple tokens. We discard the intuitive but useless solution to write the expression $\overline{\overline{\mathcal{N}}}$ to denote a term $\mathcal{N}$ that is marked twice since it can result in overwhelming unmanageable marked AC terms if the number of tokens grows. Thus, we augment the "overbar" operator with an integer n such that $\overline{\mathcal{N}}^n$ denotes a term marked with n tokens. This allows us to consider loops in activity diagrams and so multiple instances.

Referring to Fig. 11.1, the definition of the term $\mathcal{B}$ is based on $\mathcal{A}$, since $\mathcal{B}$ represents all valid sub-terms with all possible locations of the overbar symbol on top of $\mathcal{A}$ sub-terms. $\mathcal{N}$ defines an unmarked sub-term and $\mathcal{M}$ represents a marked sub-term of $\mathcal{A}$. An AC term $\mathcal{A}$ is either ϵ, to denote an empty activity, or $\iota \rightarrowtail \mathcal{N}$, where ι specifies the initial node and $\mathcal{N}$ can be any labeled activity node (or control flows of nodes). The symbol $\rightarrowtail$ is used to specify the activity control flow edge. The derivation of an AC term is based on a depth-first traversal of the corresponding activity diagram. Thus, the mapping of activity diagrams into AC terms is achieved systematically. It is important to note that, as a syntactic convention, each time a new merge (or join) node is met, the definition of the node and its newly assigned label are considered. If the node is encountered later in the traversal process, only its corresponding label is used. This convention is important to ensure well formedness of the AC terms.

Among the basic constructs of $\mathcal{N}$, we have the following:

- The term $l: \otimes$ (resp. $l: \odot$) specifies the flow final node (resp. the activity final node).
- The term $l: Merge(\mathcal{N})$ (resp. $l: x.Join(\mathcal{N})$) represents the definition of the merge (resp. join) node. This notation is used only when the corresponding node is first encountered during the depth-first traversal of the activity diagram. The parameter $\mathcal{N}$ inside the merge (resp. join) refers to the subsequent destination nodes (or flow) connected to the outgoing edge of the merge (resp. join) node. With respect to the join node, the entity x represents an integer specifying the number of incoming edges into this specific join node.
- The term $l: Fork(\mathcal{N}_1, \mathcal{N}_2)$ is the construct referring to the fork node. The parameters $\mathcal{N}_1$ and $\mathcal{N}_2$ represent the sub-terms corresponding to the destination of the outgoing edges of the fork node (i.e., the flows split in parallel).
- The term $l: Decision_p(\langle g \rangle \mathcal{N}_1, \langle \neg g \rangle \mathcal{N}_2)$ (resp. $l: Decision(\langle g \rangle \mathcal{N}_1, \langle \neg g \rangle \mathcal{N}_2)$) specifies the probabilistic (resp. non-probabilistic) decision node. It denotes a probabilistic (resp. non-probabilistic guarded) choice between alternative flows $\mathcal{N}_1$ and $\mathcal{N}_2$. For the probabilistic case, the sub-term $\mathcal{N}_1$ is selected with a probability p, whereas $\mathcal{N}_2$ is selected with probability $1 - p$.
- The term $l: a \rightarrowtail \mathcal{N}$ is the construct representing the prefix operator: The labeled action $l: a$ is connected to $\mathcal{N}$ using a control flow edge.
- The term l is a reference to a node labeled with l.

A marked term $\mathcal{B}$ is either $\overline{\mathcal{A}}$ or $\overline{\iota} \rightarrowtail \mathcal{N}$, which denotes the initial node ι marked with one token and connected to the unmarked sub-term $\mathcal{N}$, or $\iota \rightarrowtail \mathcal{M}$ that denotes an unmarked initial node that is connected to the marked sub-term $\mathcal{M}$. Among the basic constructs of $\mathcal{M}$, we have the following:

- The term $\mathcal{N}$ is a special case of an AC marked term where $n = 0$.
- The term $\overline{\mathcal{M}}^n$ denotes a term $\mathcal{M}$ that is marked with n other tokens such that $n \geq 0$.
- The term $l: Merge(\mathcal{M})$ (resp. $l: x.Join(\mathcal{M})$) represents the definition of an unmarked merge (resp. join) term with a marked sub-term $\mathcal{M}$.
- The term $l: Fork(\mathcal{M}_1, \mathcal{M}_2)$ represents an unmarked fork term with two marked sub-terms $\mathcal{M}_1$ and $\mathcal{M}_2$.
- The term $l: Decision(\langle g \rangle \mathcal{M}_1, \langle \neg g \rangle \mathcal{M}_2)$ (resp. $l: Decision_p(\langle g \rangle \mathcal{M}_1, \langle \neg g \rangle \mathcal{M}_2)$) denotes an unmarked decision (resp. probabilistic decision) term having two marked sub-terms $\mathcal{M}_1$ and $\mathcal{M}_2$.
- The term $\overline{l: a}^n \rightarrowtail \mathcal{M}$ denotes a prefix operator with n-times marked action connected to a marked sub-term $\mathcal{M}$.

An important observation has to be made. Since the "overbar" symbol represents the presence (and eventually the location) of tokens, one may picture these tokens graphically on the activity diagram using small solid squares (to not mix with initial node notation) similar to the Petri-net tokens. This is not part of the UML notation, but it is only meant for illustration purposes. This exercise may reveal that two marked expressions may refer to the same activity diagram structure annotated with tokens that can be considered to be in the same locations. For instance, this is the case for the marked expressions $\iota \rightarrowtail \mathcal{N}$ and $\overline{\iota} \rightarrowtail \mathcal{N}$. More precisely, the term $\overline{\iota \rightarrowtail \mathcal{N}}$ denotes an activity diagram with a token on the top of the whole diagram. This configuration is exactly the same as having the token placed in the initial element of the diagram, which is represented by the term $\overline{\iota} \rightarrowtail \mathcal{N}$. This is also the case of $\overline{l : a \rightarrowtail \mathcal{N}}$ and $\overline{l : a} \rightarrowtail \mathcal{N}$. This complies with [188] stating that "when an activity starts, a control token is placed at each action or structured node that has no incoming edges."

Thus, in order to identify these pairs of marked expressions, we define a pre-order relation denoted by $\preccurlyeq_M$ over the set of marked expressions.

Definition 11.1 Let $\preccurlyeq_M \subseteq \mathcal{M} \times \mathcal{M}$ be the smallest pre-order relation defined as specified in Fig. 11.2.

This relation allows us to rewrite M_1 into M_1' in the case where $M_1 \preccurlyeq_M M_1'$ and then apply the semantic rule corresponding to M_1'. This simplifies considerably our operational semantics by keeping it concise. In these settings, we only need the pre-order concept; however, $\preccurlyeq_M$ can be extended easily to an equivalence relation using the kernel of this pre-order.

Before discussing the operational semantics, we present first the translation of activity diagram constructs into their corresponding AC syntactic elements then, we express an activity diagram example using AC. The correspondence between the concrete syntax of activity diagrams and the syntax of the calculus is summarized in Fig. 11.3.

Example 11.1 The SysML activity diagram illustrated in Fig. 11.4 denotes the design of a withdraw money banking operation. It can be expressed using the unmarked term $\mathcal{A}_{\texttt{withdraw}}$ as follows:

$$\mathcal{A}_{\texttt{withdraw}} = \iota \rightarrowtail l_1 : \texttt{Enter} \rightarrowtail l_2 : \texttt{Check} \rightarrowtail \mathcal{N}_1$$
$$\mathcal{N}_1 = l_3 : \texttt{Decision}_{0.1}(\langle \texttt{not enough} \rangle \mathcal{N}_2, \langle \texttt{enough} \rangle \mathcal{N}_3)$$
$$\mathcal{N}_2 = l_4 : \texttt{Notify} \rightarrowtail l_5 : \texttt{Merge}(l_6 : \odot)$$
$$\mathcal{N}_3 = l_7 : \texttt{Fork}(\mathcal{N}_4, l_{13} : \texttt{Fork}(l_{14} : \texttt{Disp} \rightarrowtail l_{10}, l_{15} : \texttt{Print} \rightarrowtail l_{12}))$$
$$\mathcal{N}_4 = l_8 : \texttt{Debit} \rightarrowtail l_9 : \texttt{Record} \rightarrowtail l_{10} : 2.\texttt{Join}(l_{11} : \texttt{Pick} \rightarrowtail l_{12} : 2.\texttt{Join}(l_5))$$

The $\mathcal{A}_{\texttt{withdraw}}$ term expresses the structure of the activity diagram. One can draw exactly the same activity diagram from its corresponding AC term.

(M1)	$\iota \rightarrowtail \mathcal{N} \preccurlyeq_M \overline{\iota} \rightarrowtail \mathcal{N}$
(M2)	$\overline{l : a^k}^n \rightarrowtail \mathcal{M} \preccurlyeq_M \overline{l : a}^{n+k} \rightarrowtail \mathcal{M}$
(M3)	$\overline{l : \otimes}^n \preccurlyeq_M l : \otimes$
(M4)	$\overline{\overline{\mathcal{M}}^k}^n \preccurlyeq_M \overline{\mathcal{M}}^{n+k}$
(M5)	$\mathcal{B}[l : Merge(\mathcal{M})^n, \overline{l}^k] \preccurlyeq_M \mathcal{B}[\overline{l : Merge(\mathcal{M})}^{n+k}, l]$

Fig. 11.2 Marking pre-order definition

	AD Constructs	AC Syntax
$\mathscr{A}$	● → $\mathcal{N}$	$\imath \rightarrowtail \mathcal{N}$
	◉	$l : \odot$
	⊗	$l : \otimes$
$\mathcal{N}$	a → $\mathcal{N}$	$l : a \rightarrowtail \mathcal{N}$
	◇ [¬g] $\mathcal{N}_2$, [g] $\mathcal{N}_1$	$l : Decision(\langle g \rangle \, \mathcal{N}_1, \langle \neg g \rangle \, \mathcal{N}_2)$
	◇ [¬g] {1-p} $\mathcal{N}_2$, [g] {p} $\mathcal{N}_1$	$l : Decision_p(\langle g \rangle \, \mathcal{N}_1, \langle \neg g \rangle \, \mathcal{N}_2)$
	◇ → $\mathcal{N}$	$l : Merge(\mathcal{N})$ or l
	$\mathcal{N}_1 \quad \mathcal{N}_2$	$l : Fork(\mathcal{N}_1, \mathcal{N}_2)$
	$\mathcal{N}$	$l : x.Join(\mathcal{N})$ or l (x is the number of incoming edges)

Fig. 11.3 Mapping activity diagram constructs into AC syntax

11.1.2 Operational Semantics

In this section, we present the operational semantics of the activity calculus in the structural operational semantics (SOS) style [201]. The latter is a well-established approach that provides a framework to give an operational semantics to many programming and specification languages [201]. It is also considerably applied in the study of the semantics of concurrent processes. Defining such a semantics (small-step semantics) consists in defining a set of axioms and inference rules that are used to describe the operational evolution. Since the propagation of the tokens within the diagram denotes its execution steps, the axioms and rules specify the tokens progress within the corresponding marked AC term. Each axiom and rule specifies the possible transitions between two marked terms of the activity diagram. In some cases, we might have more than one token present in the activity at a given instant. The selection of the progressing token is then performed non-deterministically.

The operational semantics is given by a probabilistic transition system (PTS) as presented in Definition 11.2. The initial state of the PTS corresponds to place a unique token on the initial node. The initially marked AC term corresponding

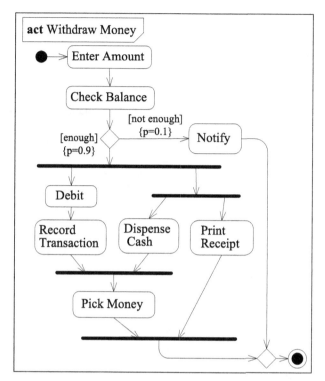

Fig. 11.4 Case study: activity diagram of money withdrawal

to $\mathcal{A}$ is the term $\overline{\mathcal{A}}$ where the one overbar is placed on the sub-term ι (i.e., $\overline{\iota} \rightarrowtail \mathcal{N}$) according to (M1) in Fig. 11.2. We denote this marked term by $\mathcal{B}_o$. The general form of a transition is $\mathcal{B} \xrightarrow{\alpha}_p \mathcal{B}'$ or $\mathcal{B} \xrightarrow{\alpha}_p \mathcal{A}$, such that $\mathcal{B}$ and $\mathcal{B}'$ are marked activity calculus terms, $\mathcal{A}$ is the unmarked activity calculus term, $\alpha \in \Sigma \cup \{o\}$, the set of actions ranged over by $a, a_1, \ldots, b, o$ denotes the empty action, and $p, q \in [0, 1]$ are probabilities of transitions' occurrences. This transition relation shows the marking evolution and means that a marked term $\mathcal{B}$ can be transformed into another marked term $\mathcal{B}'$ or to an unmarked term $\mathcal{A}$ by executing α with a probability p. If a marked term is transformed into an unmarked term, the transition denotes the loss of the marking. This is the case when either a flow final or an activity final node is reached. For simplicity, we omit the label o on the transition relation, if no action is executed, i.e., $\mathcal{B} \longrightarrow_p \mathcal{B}'$ or $\mathcal{B} \longrightarrow_p \mathcal{A}$. The transition relation is defined using the semantic rules from Figs. 11.5, 11.6, 11.7, 11.8, 11.9, 11.10, 11.11, and 11.12.

Definition 11.2 The probabilistic transition system of the activity calculus term $\mathcal{A}$ is the tuple $\mathcal{T} = (S, s_0, \xrightarrow{\alpha}_p)$ where

- S is the set of states, ranged over by s, each of which represents an AC term $\mathcal{B}$ corresponding to the unmarked term $\mathcal{A}$;
- $s_0 \in S$, the initial state representing the term $\mathcal{B}_o = \overline{\mathcal{A}}$;

- $\xrightarrow{\alpha}_p \subseteq S \times \Sigma \cup \{o\} \times [0, 1] \times S$ is the probabilistic transition relation and it is the least relation satisfying the AC operational semantics rules. We write $s_1 \xrightarrow{\alpha}_p s_2$ in order to specify a probabilistic transition of the form $(s_1, (\alpha, p), s_2)$ for $s_1, s_2 \in S$ and (α, p) in $\Sigma \cup \{o\} \times [0, 1]$.

Let e be a marked term and $f, f_1, \ldots, f_n$ specify marked (or unmarked) sub-terms. The term f is a sub-term (or a sub-expression) of e, denoted by $e[f]$, if f is a valid activity calculus term occurring once in the definition of e. We also use the notation $e[f\{x\}]$ to denote that f occurs exactly x times in the expression e. For simplification $e[f\{1\}] = e[f]$. We may generalize this notation to more than one sub-term, i.e., $e[f_1, f_2, \ldots, f_n]$. For instance, given a marked term $\mathcal{B} = \iota \rightarrowtail \overline{l_1 : a_1} \rightarrowtail l_2 : a_2 \rightarrowtail l_3 : \odot$. We write $\mathcal{B}[\overline{l_1 : a_1}]$ to specify that $\overline{l_1 : a_1}$ is a sub-term of $\mathcal{B}$. Furthermore, we use the notation $|\mathcal{B}|$ to denote the unmarked activity calculus term obtained by removing the marking (all overbars) from the marked term $\mathcal{B}$.

The AC operational semantics rules are presented in next section.

INIT-1 $$\overline{\iota} \rightarrowtail \mathcal{N} \longrightarrow_1 \iota \rightarrowtail \overline{\mathcal{N}}$$

INIT-2 $$\frac{\mathcal{M} \xrightarrow{\alpha}_q \mathcal{M}'}{\iota \rightarrowtail \mathcal{M} \xrightarrow{\alpha}_q \iota \rightarrowtail \mathcal{M}'}$$

Fig. 11.5 Semantic rules for initial

ACT-1 $$\overline{l : a}^n \rightarrowtail \mathcal{M} \xrightarrow{a}_1 \overline{l : a}^{n-1} \rightarrowtail \overline{\mathcal{M}} \quad \forall n > 0$$

ACT-2 $$\frac{\mathcal{M} \xrightarrow{\alpha}_q \mathcal{M}'}{\overline{l : a}^n \rightarrowtail \mathcal{M} \xrightarrow{\alpha}_q \overline{l : a}^n \rightarrowtail \mathcal{M}'}$$

Fig. 11.6 Semantic rules for action prefixing

FINAL $$\mathcal{B}[\overline{l : \odot}] \longrightarrow_1 |\mathcal{B}|$$

Fig. 11.7 Semantic rules for final

FORK-1 $$\overline{l : Fork(\mathcal{M}_1, \mathcal{M}_2)}^n \longrightarrow_1 \overline{l : Fork(\overline{\mathcal{M}_1}, \overline{\mathcal{M}_2})}^{n-1} \quad \forall n > 0$$

FORK-2 $$\frac{\mathcal{M}_1 \xrightarrow{\alpha}_q \mathcal{M}_1'}{\begin{array}{c}\overline{l : Fork(\mathcal{M}_1, \mathcal{M}_2)}^n \xrightarrow{\alpha}_q \overline{l : Fork(\mathcal{M}_1', \mathcal{M}_2)}^n \\ \overline{l : Fork(\mathcal{M}_2, \mathcal{M}_1)}^n \xrightarrow{\alpha}_q \overline{l : Fork(\mathcal{M}_2, \mathcal{M}_1')}^n\end{array}}$$

Fig. 11.8 Semantic rules for fork

$$
\textbf{DEC-1}\quad \dfrac{\overline{l:Decision(\langle g\rangle \mathscr{M}_1,\langle \neg g\rangle \mathscr{M}_2)}^{\,n}\longrightarrow_1}{\overline{l:Decision(\langle tt\rangle \overline{\mathscr{M}_1},\langle ff\rangle \mathscr{M}_2)}^{\,n-1}}\ \forall n>0
$$

$$
\textbf{DEC-2}\quad \dfrac{\overline{l:Decision(\langle g\rangle \mathscr{M}_1,\langle \neg g\rangle \mathscr{M}_2)}^{\,n}\longrightarrow_1}{\overline{l:Decision(\langle ff\rangle \mathscr{M}_1,\langle tt\rangle \overline{\mathscr{M}_2})}^{\,n-1}}\ \forall n>0
$$

$$
\textbf{DEC-3}\quad \dfrac{\mathscr{M}_1\xrightarrow{\alpha}_q \mathscr{M}_1'}{\begin{array}{c}\overline{l:Decision(\langle g\rangle \mathscr{M}_1,\langle \neg g\rangle \mathscr{M}_2)}^{\,n}\xrightarrow{\alpha}_q \overline{l:Decision(\langle g\rangle \mathscr{M}_1',\langle \neg g\rangle \mathscr{M}_2)}^{\,n}\\[4pt]\hline\\[-6pt]\overline{l:Decision(\langle g\rangle \mathscr{M}_2,\langle \neg g\rangle \mathscr{M}_1)}^{\,n}\xrightarrow{\alpha}_q \overline{l:Decision(\langle g\rangle \mathscr{M}_2,\langle \neg g\rangle \mathscr{M}_1')}^{\,n}\end{array}}
$$

Fig. 11.9 Semantic rules for non-probabilistic guarded decision

$$
\textbf{PDEC-1}\quad \dfrac{\overline{l:Decision_p(\langle g\rangle \mathscr{M}_1,\langle \neg g\rangle \mathscr{M}_2)}^{\,n}\longrightarrow_p}{\overline{l:Decision_p(\langle tt\rangle \overline{\mathscr{M}_1},\langle ff\rangle \mathscr{M}_2)}^{\,n-1}}\ \forall n>0
$$

$$
\textbf{PDEC-2}\quad \dfrac{\overline{l:Decision_p(\langle g\rangle \mathscr{M}_1,\langle \neg g\rangle \mathscr{M}_2)}^{\,n}\longrightarrow_{1-p}}{\overline{l:Decision_p(\langle ff\rangle \mathscr{M}_1,\langle tt\rangle \overline{\mathscr{M}_2})}^{\,n-1}}\ \forall n>0
$$

$$
\textbf{PDEC-3}\quad \dfrac{\mathscr{M}_1\xrightarrow{\alpha}_q \mathscr{M}_1'}{\begin{array}{c}\overline{l:Decision_p(\langle g\rangle \mathscr{M}_1,\langle \neg g\rangle \mathscr{M}_2)}^{\,n}\xrightarrow{\alpha}_q \overline{l:Decision_p(\langle g\rangle \mathscr{M}_1',\langle \neg g\rangle \mathscr{M}_2)}^{\,n}\\[4pt]\hline\\[-6pt]\overline{l:Decision_p(\langle g\rangle \mathscr{M}_2,\langle \neg g\rangle \mathscr{M}_1)}^{\,n}\xrightarrow{\alpha}_q \overline{l:Decision_p(\langle g\rangle \mathscr{M}_2,\langle \neg g\rangle \mathscr{M}_1')}^{\,n}\end{array}}
$$

Fig. 11.10 Semantic rules for probabilistic decision

$$
\textbf{MERG-1}\quad \dfrac{\overline{l:Merge(\mathscr{M})}^{\,n}\longrightarrow_1 \overline{l:Merge(\overline{\mathscr{M}})}^{\,n-1}}{}\ \forall n\geq 1
$$

$$
\textbf{MERG-2}\quad \dfrac{\mathscr{M}\xrightarrow{\alpha}_q \mathscr{M}'}{\overline{l:Merge(\mathscr{M})}^{\,n}\xrightarrow{\alpha}_q \overline{l:Merge(\mathscr{M}')}^{\,n}}
$$

Fig. 11.11 Semantic rules for merge

$$
\textbf{JOIN-1}\quad \mathscr{B}[\overline{l:x.Join(\mathscr{M})}^{\,n},\overline{l}^{\,k_x}\{x-1\}]\longrightarrow_1 \mathscr{B}[\overline{l:x.Join(\overline{\mathscr{M}})},l\{x-1\}]\ x>1;\ n,k_x\geq 1
$$

$$
\textbf{JOIN-2}\quad \dfrac{}{\overline{l:1.Join(\mathscr{M})}^{\,n}\longrightarrow_1 \overline{l:1.Join(\overline{\mathscr{M}})}^{\,n-1}}\ n\geq 1
$$

$$
\textbf{JOIN-3}\quad \dfrac{\mathscr{M}\xrightarrow{\alpha}_q \mathscr{M}'}{\overline{l:x.Join(\mathscr{M})}^{\,n}\xrightarrow{\alpha}_q \overline{l:x.Join(\mathscr{M}')}^{\,n}}
$$

Fig. 11.12 Semantic rules for join

11.1.2.1 Rules for Initial

The first set of rules in Fig. 11.5 refers to the transitions related to the term $\iota \rightarrowtail \mathcal{N}$. "Tokens in an initial node are offered to outgoing edges" [188]. This is interpreted by our semantics using the axiom INIT-1, which means that if ι is marked, the marking propagates to the rest of the term $\mathcal{N}$ throughout its outgoing edge, with no observable action and a probability $q = 1$. Rule INIT-2 allows the marking to evolve in the rest of the activity term from $\iota \rightarrowtail \mathcal{M}$ to $\iota \rightarrowtail \mathcal{M}'$ with a probability q, by executing the action α if the marking on the sub-term $\mathcal{M}$ can evolve to another marking $\mathcal{M}'$ using the same transition.

11.1.2.2 Rules for Action Prefixing

The second set of rules in Fig. 11.6 concerns action prefixing. These rules illustrate the possible progress of the tokens in the expression $\overline{l : a}^n \rightarrowtail \mathcal{M}$. "The completion of the execution of an action may enable the execution of successor node" [188]. Accordingly, the axiom ACT-1 specifies the progress of a token from $\overline{l : a}^k$, where action a terminates its execution, to the sub-term $\mathcal{M}$. Note that ACT-1 supports the case of multiple tokens, which is compliant with the specification stating that "start a new execution of the behavior with newly arrived tokens, even if the behavior is already executing from tokens arriving at the invocation earlier" [188]. Rule ACT-2 allows the marking to evolve in the rest of the activity term from $\overline{l : a}^n \rightarrowtail \mathcal{M}$ to $\overline{l : a}^n \rightarrowtail \mathcal{M}'$ by executing the action α and with a probability q, if the marked sub-term $\mathcal{M}$ can evolve to $\mathcal{M}'$.

11.1.2.3 Rules for Final

The rules for activity final are given in Fig. 11.7. "A token reaching an activity final node terminates the activity. In particular, it stops all executing actions in the activity, and destroys all tokens" [188]. Once marked (one token is enough), the activity final node imposes the abrupt termination of all the other normal flows in the activity. Accordingly, the axiom FINAL states that if $\overline{l : \odot}$ is a subterm of a marked term $\mathcal{B}$, the latter can do a transition with a probability $q = 1$ and no action, which results in the deletion of all overbars (tokens) from the marked activity term $\mathcal{B}$.

11.1.2.4 Rules for Fork

The rules for fork are listed in Fig. 11.8. "Tokens arriving at a fork are duplicated across the outgoing edges" [188]. Accordingly, the axiom FORK-1 shows the propagation of the tokens to the sub-terms of the fork in the case where the fork expression is marked. A fork expression is marked means that one or many tokens are offered at the incoming edge of the fork node. Rule FORK-2 illustrates two symmetric rules showing the evolution of the marking within the sub-terms of the fork expression. According to the activity diagram specification, "UML 2.0 activity forks model unrestricted parallelism," which is contrasted with the earlier semantics of UML

1.x, where there is a required synchronization between parallel flows [188]. Thus, the marking evolves asynchronously according to an interleaving semantics on both left and right sub-terms.

11.1.2.5 Rules for Decision

The next set of rules concerns the non-probabilistic decision shown in Fig. 11.9 and the probabilistic decision provided in Fig. 11.10. With respect to non-probabilistic decision nodes, the specification document states the following: "Each token arriving at a decision node can traverse only one outgoing edge. Guards of the outgoing edges are evaluated to determine which edge should be traversed" [188]. Axioms DEC-1 and DEC-2 describe the evolution of tokens reaching a non-probabilistic decision node. For the probabilistic counterpart, the axioms PDEC-1 and PDEC-2 specify the likelihood of a token reaching a probabilistic decision node to traverse one of its branches. The choice is probabilistic. The marking will propagate either to the first branch with a probability p (PDEC-1) or to the second branch with a probability $1-p$ (PDEC-2). This complies with the specification [187].

Rule PDEC-3 (respectively, DEC-3) groups two symmetric cases that are related to the marking evolution through the decision sub-terms. If a possible transition $\mathcal{M}_1 \xrightarrow{\alpha}_q \mathcal{M}_1'$ exists and $\mathcal{M}_1$ is a subexpression of $\overline{l: Decision_p(\langle g \rangle \mathcal{M}_1, \langle \neg g \rangle \mathcal{M}_2))}^n$, then we can deduce the transition $\overline{l: Decision_p(\langle g \rangle \mathcal{M}_1, \langle \neg g \rangle \mathcal{M}_2)}^n \xrightarrow{\alpha}_q \overline{l: Decision_p(\langle g \rangle \mathcal{M}_1', \langle \neg g \rangle \mathcal{M}_2)}^n$.

11.1.2.6 Rules for Merge

Rules for merge are presented in Fig. 11.11. The semantics of merge node according to Ref. [188] is defined as follows: "All tokens offered on incoming edges are offered to the outgoing edge. There is no synchronization of flows or joining of tokens." Thus, the axiom MERG-1 states that the marking on top of the merge evolves with a probability 1 and no action to its sub-term $\mathcal{M}$. Rule MERG-2 allows the marking to evolve in $\overline{l: Merge(\mathcal{M})}^n$ if there is a possible transition such that $\mathcal{M} \xrightarrow{\alpha}_q \mathcal{M}'$.

11.1.2.7 Rules for Join

Rules for join are presented in Fig. 11.12. "If there is a token offered on all incoming edges, then one control token is offered on the outgoing edge" [188]. Axioms JOIN-1 and JOIN-2 describe the propagation of a token on the top of the join definition expression, namely $\overline{l: x.Join(\mathcal{M})}^n$ and the referencing labels. Unlike the merge node, the join traversal requires all references to itself to be marked, which is described using the "join specification" requirement in [188]. More precisely, all the sub-terms l corresponding to a given join node in the AC term, including the definition of the join itself, have to be marked so that the token can progress to the rest of the expression. The number of occurrences of the sub-term $\bar{l}$ in the whole marked term is known and it corresponds to the value of $x-1$. If so, only one control token propagates to the subsequent subterm $\mathcal{M}$ with a probability $q = 1$. Moreover, Ref. [188] states that "Multiple control tokens offered on the same incoming edge are combined into one before" the traversal, which is specified in axiom JOIN-1. Axiom JOIN-2 corresponds to the special case where $x = 1$. According to [188], there is no restriction on the use of a join node with a single incoming edge even though this is qualified therein as not useful. Rule JOIN-3 shows the possible evolution of the marking in $\overline{l:x.Join(\mathcal{M})}^n$ to $\overline{l:x.Join(\mathcal{M}')}^n$, if the marking in $\mathcal{M}$ evolves to $\mathcal{M}'$ with the same transition.

11.2 Case Study

We present a SysML activity diagram case study depicting a hypothetical design of the behavior corresponding to banking operations on an ATM system illustrated in Fig. 11.13. We first show how we can express the activity diagram using the AC language and then demonstrate the benefit and usefulness of the proposed formal semantics.

The actions in an activity diagram can be refined using structured activity nodes in order to expand their internal behavior. For instance, the node labeled Withdraw in Fig. 11.13 is actually a structured node that calls the activity diagram pictured in Fig. 11.4. Using the operational semantics defined earlier, a compositional assessment of the design can be performed. For instance, the detailed activities are abstracted away at a first step and the global behavior is validated. Then, the assessment of the refined behavior can be performed. The compositionality and

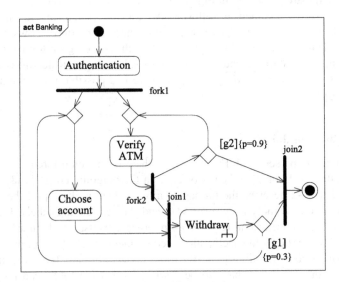

Fig. 11.13 Case study: activity diagram of a banking operation

abstraction features allow handling real-world systems without compromising the validation process. For instance, we consider the activity diagram of Fig. 11.13 and assume that Withdraw action is an atomic action denoted by the abbreviation d. Moreover, considering the actions a, b, and c as the abbreviations of the actions Authentication, Verify ATM, and Choose account, respectively, the corresponding unmarked term $\mathcal{A}_1$ is as follows:

$$\mathcal{A}_1 = \iota \rightarrowtail l_1 : a \rightarrowtail l_2 : \mathtt{Fork}(\mathcal{N}_1, l_{12})$$
$$\mathcal{N}_1 = l_3 : \mathtt{Merge}(l_4 : b \rightarrowtail l_5 : \mathtt{Fork}(\mathcal{N}_2, \mathcal{N}_3))$$
$$\mathcal{N}_2 = l_6 : \mathtt{Decision}_{0.9}(\langle g2 \rangle\, l_3, \langle \neg g2 \rangle\, l_7 : 2.\mathtt{Join}(l_8 : \odot))$$
$$\mathcal{N}_3 = l_9 : 2.\mathtt{Join}(l_{10} : d \rightarrowtail \mathcal{N}_4)$$
$$\mathcal{N}_4 = l_{11} : \mathtt{Decision}_{0.3}(\langle g1 \rangle\, \mathcal{N}_5, \langle \neg g1 \rangle\, l_7)$$
$$\mathcal{N}_5 = l_{12} : \mathtt{Merge}(l_{13} : c \rightarrowtail l_9)$$

The abbreviations are used to simplify the presentation of the AC term. The guard $g1$ denotes the possibility of triggering a new operation if evaluated to *true* and guard $g2$ denotes the result of evaluating the status of the connection. Applying the operational rules on the marked $\overline{\mathcal{A}_1}$, we can derive a run that leads to a deadlock, which means that we reached a configuration where the expression is marked but no progress can be made (no operational rule can be applied). This derivation may reveal a design error in the activity diagram, which is not obvious using only inspection. Even though one may suspect the join2 to cause the deadlock due to the presence of a prior decision node, the deadlock actually occurs due to the other join node (i.e., node join1).

$$\overline{\mathcal{A}_1} = \overline{\iota} \rightarrowtail l_1 : a \rightarrowtail l_2 : \mathtt{Fork}(\mathcal{N}_1, l_{12})$$

$$\rightarrow_1 \iota \rightarrowtail \overline{l_1} : a \rightarrowtail l_2 : \mathtt{Fork}(\mathcal{N}_1, l_{12})$$

$$\xrightarrow{a}_1 \iota \rightarrowtail l_1 : a \rightarrowtail \overline{l_2} : \mathtt{Fork}(\mathcal{N}_1, l_{12})$$

$$\rightarrow_1 \iota \rightarrowtail l_1 : a \rightarrowtail l_2 : \mathtt{Fork}(\overline{\mathcal{N}_1}, \overline{l_{12}})$$

$$\rightarrow_1 \iota \rightarrowtail l_1 : a \rightarrowtail l_2 : \mathtt{Fork}(l_3 : \mathtt{Merge}(\overline{l_4 : b} \rightarrowtail l_5 : \mathtt{Fork}(\mathcal{N}_2, \mathcal{N}_3)), \overline{l_{12}})$$

$$\xrightarrow{b}_1 \iota \rightarrowtail l_1 : a \rightarrowtail l_2 : \mathtt{Fork}(l_3 : \mathtt{Merge}(l_4 : b \rightarrowtail \overline{l_5 : \mathtt{Fork}(\mathcal{N}_2, \mathcal{N}_3)}), \overline{l_{12}})$$

$$\rightarrow_1 \iota \rightarrowtail l_1 : a \rightarrowtail l_2 : \mathtt{Fork}(l_3 : \mathtt{Merge}(l_4 : b \rightarrowtail l_5 : \mathtt{Fork}(\overline{\mathcal{N}_2}, \overline{\mathcal{N}_3})), \overline{l_{12}})$$

$$\rightarrow_{0.1} \iota \rightarrowtail l_1 : a \rightarrowtail l_2 : \mathtt{Fork}(l_3 : \mathtt{Merge}(l_4 : b \rightarrowtail l_5 : \mathtt{Fork}($$
$$l_6 : \mathtt{Decision}_{0.9}(\langle g2 \rangle\, l_3, \langle \neg g2 = tt \rangle\, \overline{l_7} : 2.\mathtt{Join}(l_8 : \odot)), \mathcal{N}_3)), \overline{l_{12}})$$

$$\rightarrow_1 \iota \rightarrowtail l_1 : a \rightarrowtail l_2 : \mathtt{Fork}(l_3 : \mathtt{Merge}(l_4 : b \rightarrowtail l_5 : \mathtt{Fork}($$
$$l_6 : \mathtt{Decision}_{0.9}(\langle g2 \rangle\, l_3, \langle \neg g2 \rangle\, \overline{l_7} : 2.\mathtt{Join}(l_8 : \odot)), l_9 : 2.\mathtt{Join}($$
$$l_{10} : d \rightarrowtail l_{11} : \mathtt{Decision}_{0.3}(\langle g1 \rangle\, l_{12} : \mathtt{Merge}(\overline{l_{13} : c} \rightarrowtail l_9), \langle \neg g1 \rangle\, l_7)))), l_{12})$$

Fig. 11.14 Derivation run leading to a deadlock – part 1

More precisely, the run consists in executing the action c twice (because the guard $g1$ is true) and the action b once ($g2$ evaluated to false). The deadlocked configuration reached by the derivation run has the following marked sub-terms:

$$\mathcal{M}_2 = l_6:\texttt{Decision}_{0.9}(\langle g2 \rangle\, l_3, \langle \neg g2 \rangle\, \overline{l_7}:\texttt{Join}(l_8:\odot))$$
$$\mathcal{M}_5 = l_{12}:\texttt{Merge}(l_{13}:c \rightarrowtail \overline{l_9})$$

A possible derivation run leading to this deadlocked configuration is presented in Fig. 11.14 and 11.15. This has been obtained by applying the AC operational semantic rules on the term $\overline{\mathcal{A}_1}$, which corresponds to the initial state of the probabilistic transition system. This run represents a single path in the probabilistic transition system corresponding to the semantic model of the activity diagram of Fig. 11.13. Informally, the deadlock occurs because both join nodes $\texttt{join1}$ and $\texttt{join2}$ are waiting for a token that will never be delivered on one of their incoming edges. There is no possible token progress from the deadlocked configuration since no rule can be applied.

$$\xrightarrow{c}_1 \iota \rightarrowtail l_1:a \rightarrowtail l_2:\texttt{Fork}(l_3:\texttt{Merge}(l_4:b \rightarrowtail l_5:\texttt{Fork}(\underline{}$$
$$l_6:\texttt{Decision}_{0.9}(\langle g2 \rangle\, l_3, \langle \neg g2 \rangle\, \overline{l_7}:2.\texttt{Join}(l_8:\odot)), l_9:2.\texttt{Join}(\underline{}$$
$$l_{10}:d \rightarrowtail l_{11}:\texttt{Decision}_{0.3}(\langle g1 \rangle\, l_{12}:\texttt{Merge}(l_{13}:c \rightarrowtail \overline{l_9}),$$
$$\langle \neg g1 \rangle\, l_7)))), l_{12})$$

$$\xrightarrow{}_1 \iota \rightarrowtail l_1:a \rightarrowtail l_2:\texttt{Fork}(l_3:\texttt{Merge}(l_4:b \rightarrowtail l_5:\texttt{Fork}(\underline{}$$
$$l_6:\texttt{Decision}_{0.9}(\langle g2 \rangle\, l_3, \langle \neg g2 \rangle\, \overline{l_7}:2.\texttt{Join}(l_8:\odot)), l_9:2.\texttt{Join}(\underline{}$$
$$\overline{l_{10}:d} \rightarrowtail l_{11}:\texttt{Decision}_{0.3}(\langle g1 \rangle\, l_{12}:\texttt{Merge}(l_{13}:c \rightarrowtail l_9),$$
$$\langle \neg g1 \rangle\, l_7)))), l_{12})$$

$$\xrightarrow{d}_1 \iota \rightarrowtail l_1:a \rightarrowtail l_2:\texttt{Fork}(l_3:\texttt{Merge}(l_4:b \rightarrowtail l_5:\texttt{Fork}(\underline{}$$
$$l_6:\texttt{Decision}_{0.9}(\langle g2 \rangle\, l_3, \langle \neg g2 \rangle\, \overline{l_7}:2.\texttt{Join}(l_8:\odot)), l_9:2.\texttt{Join}(\underline{}$$
$$l_{10}:d \rightarrowtail \overline{l_{11}}:\texttt{Decision}_{0.3}(\langle g1 \rangle\, l_{12}:\texttt{Merge}(l_{13}:c \rightarrowtail l_9),$$
$$\overline{\langle \neg g1 \rangle\, l_7)}))), l_{12})$$

$$\xrightarrow{}_{0.3} \iota \rightarrowtail l_1:a \rightarrowtail l_2:\texttt{Fork}(l_3:\texttt{Merge}(l_4:b \rightarrowtail l_5:\texttt{Fork}(\underline{}$$
$$l_6:\texttt{Decision}_{0.9}(\langle g2 \rangle\, l_3, \langle \neg g2 \rangle\, \overline{l_7}:2.\texttt{Join}(l_8:\odot)), l_9:2.\texttt{Join}(\underline{}$$
$$l_{10}:d \rightarrowtail l_{11}:\texttt{Decision}_{0.3}(\langle g1 \rangle\, l_{12}:\texttt{Merge}(l_{13}:c \rightarrowtail l_9),$$
$$\langle \neg g1 \rangle\, l_7)))), l_{12})$$

$$\xrightarrow{}_1 \iota \rightarrowtail l_1:a \rightarrowtail l_2:\texttt{Fork}(l_3:\texttt{Merge}(l_4:b \rightarrowtail l_5:\texttt{Fork}(\underline{}$$
$$l_6:\texttt{Decision}_{0.9}(\langle g2 \rangle\, l_3, \langle \neg g2 \rangle\, \overline{l_7}:2.\texttt{Join}(l_8:\odot)), l_9:2.\texttt{Join}(\underline{}$$
$$l_{10}:d \rightarrowtail l_{11}:\texttt{Decision}_{0.3}(\langle g1 \rangle\, l_{12}:\texttt{Merge}(\overline{l_{13}}:c \rightarrowtail l_9),$$
$$\langle \neg g1 \rangle\, l_7)))), l_{12})$$

$$\xrightarrow{c}_1 \iota \rightarrowtail l_1:a \rightarrowtail l_2:\texttt{Fork}(l_3:\texttt{Merge}(l_4:b \rightarrowtail l_5:\texttt{Fork}(\underline{}$$
$$l_6:\texttt{Decision}_{0.9}(\langle g2 \rangle\, l_3, \langle \neg g2 \rangle\, \overline{l_7}:2.\texttt{Join}(l_8:\odot)), l_9:2.\texttt{Join}(\underline{}$$
$$l_{10}:d \rightarrowtail l_{11}:\texttt{Decision}_{0.3}(\langle g1 \rangle\, l_{12}:\texttt{Merge}(l_{13}:c \rightarrowtail \overline{l_9}),$$
$$\langle \neg g1 \rangle\, l_7)))), l_{12})$$

Fig. 11.15 Derivation run leading to a deadlock – part 2

11.3 Markov Decision Process

The MDP underlying the PTS corresponding to the semantic model of a given SysML activity diagram can be described using the following definition.

Definition 11.3 The Markov decision process $\mathcal{M}_T$ underlying the probabilistic transition system $T=(S, s_0, \xrightarrow{\alpha}_p)$ is the tuple $\mathcal{M}_T=(S, s_0, Act, Steps)$ such that

- $Act=\Sigma \cup \{o\}$,
- $Steps: S \rightarrow 2^{Act \times Dist(S)}$ is the probabilistic transition function defined over S such that for each $s \in S$, $Steps(s)$ is defined as follows:

  - For each set of transitions $\Gamma_\alpha=\{s \xrightarrow{\alpha}_{p_j} s_j, j \in J, p_j < 1, \text{and} \sum_j p_j = 1\}$, $(\alpha, \mu_\Gamma) \in Steps(s)$ such that $\mu_\Gamma(s_j) = p_j$ and $\mu_\Gamma(s') = 0$ for $s' \in S \setminus \{s_j\}_{j \in J}$.
  - For each transition $\tau = s \xrightarrow{\alpha}_1 s'$, $(\alpha, \mu_\tau) \in Steps(s)$ such that $\mu_\tau(s') = 1$ and $\mu_\tau(s) = 0$ for $s \neq s'$.

11.4 Conclusion

In this chapter, we defined a probabilistic calculus that we called activity calculus (AC). The latter allows expressing algebraically SysML activity diagrams and providing its formal semantic foundations using operational semantics framework. Our calculus not only serves proving the soundness of the translation algorithm that we presented in the previous chapter but also opens up new directions to explore other properties and applications using the formal semantics of SysML activity diagrams. The next chapter defines a formal syntax and semantics for PRISM specification language and examines the soundness of the proposed translation algorithm that maps SysML activity diagrams into PRISM MDP.

Chapter 12
Soundness of the Translation Algorithm

In this chapter, our main objective is to closely examine the correctness of the translation procedure proposed earlier that maps SysML activity diagrams into the input language of the probabilistic model checker PRISM. In order to provide a systematic proof, we rely on formal methods, which enable us with solid mathematical basis. To do so, four main ingredients are needed. First, we need to express formally the translation algorithm. This enables its manipulation forward deriving the corresponding proofs. Second, the formal syntax and semantics for SysML activity diagrams need to be defined. This has been proposed in the previous chapter by the means of the activity calculus language. Third, the formal syntax and semantics of PRISM input language have to be defined. Finally, a suitable relation is needed in order to compare the semantics of the diagram with the semantics of the resulting PRISM model.

We start by exposing the notation that we use in Sect. 12.1. Then, in Sect. 12.2 we explain the followed methodology for establishing the correctness proof. After that, we describe in Sect. 12.3 the formal syntax and semantics definitions of PRISM input language. Section 12.4 is dedicated for formalizing the translation algorithm using a functional core language. Section 12.6 defines a simulation relation over Markov decision processes, which can be used in order to compare the semantics of both SysML activity diagrams and their corresponding PRISM models. Finally, Sect. 12.7 presents the soundness theorem, which formally defines the soundness property of the translation algorithm. Therein, we provide the details of the related proof.

12.1 Notation

In the following, we present the notation that we are going to use in this chapter. A multiset is denoted by (A, m), where A is the underlying set of elements and $m: A \longrightarrow \mathbb{N}$ is the multiplicity function that associates a positive natural number in $\mathbb{N}$ with each element of A. For each element $a \in A$, $m(a)$ is the number of occurrences of a. The notation $\{\!|\ |\!\}$ is used to designate the empty multiset and $\{\!| (a \hookrightarrow n) |\!\}$ denotes the multiset containing the element a occurring $m(a) = n$ times. The operator $\uplus$ denotes the union of two multisets, such that if (A_1, m_1)

M. Debbabi et al., *Verification and Validation in Systems Engineering*,
DOI 10.1007/978-3-642-15228-3_12, © Springer-Verlag Berlin Heidelberg 2010

and (A_2, m_2) are two multisets, the union of these two multisets is a multiset $(A, m) = (A_1, m_1) \uplus (A_2, m_2)$ such that $A = A_1 \cup A_2$ and $\forall a \in \mathcal{A}$, we have $m(a) = m_1(a) + m_2(a)$.

A discrete probability distribution over a countable set S is a function $\mu : S \to [0, 1]$ such that $\sum_{s \in S} \mu(s) = 1$ where $\mu(s)$ denotes the probability for s under the distribution μ. The support of the distribution μ is the set $Supp(\mu) = \{s \in S : \mu(s) > 0\}$. We write μ_s^1 for $s \in S$ to designate a distribution that assigns a probability 1 to s and 0 to any other element in S. Also, sub-distributions μ are considered where $\sum_{s \in S} \mu(s) < 1$ and μ_s^λ denotes a probability distribution that assigns λ probability to s and 0 to any other element in S. The set of probability distributions over S is denoted by $Dist(S)$.

12.2 Methodology

Let $\mathcal{A}$ be the unmarked AC term corresponding to a given SysML activity diagram. Let $\mathcal{P}$ be the corresponding PRISM model description written in the PRISM input language. We denote by $\mathcal{T}$ the translation algorithm that maps $\mathcal{A}$ into $\mathcal{P}$, i.e., $\mathcal{T}(\mathcal{A}) = \mathcal{P}$. If we denote by $\mathcal{S}$ the semantic function that associates for each SysML activity diagram its formal meaning $\mathcal{S}(\mathcal{A})$ denotes the corresponding semantic model. According to our previous results, the semantics of the activity diagram can be expressed as an MDP as defined in Definition 11.3. Let us denote it by $\mathcal{S}(\mathcal{A}) = M_{\mathcal{A}}$. Similarly, let $\mathcal{S}'$ be the semantic function that associates with a PRISM model description its formal semantics. Since we are dealing with MDP models, $\mathcal{S}'(\mathcal{P}) = M_{\mathcal{P}}$ represents the MDP semantics of $\mathcal{P}$.

Our main objective is to prove the correctness of the translation algorithm with respect to the SysML activity diagram semantics. This can be reduced to prove the commutativity of the diagram presented in Fig. 12.1. To this end, we aim at defining a relation that we can use to compare $M_{\mathcal{P}}$ with $M_{\mathcal{A}}$. Let $\approx$ denote this relation, we aim at proving that there exists such a relation so that $M_{\mathcal{P}} \approx M_{\mathcal{A}}$.

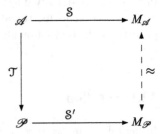

Fig. 12.1 Approach to prove the correctness of the translation

12.3 Formalization of the PRISM Input Language

We describe in this section the formal syntax and the semantics of the PRISM input language. By doing so, we greatly simplify the manipulation of the output of our translation algorithm for the sake of proofs. Moreover, defining a formal semantics for the PRISM language itself leads to more precise soundness concepts and more rigorous proofs. While reviewing the literature, there were no initiatives in this direction.

12.3.1 Syntax

The formal syntax of PRISM input language is presented in a BNF style in Figs. 12.2 and 12.3. A PRISM model, namely *prism_model*, starts with the specification of the model type *model_type* (i.e., MDP, CTMC, or DTMC). A model consists of two main parts:

- The declaration of the constants, the formulas, and the global variables corresponding to the model.
- The specification of the modules composing the model each consisting of a set of local variables declaration followed by a set of commands.

We focus on the commands since they describe the intrinsic behavior of the model. The formal descriptions of constants, formulas, and local and global variable declarations are not provided in detail since they are supposed to be pre-determined and generated before the actual definition of the commands. In addition, we assume that each variable declaration contains an initial value. We denote by x_0 the initial value of the variable x.

A command c is of the form $[\alpha]\ w \rightharpoonup u$ where α represents the action label of the command, w is the corresponding (boolean) guard, and u is its update representing the effect of the command on the values of the variables. An update is build as the probabilistic choice over unit updates d_i, denoted by $\sum_{i \in I} \lambda_i : d_i$ such that

$$
\begin{array}{rll}
prism\_model ::= & model\_type & \\
& global\_declaration & \text{(Global Declarations)} \\
& modules & \text{(Modules Specification)} \\
& & \\
modules ::= & \textbf{module}\ module\_name & \\
& localvar\_dec & \text{(Local Variables Declarations)} \\
& c & \text{(Commands)} \\
& \textbf{endmodule} & \\
& |\ modules \parallel modules & \text{(Modules Composition)} \\
& & \\
global\_declaration ::= & const\_dec & \text{(Constants Declarations)} \\
& formula\_dec & \text{(Formulas Declarations)} \\
& globalvar\_dec & \text{(Global Variables Declarations)} \\
& & \\
model\_type ::= & \textbf{mdp} & \\
& |\ \textbf{ctmc} & \\
& |\ \textbf{dtmc} & \\
\end{array}
$$

Fig. 12.2 Syntax of the PRISM input language – part 1

$\sum_{i \in I} \lambda_i = 1$. A given unit update d is the conjunction of assignments of the form $x' = e$, where x' represents the new value of the variable x and e is an expression over the variables, constants, and/or formulas of the model. Thus, we require type consistency of the variable x and the expression e. A trivial update unit $skip$ stands for the update that does not affect the values of the variables. Finally, a guard w is built using a logical expression over the variables and formulas of the model.

12.3.2 Operational Semantics

In this section, we focus on the semantics of a program written in PRISM input language limiting ourselves to the fragment that has an MDP semantics. We define the operational semantics of the PRISM language following the style of SOS [201]. We consider PRISM models consisting of a single system module, since any PRISM model described as a composition of a set of modules can be reduced to a single module system according to a set of construction rules described in [203]. In the case of a single module, actions labeling the commands are not as much useful as in the case of multiple modules.

$$
\begin{array}{ll}
\mathscr{C} \ni c ::= [\alpha]\, w \rightharpoonup u & \text{(Command)} \\
\quad\ |\ c \cup c & \\[4pt]
\mathscr{W} \ni w ::= e & \text{(Guard)} \\[4pt]
\mathscr{U} \ni u ::= \lambda : d & \text{(Update)} \\
\quad\ |\ u_1 + u_2 & \\[4pt]
\mathscr{D} \ni d ::= skip & \text{(Update unit)} \\
\quad\ |\ x' = e & \\
\quad\ |\ d_1 \wedge d_2 & \\[4pt]
\mathscr{E} \ni e ::= x & \text{(Expression)} \\
\quad\ |\ v & \\
\quad\ |\ e_1\, op\, e_2 & \\
\quad\ |\ \neg e_1 & \\[4pt]
\mathscr{V} \ni v ::= i & \text{(Value)} \\
\quad\ |\ d & \\
\quad\ |\ b & \\[6pt]
op \in \{*, \vartriangleleft, +, -, <, \leq, >, \geq, =, \neq, \wedge, \vee\} & \text{(Operators)} \\
\lambda \in [0,1] & \text{(Probability Value)} \\
x \in variables & \text{(Variable)} \\
\alpha \in actions & \text{(Action)} \\
i \in integer & \text{(Integer)} \\
d \in double & \text{(Double)} \\
b \in boolean & \text{(Boolean)}
\end{array}
$$

Fig. 12.3 Syntax of the PRISM input language – part 2

A configuration represents the state of the system at a certain moment during its evolution. It is build as a pair $\langle \mathcal{C}, s \rangle$ where $\mathcal{C}$ denotes the set of commands to be executed and s the associated store, which models the memory used in order to keep track of the current values associated with the variables of the system. Let $\mathcal{V}$ be the set of values and $\mathcal{S}$ be the set of stores ranged over by s, s_1, s_2, etc. We write $s[x \mapsto v_x]$ to denote the store s that assigns to the variable x the value v_x and the value $s(y)$ to the variable $y \neq x$. We denote by $[\![\_]\!](\_)$ the semantic function used to evaluate expressions or guards defined in Fig. 12.3. Let E be the set of expressions and W the set of guards. We have $[\![\_]\!](\_): E \cup W \to \mathcal{S} \to \mathcal{V}$ a function that takes as argument an expression e (or a guard) and a store s and returns the value of the expression e where each variable x is interpreted by $s(x)$.

We define an auxiliary function $f(\_)(\_): Dist(\mathcal{S}) \to Dist(\mathcal{S}) \to Dist(\mathcal{S})$ such that $\forall \mu_1, \mu_2 \in Dist(\mathcal{S})$,

$$f(\mu_1)(\mu_2) = \mu = \begin{cases} \sum_{\substack{i \in I \\ s_i = s}} \mu_1(s_i) + \sum_{\substack{j \in J \\ s_j = s}} \mu_2(s_j) \\ 0 \qquad\qquad\qquad\qquad\qquad \text{otherwise} \end{cases}$$

The inference rules corresponding to the operational semantics of PRISM model are listed in Fig. 12.4. Basically, rule (SKIP) denotes that the trivial unit update $skip$ does not affect the store (i.e., the values of the variables). Rule (UPD-EVAL) expresses the effect on the store s of a new value assignment to the variable x using the evaluation of the expression e. Rule (UPD-PROCESSING) is used to process a conjunction of updates $\langle d_1 \wedge d_2, s \rangle$ given the evaluation of $\langle d_1, s \rangle$. The unit update d_2 is applied on the store s_1 resulting from applying the unit update d_1. This rule allows a recursive application of unit updates until processing all the components of

(SKIP)	$\langle skip, s \rangle \to s$
(UPD-EVAL)	$\langle x' = e, s \rangle \to s[x \mapsto [\![e]\!](s)]$
(UPD-PROCESSING)	$\dfrac{\langle d_1, s \rangle \to s_1}{\langle d_1 \wedge d_2, s \rangle \to \langle d_2, s_1 \rangle}$
(PROB-UPD)	$\dfrac{\langle d, s \rangle \to s_1}{\langle \lambda : d, s \rangle \to \mu_{s_1}^{\lambda}}$
(PROBCHOICE-UPD)	$\dfrac{\langle u_1, s \rangle \to \mu_1 \qquad \langle u_2, s \rangle \to \mu_2}{\langle u_1 + u_2, s \rangle \to f(\mu_1)(\mu_2)}$
(ENABLED-CMD)	$\dfrac{[\![w]\!](s) = true}{\langle [\alpha]\, w \to u, s \rangle \xrightarrow{\alpha} \langle u, s \rangle}$
(CMD-PROCESSING)	$\dfrac{\langle c, s \rangle \xrightarrow{\alpha} \langle u, s \rangle \qquad \langle u, s \rangle \to \mu}{\langle \{c\} \cup C, s \rangle \xrightarrow{\alpha} \langle \{c\} \cup C, \mu \rangle}$

Fig. 12.4 Semantic inference rules for PRISM's input language

an update of the form $\lambda : d$, which results in a new state of the system, i.e., a new store reflecting the new variable values of the system. Rule (PROB-UPD) denotes the processing of a probabilistic update on the system. The result of processing $\langle \lambda : d, s \rangle$ is a probability sub-distribution that associates a probability λ with a store s_1 obtained by applying the update. If $\lambda < 1$, the definition of the probability distribution is partial since it is a part of a probabilistic choice over the related command's updates.

Rule (PROBCHOICE-UPD) processes the probabilistic choice between different updates as a probability distribution over the set of resulting stores. It uses the function f in order to build the resulting probability distribution from partial probability distribution definitions taking into account the possibility that different updates may lead to the same store. Rule (ENABLED-CMD) is used to evaluate the guard of a given command and thus enabling its execution if its corresponding guard is true. Finally, rule (CMD-PROCESSING) states that if a command is non-deterministically selected from the set of available enabled commands (since their guards are true) for a given store s (first premise) and if the set of corresponding updates leads to the probability distribution μ (second premise), then a transition can be fired from the configuration $\langle \{c\} \cup C, s \rangle$ resulting in a set of new possible configurations where all reachable states are defined using the probability distribution μ.

An operational semantics of a PRISM MDP program $\mathcal{P}$ is provided by means of the MPD $M_{\mathcal{P}}$ where the states are of the form $\langle \mathcal{C}, s \rangle$, the initial state is $\langle \mathcal{C}, s_0 \rangle$ such that s_0 is the store where each variable is assigned its default value, the set of actions are the action labeling the commands, and the probabilistic transition relation is obtained by the rule (CMD-PROCESSING) in Fig. 12.4 such that $Steps(s) = (\alpha, \mu)$. We omit the set of commands $\mathcal{C}$ from the configuration and write simply $s \xrightarrow{\alpha} \mu$ to denote $Steps(s)$.

12.4 Formal Translation

We focus hereafter on the formal translation of SysML activity diagrams into their corresponding MDP using the input language of PRISM. We presented in Chap. 9 the translation algorithm written in an imperative language representing an abstraction of the implementation code. In order to simplify the analysis of the translation algorithm, we need to express it in some functional core language. The latter allows making assertions about programs and prove their correctness easier than having them written in an imperative language. Thus, we use the ML functional language [101]. The input to the translation algorithm corresponds to the AC term expressing formally the structure of the SysML activity diagram. The output of the translation algorithm represents the PRISM MDP model. The latter contains two parts: variable declarations and the set of PRISM commands enclosed in the main module. We suppose that the declarations of variables, constants, and formulas are performed separately of the actual translation using our algorithm.

Before detailing the translation algorithm, we first clarify our choices for the constants, the formulas, and the variables in the model and their correspondences with the elements of the diagram. First, we need to define a constant of type integer, namely *max_inst*, that specifies the maximum number of supported execution instances (i.e., the maximum number of control tokens). Each node (action or control) that might receive tokens is associated with a variable of type integer, which values range over the interval [0, *max_inst*]. Exceptionally, the flow final nodes are the only nodes that are not represented in the PRISM model since they only absorb the tokens reaching them. The value assigned to each variable at a point in the time denotes the number of active instances of the corresponding activity node. An activity node that is not active will have its corresponding variable assigned the value 0. An activity node that reached the maximum supported number of active instances will have its corresponding variable assigned the maximum value *max_inst*. However, there are two exceptions to this rule: the first corresponds to the initial and the final nodes and the second to the join nodes.

First, each of the initial and final nodes is associated with an integer variable that takes two possible values 0 or 1. This is because these nodes are supposed to have a boolean state (active or inactive). Second, the join node represents also an exceptional case because of the specific processing of the join condition. The latter states that each of the incoming edges has to receive at least one control token in order to produce a single token that traverses the join node. Thus, we assign an integer variable for each incoming edge of a join node. Their values range over the interval [0, *max_inst*]. Then, we also assign a boolean formula to the join node in order to express the join condition. This formula is a conjunction of boolean conditions stating that each variable associated with an incoming edge has a value greater than or equal to 1. Finally, we also consider the guards of all decision nodes. These are helpful in describing properties to be verified on the model. Thus, we assign a boolean PRISM variable for each boolean guard of a decision node.

We use the labels associated with the activity nodes as defined in the activity calculus term as the identifiers of their corresponding PRISM variables. For the exceptional cases (meaning the initial, final, and join nodes), we use other adequate notation. As for the initial and final nodes, we use, respectively, the variable identifiers l_i and l_f. Concerning the join nodes denoted in the AC term either as the subterm $l : x.join(\mathcal{N})$ for the definition of the join or as l for referencing each of its incoming edges, we need to assign x distinct variables. Thus, we use the label l concatenated with an integer number k such that $k \in [1, x]$, which results in a variable $l[k]$ associated with each incoming edge. By convention, we use $l[1]$ for specifying the variable related to $l : x.\text{join}(\mathcal{N})$. We denote by $\mathcal{L}_A$ the set of labels associated with the AC term $\mathcal{A}$ representing the identifiers of the variables in the corresponding MDP model.

A generated PRISM command c is expressed formally using the syntax definition presented in Fig. 12.3. The main mapping function denoted by $\mathcal{T}$ is described in Listing 12.1. It makes use of the function $\mathcal{E}$ described in Listing 12.2. It also employs an utility function $\mathcal{L}$ in order to identify the label of an element of the AC term. The signatures of the two main functions are provided in their respective listings. We denote by $\mathcal{AC}$ the set of unmarked AC terms and $\overline{\mathcal{AC}}$ the set of marked AC terms. Let $\mathcal{L}$ be the universal set of labels ranged over by l. Moreover, let C be the set of commands ranged over by c, W be the set of guard expressions ranged over by w, Act be the set of actions ranged over by α, and D be the set of update units ranged over by d.

Listing 12.1 Formal SysML activity diagram translation algorithm

$$\mathcal{T}:\ AC \to C$$
$$\mathcal{T}(\mathcal{N})\ =\ \text{Case}\ (\mathcal{N})\ \textbf{of}$$

$\iota \mapsto \mathcal{N}' \quad \Rightarrow\ \textbf{let}$

$$c\ =\ \mathcal{E}(\mathcal{N}')(l_\iota = 1)(l'_\iota = 0)(1.0)(l_\iota)$$

$\textbf{in}$

$$\{c\}\ \bigcup\ \mathcal{T}(\mathcal{N}')$$

$\textbf{end}$

$l:a \mapsto \mathcal{N}' \Rightarrow\ \textbf{let}$

$$c\ =\ \mathcal{E}(\mathcal{N}')(l > 0)(l' = l - 1)(1.0)(l)$$

$\textbf{in}$

$$\{c\}\ \bigcup\ \mathcal{T}(\mathcal{N}')$$

$\textbf{end}$

$l:Merge(\mathcal{N}') \Rightarrow\ \textbf{let}$

$$c\ =\ \mathcal{E}(\mathcal{N}')(l > 0)(l' = l - 1)(1.0)(l)$$

$\textbf{in}$

$$\{c\}\ \bigcup\ \mathcal{T}(\mathcal{N}')$$

$\textbf{end}$

$l:x.Join(\mathcal{N}') \Rightarrow\ \textbf{let}$

$$c = \mathcal{E}(\mathcal{N}')(\textstyle\bigwedge_{1 \le k \le x}(l[k] > 0))(\textstyle\bigwedge_{1 \le k \le x}(l[k]' = 0))(1.0)(l[1])$$

$\textbf{in}$

$$\{c\}\ \bigcup\ \mathcal{T}(\mathcal{N}')$$

$\textbf{end}$

$l:Fork(\mathcal{N}_1, \mathcal{N}_2) \Rightarrow\ \textbf{let}$

$$[\alpha]\,w \rightharpoonup \lambda : d\ =\ \mathcal{E}(\mathcal{N}_1)(l > 0)(l' = l - 1)(1.0)(l)$$

$\textbf{in}$

$\textbf{let}$

$$c\ =\ \mathcal{E}(\mathcal{N}_2)(w)(d)(\lambda)(\alpha)$$

$\textbf{in}$

$$\{c\}\ \bigcup\ \mathcal{T}(\mathcal{N}_1)\ \bigcup\ \mathcal{T}(\mathcal{N}_2)$$

$\textbf{end}$

$\textbf{end}$

$l:Decision_p(\langle g \rangle\,\mathcal{N}_1,\ \langle \neg g \rangle\,\mathcal{N}_2) \Rightarrow\ \textbf{let}$

$$[\alpha_1]\,w_1 \rightharpoonup \lambda_1 : d_1 = \mathcal{E}(\mathcal{N}_1)(l > 0)((l' = l - 1) \wedge (g' = tt))(p)(l)$$
$$[\alpha_2]\,w_2 \rightharpoonup \lambda_2 : d_2 =$$
$$\mathcal{E}(\mathcal{N}_2)(tt)((l' = l - 1) \wedge (g' = ff))(1 - p)(l)$$

$\textbf{in}$

$$([l]\,w_1 \wedge w_2 \rightharpoonup \lambda_1 : d_1 + \lambda_2 : d_2)\ \bigcup\ \mathcal{T}(\mathcal{N}_1)\ \bigcup\ \mathcal{T}(\mathcal{N}_2)$$

$\textbf{end}$

$l:Decision(\langle g \rangle\,\mathcal{N}_1,\ \langle \neg g \rangle\,\mathcal{N}_2) \Rightarrow\ \textbf{let}$

$$[\alpha_1]\,w_1 \rightharpoonup \lambda_1 : d_1 = \mathcal{E}(\mathcal{N}_1)(l > 0)((l' = l - 1) \wedge (g' = tt))(1.0)(l)$$
$$[\alpha_2]\,w_2 \rightharpoonup \lambda_2 : d_2 = \mathcal{E}(\mathcal{N}_2)(l > 0)((l' = l - 1) \wedge (g' = ff))(1.0)(l)$$

$\textbf{in}$

$$([l]\,w_1 \rightharpoonup \lambda_1 : d_1)\ \bigcup\ \mathcal{T}(\mathcal{N}_1)\ \bigcup\ ([l]\,w_2 \rightharpoonup \lambda_2 : d_2)\ \bigcup\ \mathcal{T}(\mathcal{N}_2)$$

$\textbf{end}$

$l_f:\odot \qquad\qquad \Rightarrow\ \textbf{let}$

$$w\ =\ (l_f = 1)$$
$$d\ =\ \textstyle\bigwedge_{l \in \mathcal{L}_A}(l' = 0)$$
$$\lambda = 1.0$$

$\textbf{in}$

$$([l_f]\,w \rightharpoonup \lambda : d)$$

otherwise $\qquad\qquad \Rightarrow\ \textbf{skip}$

Listing 12.2 Definition of the $\mathcal{E}$ function

$$\mathcal{E}: \ \mathcal{AC} \to W \to D \to [0,1] \to Act \to C$$
$$\mathcal{E}(\mathcal{N})(w)(d)(\lambda)(\alpha) \ = \ \text{Case}(\mathcal{N}) \ \textbf{of}$$

$$l:\otimes \qquad\qquad \Rightarrow \ ([\alpha]\,w \wedge (l_f = 0) \rightharpoonup \lambda : d\,)$$
$$l_f:\odot \qquad\qquad \Rightarrow \ ([\alpha]\,w \wedge (l_f = 0) \rightharpoonup \lambda : (l'_f = 1) \wedge d\,)$$
$$l:x.Join(\mathcal{N}') \Rightarrow \ \textbf{let}$$

$$w_1 \ = \ w \wedge (l_f = 0) \wedge \neg(\textstyle\bigwedge_{1 \leq k \leq x}(l[k] > 0)) \wedge (l[1] < max\_inst)$$
$$d_1 \ = \ (l[1]' = l[1] + 1) \ \wedge \ d$$

$$\textbf{in}$$
$$([\alpha]\,w_1 \rightharpoonup \lambda : d_1\,)$$
$$\textbf{end}$$

$$l \qquad\qquad \Rightarrow \ \textbf{if} \ \ l \ = \ \mathcal{L}(l:x.Join(\mathcal{N}')) \ \ \textbf{then}$$
$$\textbf{let}$$
$$w_1 = w \wedge (l_f = 0) \ \wedge \ \neg(\textstyle\bigwedge_{1 \leq k \leq x}(l[k] > 0)) \ \wedge \ (l[j] < max\_inst)$$
$$d_1 \ = \ (l[j]' = l[j] + 1) \ \wedge \ d$$
$$\textbf{in}$$
$$([\alpha]\,w_1 \rightharpoonup \lambda : d_1\,)$$
$$\textbf{end}$$
$$\textbf{end}$$
$$\textbf{if} \ \ l \ = \ \mathcal{L}(l:Merge(\mathcal{N}')) \ \ \textbf{then}$$
$$\textbf{let}$$
$$w_1 = w \wedge \ (l_f = 0) \ \wedge \ (l < max\_inst)$$
$$d_1 \ = \ (l' = l + 1) \ \wedge \ d$$
$$\textbf{in}$$
$$([\alpha]\,w_1 \rightharpoonup \lambda : d_1\,)$$
$$\textbf{end}$$
$$\textbf{end}$$
$$otherwise \quad \Rightarrow \ \textbf{let}$$
$$w_1 \ = \ w \wedge (l_f = 0) \ \wedge \ (l < max\_inst)$$
$$d_1 \ = \ (l' = l + 1) \ \wedge \ d$$
$$\textbf{in}$$
$$([\alpha]\,w_1 \rightharpoonup \lambda : d_1\,)$$
$$\textbf{end}$$

12.5 Case Study

In this section, we present a SysML activity diagram case study depicting a hypothetical design of the behavior corresponding to banking operations on an ATM system illustrated in Fig. 11.13. It is designed intentionally with flaws in order to demonstrate the viability of our approach. The activity starts by Authentication then a fork node indicates the initiation of concurrent behavior. Thus, Verify ATM, and Choose account are triggered together. This activity diagram presents mixed disposition of fork and join nodes. Thus, Withdraw money action cannot start until both Verify ATM and Choose account terminate. The guard $g1$, if evaluated to *true*, denotes the possibility of triggering a new operation. The probability on the latter decision node models the probabilistic user behavior. The guard $g2$ denotes the result of evaluating the status of the connection presenting functional uncertainty.

We first present the corresponding AC term $\mathcal{A}_1$ explained earlier and then explain its mapping into PRISM code.

The corresponding unmarked term $\mathcal{A}_1$ is as follows:

$\mathcal{A}_1 = \iota \rightarrowtail l_1 : a \rightarrowtail l_2 : \mathtt{Fork}(\mathcal{N}_1, l_{12})$
$\mathcal{N}_1 = l_3 : \mathtt{Merge}(l_4 : b \rightarrowtail l_5 : \mathtt{Fork}(\mathcal{N}_2, \mathcal{N}_3))$
$\mathcal{N}_2 = l_6 : \mathtt{Decision}_{0.9}(\langle g2 \rangle\, l_3, \langle \neg g2 \rangle\, l_7 : 2.\mathtt{Join}(l_8 : \odot))$
$\mathcal{N}_3 = l_9 : 2.\mathtt{Join}(l_{10} : d \rightarrowtail \mathcal{N}_4)$
$\mathcal{N}_4 = l_{11} : \mathtt{Decision}_{0.3}(\langle g1 \rangle\, \mathcal{N}_5, \langle \neg g1 \rangle\, l_7)$
$\mathcal{N}_5 = l_{12} : \mathtt{Merge}(l_{13} : c \rightarrowtail l_9)$

First, PRISM variable identifiers are deduced from the AC term. We use li and lf as variable identifiers for, respectively, the initial node ι and the final node $l_8 : \odot$. For the join node $l_7 : 2.\mathtt{Join}$ (resp. $l_9 : 2.\mathtt{Join}$), we use $l7$ (resp., $l9$) as identifier for the formula specifying the join conditions and we use the PRISM variables $l7\_1$ and $l7\_2$ (resp. $l9\_1$ and $l9\_2$) as variable identifiers for the incoming edges of the join node. Once the declaration of variables and formulas is done, the module commands are generated using the algorithm $\mathcal{T}$ described in Listing 12.1. For instance, the first command labeled $[li$ is generated in the first iteration while calling $\mathcal{T}(\mathcal{A}_1)$. It corresponds to the first case such that $\mathcal{A}_1 = \iota \rightarrowtail \mathcal{N}'$ and $\mathcal{N}' = l_1 : a \rightarrowtail l_2 : \mathtt{Fork}(\mathcal{N}_1, l_{12})$. Thus, the function $\mathcal{E}$ described in Listing 12.2 is called $\mathcal{E}(\mathcal{N}')((li = 1))((li' = 0))(1.0)(li)$. The last case of the latter function is triggered since $\mathcal{N}'$ is of the form $l : a \rightarrowtail \mathcal{N}$. This allows to generate the first command and then a call of $\mathcal{T}(\mathcal{N}')$ is triggered which launches the algorithm again. The translation halts when all the nodes are visited and all instances of the algorithm $\mathcal{T}$ stop their executions. The PRISM MDP code obtained for the activity diagram $\mathcal{A}_1$ is shown in Fig. 12.5. Once, the PRISM code is generated, one can input the code to PRISM model checker for assessment. However, the properties that have to be verified on the model need to be expressed in adequate temporal logic. The property specification language of PRISM subsumes several well-known probabilistic temporal logics, including PCTL [44], CSL [11], LTL [248], and PCTL* [204]. Moreover, PRISM also extend and customize this logics with additional features. For instance, PRISM adds the ability to determine the actual probability of satisfying a formula, rather than only placing a bound on it.

In order to verify MDP model, we use PCTL* temporal logic. A property that can verify on the model is the presence/absence of a deadlock. Property (12.1) specifying the eventuality of reaching a deadlock state (with probability $P > 0$) from any configuration starting at the initial state can be expressed as follows:

$$\textit{"init"} \Rightarrow \mathtt{P} > 0\,[\,\mathtt{F}\,\text{"deadlock"}\,] \tag{12.1}$$

Using PRISM model checker, this property returns $true$. In fact, the execution of the action $\mathtt{Choose\ account}$ twice (because the guard $g1$ is true) and the action $\mathtt{Verify\ ATM}$ only once (because $g2$ evaluated to false) result in a deadlock configuration where the condition of the join node $\mathtt{join1}$ is never fulfilled. This confirms the findings using the operational semantics of AC (see the corresponding case study in Sect. 11.2).

```
mdp

const int max_inst=1;
formula l9 = l9_1>0 & l9_2>0 ;
formula l7 = l7_1> 0 & l7_2>0;


module mainmod

g1 :bool init false;
g2 :bool init false;
li : [0..1] init 1; lf : [0..1] init 0;
l1 : [0..max_inst] init 0; l2 : [0..max_inst] init 0;
l3 : [0..max_inst] init 0;l4 : [0..max_inst] init 0;
l5 : [0..max_inst] init 0;l6 : [0..max_inst] init 0;
l7_1 : [0..max_inst] init 0; l7_2 : [0..max_inst] init 0;
l9_1 : [0..max_inst] init 0;l9_2 : [0..max_inst] init 0;
l10 : [0..max_inst] init 0;
l11 : [0..max_inst] init 0;l12 : [0..max_inst] init 0;
l13 : [0..max_inst] init 0;

[li] li=1 & l1<max_inst & lf=0 → 1.0 : (l1'=l1 + 1) & (li'=0);
[l1] l1>0 & l2<max_inst & lf=0 → 1.0 : (l2'=l2+1) & (l1'=l1 − 1);
[l2] l2>0 & l3<max_inst & l12<max_inst & lf=0
                      → 1.0 : (l3'=l3 + 1) & (l12'=l12 + 1) & (l2'=l2 − 1);
[l3] l3>0 & l4<max_inst & lf=0 → 1.0 : (l4'=l4 + 1)&(l3'=l3 − 1);
[l4] l4>0 & l5<max_inst & lf=0 → 1.0 : (l5'=l5 + 1)&(l4'=l4 − 1);
[l5] l5>0 & l6<max_inst & !l9 & l9_1<max_inst & lf=0
                      → 1.0 : (l6'=l6 + 1) &(l9_1'=l9_1 + 1) & (l5'=l5 − 1);
[l6] l6>0 & l3<max_inst & !l7 & l7_1<max_inst &lf=0 →
                      0.9 : (l3'=l3 + 1) & (l6'=l6 − 1) & (g2'=true)
                      +0.1 : (l7_1'=l7_1 + 1) & (l6'=l6 − 1) & (g2'=false);
[l7] l7 & lf=0 → 1.0 : (l7_1'=0) & (l7_2'=0) & (lf'=1);
[l9] l9 & l10<max_inst & lf=0 → 1.0 : (l10'=l10 + 1) & (l9_1'=0) & (l9_2'=0);
[l10]l10>0 & l11<max_inst & lf=0 → 1.0 : (l11'=l11 + 1) & (l10'=l10 − 1);
[l11]l11>0 & l12<max_inst & ! l7 &l7_2<max_inst & lf=0 →
                      0.3 : (l12'=l12 + 1) & (l11'=l11 − 1) & (g1'=true)
                      + 0.7 : (l7_2'=l7_2 + 1) & (l11'=l11 − 1) & (g1'=false);
[l12] l12>0 & l13<max_inst & lf=0 → 1.0 : (l13'=l13 + 1) & (l12'=l12 − 1);
[l13] l13>0 & !l9 & l9_2<max_inst & lf=0 → 1.0 : (l9_2'=l9_2 + 1) & (l13'=l13 − 1);
[lf] lf=1 → 1.0 : (li'=0)& (lf'=0) & (l1'=0) & (l2'=0) & (l3'=0) &
               (l4'=0) & (l5'=0) & (l6'=0) & (l7_1'=0)& (l7_2'=0)& (l9_1'=0)& (l9_2'=0)&
               (l10'=0)& (l11'=0)& (l2'=0) & (l3'=0) & (g1'=false) & (g2'=false);
endmodule
```

Fig. 12.5 PRISM code for the SysML activity diagram case study

12.6 Simulation Preorder for Markov Decision Processes

Simulation preorder represents one example of relations that have been defined in both non-probabilistic and probabilistic settings in order to establish a step-by-step correspondence between two systems. Segala and Lynch have defined in their seminal work [217] several extensions of the classical simulation and bisimulation relations to the probabilistic settings. These definitions have been reused and tailored in Baier and Kwiatkowska [12] and recently in Kattenbelt and Huth [130]. Simulations are unidirectional relations that have proved to be successful in formal verification of systems. Indeed, they allow to perform abstractions of the models while preserving safe CTL properties [163]. Simulation relations are preorders on the state space such that a state s simulates state s' (written $s \sqsubseteq s'$) if and only if s' can mimic all stepwise behavior of s. However, the inverse is not always true; s' may perform steps that cannot be matched by s.

In probabilistic settings, strong simulation have been introduced, where $s \sqsubseteq s'$ (meaning s' strongly simulates s) requires that every α-successor distribution of s has a corresponding α-successor at s'. This correspondence between distributions is defined based on the concept of weight functions [128]. States related with strong simulation have to be related via weight functions on their distributions [163]. Let $\mathcal{M}$ be the class of all MDPs. A formal definition of MDP is provided in Definition 9.1. In the following, we recall the definitions related to strong simulation applied on MDPs. First, we define the concept of weight functions as follows.

Definition 12.1 Let $\mu \in Dist(S)$ and $\mu' \in Dist(S')$ and $R \subseteq S \times S'$. A weight function for (μ, μ') w.r.t. R is a function $\delta : S \times S' \to [0, 1]$ satisfying the following:

- $\delta(s, s') > 0$ implies $(s, s') \in R$.
- For all $s \in S$ and $s' \in S'$, $\sum_{s' \in S'} \delta(s, s') = \mu(s)$ and $\sum_{s \in S} \delta(s, s') = \mu'(s')$.

We write $\mu \preceq_R \mu'$ if there exists such a weight function δ for (μ, μ') with respect to R.

Definition 12.2 Let $M = (S, s_0, Act, Steps)$ and $M' = (S', s_0', Act', Steps')$ be two MDPs. We say M' simulates M via a relation $R \subseteq S \times S'$, denoted by $M \sqsubseteq_{\mathcal{M}}^R M'$, if and only if for all s and s': $(s, s') \in R$, if $s \xrightarrow{\alpha} \mu$ then there is a transition $s' \xrightarrow{\alpha} \mu'$ with $\mu \preceq_R \mu'$.

Basically, we say that M' strongly simulates M, denoted by $M \sqsubseteq_{\mathcal{M}}^R M'$, $\Longleftrightarrow$ there exists a strong simulation R between M and M' such that for every $s \in S$ and $s' \in M'$ each α-successor of s has a corresponding α-successor of s' and there exists a weight function δ that can be defined between the successor distributions of s and s'.

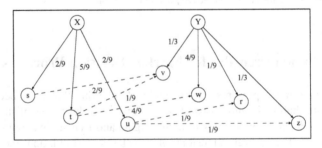

Fig. 12.6 Example of simulation relation using weight function

Example 12.1 Let us consider the example illustrated in Fig. 12.6. We consider two set of states $S = \{s, t, u\}$ destination of X and $S' = \{v, w, r, z\}$ destination states of Y. The distribution μ over S is defined as follows: $\mu(s) = 2/9$, $\mu(t) = 5/9$, and $\mu(u) = 2/9$, whereas the distribution μ' over S' is defined such that $\mu'(v) = 1/3$, $\mu'(w) = 4/9$, $\mu'(r) = 1/9$, and $\mu'(z) = 1/3$. If we consider the relation R such that $R = \{(s, v), (t, v), (t, w), (u, r), (u, z)\}$, we can find out whether R is a simulation relation provided that we can define a weight function that fulfills the constraint of being a weight function relating μ and μ'. Let δ be a weight function such that $\delta(s, v) = \frac{2}{9}$, $\delta(t, v) = \frac{1}{9}$, $\delta(t, w) = \frac{4}{9}$, $\delta(u, r) = \frac{1}{9}$, and $\delta(u, z) = \frac{1}{9}$ fulfill the constraints of being a weight function. According to Definition 12.1, the first condition is satisfied. For the second condition we have $\sum_{s' \in S'} \delta(t, s') = \delta(t, v) + \delta(t, w) = \frac{5}{9} = \mu(t)$, $\sum_{s_1 \in S} \delta(s_1, v) = \delta(s, v) + \delta(t, v) = \frac{3}{9} = \mu(t)$, and $\sum_{s' \in S'} \delta(u, s') = \delta(u, r) + \delta(u, z) = \frac{2}{9} = \mu(u)$. It follows that $\mu \preceq_R \mu'$. Thus, $X \sqsubseteq_{\mathcal{M}}^R Y'$.

12.7 Soundness of the Translation Algorithm

In this section, we aim at ensuring that the translation function $\mathcal{T}$ defined in Listing 12.1 generates a model that correctly captures the behavior of the activity diagram. More precisely, we look forward to prove the soundness of the translation. To this end, we use the operational semantics defined for both the SysML activity diagrams and the PRISM input language. Before formalizing the soundness theorem, we need first to make some important definitions.

We use the function $\lfloor\_\rfloor$ specified in Listing 12.3. The latter takes as input a term $\mathcal{B}$ in $\overline{\mathcal{AC}} \cup \mathcal{AC}$ and returns a multiset of labels $(\mathcal{L}_\mathcal{B}, m)$ corresponding to the marked nodes in the corresponding activity calculus term, i.e., $\lfloor\mathcal{B}\rfloor = \{\!\!\{ l_j \in \mathcal{L}_\mathcal{B} | m(l_j) > 0 \}\!\!\}$.

In the next definition, we make use of the function $[\![\_]\!](\_)$ defined in Sect. 12.3.2 in order to define how an activity calculus term $\mathcal{B}$ satisfies a boolean expression. This is needed in order to define a relation between a state in the semantic model of PRISM model and another state in the semantic model of the corresponding SysML activity diagram.

Definition 12.3 An activity calculus term $\mathcal{B}$ such that $\lfloor\mathcal{B}\rfloor = (\mathcal{L}_\mathcal{B}, m)$ satisfies a boolean expression e and we write $[\![e]\!](\mathcal{B}) = true \iff [\![e]\!](s[x_i \mapsto m(l_i)]) = true, \forall l_i \in \mathcal{L}_\mathcal{B}$ and $x_i \in variables$.

The evaluation of the boolean expression e using the term $\mathcal{B}$ consists of two steps. First, a store s is defined where we assign to each variable x_i the marking of the node labeled l_i. The second step is to replace in the boolean expression e each variable x_i with $s(x_i)$.

Let $M_{\mathcal{P}_\mathcal{A}} = (S_{\mathcal{P}_\mathcal{A}}, s_0, Act, Steps_{\mathcal{P}_\mathcal{A}})$ and $M_\mathcal{A} = (S_\mathcal{A}, s_0, Act, Steps_\mathcal{A})$ be the MDPs corresponding, respectively, to the PRISM model $\mathcal{P}_\mathcal{A}$ and the SysML activity diagram $\mathcal{A}$. We need to define in the following a relation $\mathcal{R} \subseteq S_{\mathcal{P}_\mathcal{A}} \times S_\mathcal{A}$.

Definition 12.4 Let $\mathcal{R} \subseteq S_{\mathcal{P}_A} \times S_A$ be a relation defined as follows.
For all $s_p \in S_{\mathcal{P}_A}$ and $\mathcal{B} \in S_A$, $s_p \ \mathcal{R} \ \mathcal{B} \iff$ for any expression $w \in \mathcal{W}$,
$[\![w]\!](s_p) = true$ implies $[\![w]\!](\mathcal{B}) = true$, $\forall l_i \in \mathcal{L}_\mathcal{B}$ and $x_i \in variables$.

Listing 12.3 Function $\lfloor - \rfloor$ definition

```
⌊−⌋ : AC ⟶ Pᴸ
⌊M⌋ = Case (M) of
    ⊤↦N        ⇒   {| (lₜ ↪ 1) |}
    ι↦M′        ⇒   ⌊M′⌋
    l_f:⊙ⁿ      ⇒   if n > 0 then {| (l_f ↪ 1) |} else {||}
    l:Merge(M′)ⁿ  ⇒  {| (l ↪ n) |} ⊎ ⌊M′⌋
    l:x.Join(M′)ⁿ ⇒  {| (l[1] ↪ n) |} ⊎ ⌊M′⌋
    l:Fork(M₁, M₂)ⁿ ⇒ {| (l ↪ n) |} ⊎ ⌊M₁⌋ ⊎ ⌊M₂⌋
    l:Decisionₚ(⟨g⟩ M₁, ⟨¬g⟩ M₂)ⁿ ⇒ {| (l ↪ n) |} ⊎ ⌊M₁⌋ ⊎ ⌊M₂⌋
    l:Decision(⟨g⟩ M₁, ⟨¬g⟩ M₂)ⁿ ⇒ {| (l ↪ n) |} ⊎ ⌊M₁⌋ ⊎ ⌊M₂⌋
    l:aⁿ ↦ M′   ⇒   {| (l ↪ n) |} ⊎ ⌊M′⌋
    ⊤ⁿ          ⇒   if l = L(l:x.join(N)) then
                        {| (l[k] ↪ n) |}
                    else
                        {| (l ↪ n) |}
                    end
    Otherwise   ⇒   {||}
```

This definition states that an AC term $\mathcal{B}$ is in relation with a state s if they both satisfy the same boolean expression. Based on this relation, we present hereafter the soundness theorem.

Theorem 12.7.1 (Soundness) *Let $\mathcal{A}$ be an AC term of a given SysML activity diagram and $M_\mathcal{A}$ its corresponding semantic model. Let $\mathcal{T}(\mathcal{A}) = \mathcal{P}_\mathcal{A}$ be the corresponding PRISM model and $M_{\mathcal{P}_A}$ be its MDP. We say that the translation algorithm $\mathcal{T}$ is sound if $M_{\mathcal{P}_A} \sqsubseteq^\mathcal{R}_\mathcal{M} M_\mathcal{A}$.*

Proof (Proof of soundness) In order to prove the theorem, we have to prove the existence of a simulation relation between both the MDPs $M_\mathcal{A}$ and $M_{\mathcal{P}_A}$. We reason by structural induction on the syntax of the AC term describing the activity diagram. The proof process consists in proving that the soundness holds for the base cases, which are $l:\otimes$ and $l:\odot$, and then proving it for the inductive cases.

- **Case of $l:\otimes$**
  The algorithm generates neither a PRISM variable nor a PRISM command associated with this element. So, there is no transition in $M_{\mathcal{P}_A}$ corresponding to this element. According to the operational semantics, we have $\overline{l:\otimes}^n \equiv_M l:\otimes$ (according to (M3) in Fig. 11.2) and there is no operational inference rule associated with this element. So there is no transition in $M_\mathcal{A}$ associated with this element. Thus, the theorem holds for this case.

- **Case of $l:\odot$**
  The algorithm generates a single PRISM command such that
  $[l_f] \, l_f = 1 \rightarrow 1.0 : l'_f = 0$.

There exists a state s_0 satisfying the corresponding guard, meaning $[\![(l_f = 1)]\!](s_0) = true$, from which emanates a transition of the form $s_0 \longrightarrow \mu_2$ where $\mu_2 = \mu_1^{s_1}$.

The AC term $\mathcal{B} = \overline{l_f : \odot}$ is related to s_0 via $\mathcal{R}$, since $[\![(l_f = 1)]\!](\overline{l_f : \odot}) = true$ (Definition 12.4). This can be justified because $\lfloor \overline{l_f : \odot} \rfloor = \{\!\mid (l_f \hookrightarrow 1) \mid\!\}$ (Listing 12.3).

According to the operational rule FINAL, we have $\overline{l_f : \odot} \longrightarrow \mu$ such that $\mu = \mu_1^{l_f : \odot}$.

For $\mathcal{R} = \{(s_0, \overline{l_f : \odot}), (s_1, l_f : \odot)\}$, it follows that $\mu \preceq_{\mathcal{R}} \mu_2$ as δ defined such that $\delta(s_1, l_f : \odot) = 1$ fulfills the constraints of being a weight function. Thus, the theorem is proved for this case.

Let $M_{\mathcal{N}}$ denote the semantics of $\mathcal{N}$ and $M_{\mathcal{P}_{\mathcal{N}}}$ denotes the semantics of the corresponding PRISM model obtained from $\mathcal{T}(\mathcal{N})$. We assume that $M_{\mathcal{P}_{\mathcal{N}}} \sqsubseteq_M^{\mathcal{R}} M_{\mathcal{N}}$. We also assume a bounded number of instances max_inst, i.e., $\forall l, l \leq max\_inst$ (ASSUMPTION 1).

- **Case of** $\iota \rightarrowtail \mathcal{N}$

  According to the translation algorithm, we have $\mathcal{T}(\iota \rightarrowtail \mathcal{N}) = \{c\} \bigcup \mathcal{T}(\mathcal{N})$. By assumption of the inductive step we have $M_{\mathcal{P}_{\mathcal{N}}} \sqsubseteq_M^{\mathcal{R}} M_{\mathcal{N}}$. Thus, we need to prove the theorem for the command c such as
  $c = \mathcal{E}(\mathcal{N})(l_\iota = 1)(l'_\iota = 0)(1.0)(l_\iota)$.
  Let w be the guard and d the update generated by $\mathcal{E}(\mathcal{N})$, the command c can be written as follows:
  $c = [l_\iota] \, w \wedge (l_\iota = 1) \wedge (l_f = 0) \rightarrow 1.0 : d \wedge (l'_\iota = 0)$.
  There exists a state s_0 satisfying the guard, i.e., $[\![w \wedge (l_\iota = 1) \wedge (l_f = 0)]\!](s_0) = true$ and a transition $s_0 \longrightarrow \mu$ where $\mu = \mu_1^{s_1}$.
  Given that $\lfloor \overline{\iota \rightarrowtail \mathcal{N}} \rfloor = \{\!\mid (l_\iota \hookrightarrow 1) \mid\!\}$, we can easily verify that $[\![(l_\iota = 1) \wedge (l_f = 0)]\!](\overline{\iota \rightarrowtail \mathcal{N}}) = true$. It remains to verify that $\forall \mathcal{N}, [\![w]\!](\overline{\iota \rightarrowtail \mathcal{N}}) = true$.
  There are two cases: $w = \neg(\bigwedge_{1 \leq k \leq x}(l[k] > 0)) \wedge (l[j] < max\_inst)$ or $w = (l < max\_inst)$. Since $\forall l \neq l_\iota, m(l) = 0$ and having ASSUMPTION 1, we can conclude that $[\![w]\!](\overline{\iota \rightarrowtail \mathcal{N}}) = true$. Thus, by Definition 12.4 $s_0 \, \mathcal{R} \, \overline{\iota \rightarrowtail \mathcal{N}}$.
  The operational semantics rule INIT-1 allows a transition $\overline{\iota \rightarrowtail \mathcal{N}} \longrightarrow \mu'$ such that $\mu'(\iota \rightarrowtail \overline{\mathcal{N}}) = 1$.
  For $\mathcal{R} = \{(s_0, \overline{\iota \rightarrowtail \mathcal{N}}), (s_1, \iota \rightarrowtail \overline{\mathcal{N}})\}$, it follows that $\mu' \preceq_{\mathcal{R}} \mu$ as δ defined such that $\delta(s_1, \iota \rightarrowtail \overline{\mathcal{N}}) = 1$ fulfills the constraints of being a weight function. Thus, the theorem is proved for this case.

- **Case of** $l : a \rightarrowtail \mathcal{N}$

  This case can be proved similar to the previous one. We need to prove the theorem for the command c expressed as follows:
  $c = \mathcal{E}(\mathcal{N})(l > 0)(l' = l - 1)(1.0)(l)$.
  Let w be the guard and d the update such that
  $c = [l] \, w \wedge (l > 0) \wedge (l_f = 0) \rightarrow 1.0 : d \wedge (l' = l - 1)$.
  The corresponding transition is $s_0 \longrightarrow \mu$ where $\mu = \mu_1^{s_1}$ and $[\![w \wedge (l > 0) \wedge (l_f = 0)]\!](s_0) = true$.
  We can verify easily that $[\![w \wedge (l > 0) \wedge (l_f = 0)]\!](\overline{l : a \rightarrowtail \mathcal{N}}) = true$.
  Let $\mathcal{R} = \{(s_0, \overline{l : a \rightarrowtail \mathcal{N}}), (s_1, l : a \rightarrowtail \overline{\mathcal{N}})\}$.

The operational semantics rule ACT-1 allows a transition $\overline{l:a} \rightarrowtail \mathcal{N} \xrightarrow{a} \mu'$ such that $\mu'(l:a \rightarrowtail \overline{\mathcal{N}}) = 1$.

It follows that $\mu' \leq_{\mathcal{R}} \mu$ as δ defined such that $\delta(s_1, l:a \rightarrowtail \overline{\mathcal{N}}) = 1$ fulfills the constraints of being a weight function. Thus, the theorem is proved for this case.

- **Case of** $l : Merge(\mathcal{N})$

  $\mathcal{T}(l : Merge(\mathcal{N})) = \{c\} \bigcup \mathcal{T}(\mathcal{N})$. In order to prove this case, we need to prove the theorem for the command c:

  $c = \mathcal{E}(\mathcal{N})(l > 0)(l' = l - 1)(1.0)(l)$.

  Let us denote by w the guard and d the update such that

  $c = [l]\, w \wedge (l > 0) \wedge (l_f = 0) \rightarrow 1.0 : d \wedge (l' = l - 1)$.

  The state s_0 such that $[\![w \wedge (l > 0) \wedge (l_f = 0)]\!](s_0) = true$ is the source of a transition of the form $s_0 \longrightarrow \mu$ where $\mu = \mu_1^{s_1}$.

  We can easily verify that $[\![w \wedge (l > 0) \wedge (l_f = 0)]\!](\overline{l : Merge(\mathcal{N})}) = true$. Thus, by Definition 12.4, $(s_0, \overline{l : Merge(\mathcal{N})}) \in \mathcal{R}$.

  Let $\mathcal{R} = \{(s_0, \overline{l : Merge(\mathcal{N})}), (s_1, l : Merge(\overline{\mathcal{N}}))\}$.

  The operational semantics rule MERGE-1 allows a transition $\overline{l : Merge(\mathcal{N})} \longrightarrow \mu'$ such that $\mu'(l : Merge(\overline{\mathcal{N}})) = 1$.

  It follows that $\mu' \leq_{\mathcal{R}} \mu$ as δ defined such that $\delta(s_1, l : Merge(\overline{\mathcal{N}})) = 1$ fulfills the constraints of being a weight function. Thus, the theorem is proved for this case.

- **Case of** $l : x.Join(\mathcal{N})$

  This case is jointly treated with the case where l is a reference of a join node.

  $\mathcal{T}(l : x.Join(\mathcal{N})) = \{c\} \bigcup \mathcal{T}(\mathcal{N})$ such that

  $c = \mathcal{E}(\mathcal{N})(\bigwedge_{1 \leq k \leq x}(l[k] > 0))(\bigwedge_{1 \leq k \leq x}(l[k]' = 0))(1.0)(l[1])$.

  Let us denote by w the guard and d the update such that

  $c = [l]\, w \wedge (\bigwedge_{1 \leq k \leq x}(l[k] > 0)) \wedge (l_f = 0) \rightarrow 1.0 : d \wedge (\bigwedge_{1 \leq k \leq x}(l[k]' = 0))$.

  The corresponding transition is $s_0 \longrightarrow \mu$ where $\mu = \mu_1^{s_1}$ and $[\![w \wedge (\bigwedge_{1 \leq k \leq x}(l[k] > 0)) \wedge (l_f = 0)]\!](s_0) = true$.

  The activity calculus term $\mathcal{B}[\overline{l : x.Join(\mathcal{N})}, \overline{l}\{x - 1\}]$ satisfies the guard $w \wedge (\bigwedge_{1 \leq k \leq x}(l[k] > 0)) \wedge (l_f = 0)$. Thus by Definition 12.4, $s_0\, \mathcal{R}\, \mathcal{B}$.

  The operational semantics rule JOIN-1 allows a transition such that

  $\mathcal{B}[\overline{l : x.Join(\mathcal{N})}, \overline{l}\{x - 1\}] \longrightarrow_1 \mathcal{B}[l : x.Join(\overline{\mathcal{N}}), l\{x - 1\}]$.

  For $\mathcal{B}' = \mathcal{B}[l : x.Join(\overline{\mathcal{N}}), l\{x - 1\}]$, we can write $\mathcal{B} \longrightarrow \mu'$ such that $\mu'(\mathcal{B}') = 1$.

  Let $\mathcal{R} = \{(s_0, \mathcal{B}), (s_1, \mathcal{B}')\}$. It follows that $\mu' \leq_{\mathcal{R}} \mu$ as δ defined such that $\delta(s_1, \mathcal{B}') = 1$ fulfills the constraints of being a weight function. Thus, the theorem is proved for this case.

- **Case of** l

  l is a reference to $l : x.Join(\mathcal{N})$ or to $l : Merge(\mathcal{N})$. Thus, the proof can be inferred from the previous corresponding cases.

Let $M_{\mathcal{N}_1}$ and $M_{\mathcal{N}_2}$, respectively, denote the semantics of $\mathcal{N}_1$ and $\mathcal{N}_2$. Also, $M_{\mathcal{P}_{\mathcal{N}_1}}$ denotes the semantics of the corresponding PRISM translation $\mathcal{T}(\mathcal{N}_1)$ and $M_{\mathcal{P}_{\mathcal{N}_2}}$ the one of $\mathcal{T}(\mathcal{N}_2)$. We assume that $M_{\mathcal{P}_{\mathcal{N}_1}} \sqsubseteq_{\mathcal{M}}^{\mathcal{R}} M_{\mathcal{N}_1}$ and $M_{\mathcal{P}_{\mathcal{N}_2}} \sqsubseteq_{\mathcal{M}}^{\mathcal{R}} M_{\mathcal{N}_2}$.

- **Case of** $l: Fork(\mathcal{N}_1, \mathcal{N}_2)$

  According to the translation algorithm, we have $\mathfrak{T}(\iota \mapsto \mathcal{N}) = \{c\} \bigcup \mathfrak{T}(\mathcal{N}_1)$ $\bigcup \mathfrak{T}(\mathcal{N}_2)$. By assumption of the inductive step we have $M_{\mathcal{P}_{\mathcal{N}_1}} \sqsubseteq^{\mathcal{R}}_{\mathcal{M}} M_{\mathcal{N}_1}$ and $M_{\mathcal{P}_{\mathcal{N}_2}} \sqsubseteq^{\mathcal{R}}_{\mathcal{M}} M_{\mathcal{N}_2}$. Thus, we need to prove the theorem for the command c.

  Let us denote by w_1 and w_2 the guards generated, respectively, for $\mathcal{N}_1$ and $\mathcal{N}_2$ and d_1 and d_2 the corresponding updates such that
  $c = [l]\, w_1 \wedge w_2 \wedge (l > 0) \wedge (l_f = 0) \rightharpoonup 1.0 : d_1 \wedge d_2 \wedge (l' = l - 1)$.

  Thus, there exists a state s_0 such that $[\![w_1 \wedge w_2 \wedge (l > 0) \wedge (l_f = 0)]\!](s_0) = true$ and a transition $s_0 \longrightarrow \mu$ where $\mu = \mu_1^{s_1}$.

  We can easily verify that $[\![w_1 \wedge w_2 \wedge (l > 0) \wedge (l_f = 0)]\!](\overline{l: Fork(\mathcal{N}_1, \mathcal{N}_2)}) = true$. So, $s_0\ \mathcal{R}\ \overline{l: Fork(\mathcal{N}_1, \mathcal{N}_2)}$.

  According to rule FORK-1, we have $\overline{l: Fork(\mathcal{N}_1, \mathcal{N}_2)} \longrightarrow_1 l: Fork(\mathcal{N}_1, \mathcal{N}_2)$, or $\overline{l: Fork(\mathcal{N}_1, \mathcal{N}_2)} \longrightarrow \mu'$, where $\mu' = \mu_1^{l: Fork(\mathcal{N}_1, \mathcal{N}_2)}$.

  Let $\mathcal{R} = \{(s_0, \overline{l: Fork(\mathcal{N}_1, \mathcal{N}_2)}), (s_1, l: Fork(\mathcal{N}_1, \mathcal{N}_2))\}$. It follows that $\mu' \preceq_{\mathcal{R}} \mu$ as δ defined such that $\delta(s_1, l: Fork(\mathcal{N}_1, \mathcal{N}_2)) = 1$ fulfills the constraints of being a weight function. Thus, the theorem is proved for this case.

- **Case of** $l: Decision_p(\langle g \rangle\, \mathcal{N}_1, \langle \neg g \rangle\, \mathcal{N}_2)$

  The translation algorithm results in the following:
  $\mathfrak{T}(l: Decision_p(\langle g \rangle\, \mathcal{N}_1, \langle \neg g \rangle\, \mathcal{N}_2)) = ([l]\, w_1 \wedge w_2 \wedge (l > 0) \wedge (l_f = 0) \rightharpoonup \lambda_1 : d_1 \wedge (l' = l - 1) \wedge (g' = true) + \lambda_2 : d_2 \wedge (l' = l - 1) \wedge (g' = false)) \bigcup \mathfrak{T}(\mathcal{N}_1) \bigcup \mathfrak{T}(\mathcal{N}_2)$.

  Given the assumption of the inductive step, we have to prove the theorem for the following command:
  $c = [l]\, w_1 \wedge w_2 \wedge (l > 0) \wedge (l_f = 0) \rightharpoonup p : d_1 \wedge (l' = l - 1) \wedge (g' = true) + (1 - p) : d_2 \wedge l' = l - 1 \wedge (g' = false)$.

  There exists a state s_0 such that the command c is enabled, i.e., $[\![w_1 \wedge w_2 \wedge (l > 0) \wedge (l_f = 0)]\!](s_0) = true$. The enabled transition is of the form $s_0 \longrightarrow \mu$ such that $\mu(s_1) = p$ and $\mu(s_2) = 1 - p$:
  $[\![w_1 \wedge w_2 \wedge (l > 0) \wedge (l_f = 0)]\!](\overline{l: Decision_p(\langle g \rangle\, \mathcal{N}_1, \langle \neg g \rangle\, \mathcal{N}_2)}) = true$.

  Thus, $s_0\ \mathcal{R}\ \overline{l: Decision_p(\langle g \rangle\, \mathcal{N}_1, \langle \neg g \rangle\, \mathcal{N}_2)}$.

  According to the operational semantics, there are two possible transitions emanating from the configuration $\overline{l: Decision_p(\langle g \rangle\, \mathcal{N}_1, \langle \neg g \rangle\, \mathcal{N}_2)}$. The transition enabled by rule PDEC-1:
  $\overline{l: Decision_p(\langle g \rangle \mathcal{N}_1, \langle \neg g \rangle \mathcal{N}_2)} \longrightarrow_p l: Decision_p(\langle tt \rangle \overline{\mathcal{N}_1}, \langle ff \rangle \mathcal{N}_2)$.

  The transition enabled by rule PDEC-2:
  $\overline{l: Decision_p(\langle g \rangle \mathcal{N}_1, \langle \neg g \rangle \mathcal{N}_2)} \longrightarrow_{1-p} l: Decision_p(\langle ff \rangle \mathcal{N}_1, \langle tt \rangle \overline{\mathcal{N}_2})$.

  Definition 11.3 defines a transition in the Markov decision process M_A such that $\overline{l: Decision_p(\langle g \rangle \mathcal{N}_1, \langle \neg g \rangle \mathcal{N}_2)} \longrightarrow \mu'$ where $\mu'(l: Decision_p(\langle tt \rangle \overline{\mathcal{N}_1}, \langle ff \rangle \mathcal{N}_2)) = p$ and $\mu'(l: Decision_p(\langle ff \rangle \mathcal{N}_1, \langle tt \rangle \overline{\mathcal{N}_2})) = 1 - p$.

  Let $\mathcal{R} = \{(s_0, \overline{l: Decision_p(\langle g \rangle \mathcal{N}_1, \langle \neg g \rangle \mathcal{N}_2)}), (s_1, l: Decision_p(\langle tt \rangle \overline{\mathcal{N}_1}, \langle ff \rangle \mathcal{N}_2)), (s_2, l: Decision_p(\langle ff \rangle \mathcal{N}_1, \langle tt \rangle \overline{\mathcal{N}_2}))\}$. It follows that $\mu' \preceq_{\mathcal{R}} \mu$ as δ defined such that $\delta(s_1, l: Decision_p(\langle tt \rangle \overline{\mathcal{N}_1}, \langle ff \rangle \mathcal{N}_2)) = p$ and

$\delta(s_2, l: Decision_p(\langle ff \rangle \mathcal{N}_1, \langle tt \rangle \overline{\mathcal{N}_2})) = 1 - p$ fulfills the constraints of being a weight function. Thus, the theorem is proved for this case.

- **Case of** $l: Decision(\langle g \rangle \ \mathcal{N}_1, \ \langle \neg g \rangle \ \mathcal{N}_2)$

  The translation algorithm results in the following:

  $\mathcal{T}(l: Decision(\langle g \rangle \ \mathcal{N}_1, \ \langle \neg g \rangle \ \mathcal{N}_2)) = ([l] \ w \rightharpoonup 1.0 : d) \bigcup \mathcal{T}(\mathcal{N}_1) \bigcup ([l] \ w' \rightharpoonup 1.0 : d') \bigcup \mathcal{T}(\mathcal{N}_2)$.

  Given the assumption of the inductive step, we have to prove the theorem for two commands c_1 and c_2:

  $c_1 = [l] \ w_1 \wedge (l > 0) \wedge (l_f = 0) \rightharpoonup 1.0 : d_1 \wedge (l' = l - 1) \wedge (g' = true)$,

  $c_2 = [l] \ w_2 \wedge (l > 0) \wedge (l_f = 0) \rightharpoonup 1.0 : d_2 \wedge (l' = l - 1) \wedge (g' = false)$.

  There exists a state s_0 such that the commands c_1 and c_2 are enabled, i.e., $[\![w_1 \wedge (l > 0) \wedge (l_f = 0)]\!](s_0) = true$ and $[\![w_2 \wedge (l > 0) \wedge (l_f = 0)]\!](s_0) = true$. Two enabled transitions from s_0 such that $s_0 \longrightarrow \mu_1$ where $\mu_1(s_1) = 1$ and $s_0 \longrightarrow \mu_2$ where $\mu_2(s_2) = 1$.

  We have $[\![w_1 \wedge (l > 0) \wedge (l_f = 0)]\!](\overline{l: Decision(\langle g \rangle \ \mathcal{N}_1, \ \langle \neg g \rangle \ \mathcal{N}_2)}) = true$.

  Also, $[\![w_2 \wedge (l > 0) \wedge (l_f = 0)]\!](\overline{l: Decision(\langle g \rangle \ \mathcal{N}_1, \ \langle \neg g \rangle \ \mathcal{N}_2)}) = true$.

  Thus, $s_0 \ \mathcal{R} \ \overline{l: Decision(\langle g \rangle \ \mathcal{N}_1, \ \langle \neg g \rangle \ \mathcal{N}_2)}$.

  According to the operational semantics, there are two possible transitions emanating from the configuration $\overline{l: Decision(\langle g \rangle \ \mathcal{N}_1, \ \langle \neg g \rangle \ \mathcal{N}_2)}$. The transition enabled by rule DEC-1:

  $\overline{l: Decision(\langle g \rangle \mathcal{N}_1, \langle \neg g \rangle \mathcal{N}_2)} \longrightarrow_1 l: Decision(\langle tt \rangle \overline{\mathcal{N}_1}, \langle ff \rangle \mathcal{N}_2)$.

  The transition enabled by rule DEC-2:

  $\overline{l: Decision(\langle g \rangle \mathcal{N}_1, \langle \neg g \rangle \mathcal{N}_2)} \longrightarrow_1 l: Decision(\langle ff \rangle \mathcal{N}_1, \langle tt \rangle \overline{\mathcal{N}_2})$.

  Definition 11.3 defines two transitions in the Markov decision process M_A emanating from the same state such that $\overline{l: Decision(\langle g \rangle \mathcal{N}_1, \langle \neg g \rangle \mathcal{N}_2)} \longrightarrow \mu'_1$ where $\mu'_1(l: Decision(\langle tt \rangle \overline{\mathcal{N}_1}, \langle ff \rangle \mathcal{N}_2)) = 1$ and $\overline{l: Decision(\langle g \rangle \mathcal{N}_1, \langle \neg g \rangle \mathcal{N}_2)} \longrightarrow \mu'_1$ where $\mu'_2(l: Decision(\langle ff \rangle \mathcal{N}_1, \langle tt \rangle \overline{\mathcal{N}_2})) = 1$.

  Let $\mathcal{R} = \{(s_0, \overline{l: Decision(\langle g \rangle \mathcal{N}_1, \langle \neg g \rangle \mathcal{N}_2)}), (s_1, l: Decision(\langle tt \rangle \overline{\mathcal{N}_1}, \langle ff \rangle \mathcal{N}_2)), (s_2, l: Decision(\langle ff \rangle \mathcal{N}_1, \langle tt \rangle \overline{\mathcal{N}_2}))\}$. It follows that $\mu'_1 \preceq_{\mathcal{R}} \mu_1$ and $\mu'_2 \preceq_{\mathcal{R}} \mu_2$ as δ_1 defined such that $\delta_1(s_1, l: Decision(\langle tt \rangle \overline{\mathcal{N}_1}, \langle ff \rangle \mathcal{N}_2)) = 1$ and δ_2 defined such that $\delta_2(s_2, l: Decision(\langle ff \rangle \mathcal{N}_1, \langle tt \rangle \overline{\mathcal{N}_2})) = 1$ fulfill both the constraints of being weight functions. Thus, the theorem is proved for this case.

12.8 Conclusion

The main result of this chapter was the proof that our translation algorithm is sound. This establishes confidence in that the PRISM code generated by our algorithm correctly captures the behavior intended by the SysML activity diagram given as input. Thus, it ensures the correctness of our probabilistic verification approach.

Chapter 13
Conclusion

Many mature technologies,[1] accompanied by ever improving and automated processes of production, brought about an increasing availability of different specialized systems and sub-systems that provide specific functionalities, such as wired and wireless data link connectivity, data storage, analog/digital signal processing, encryption. In addition, in order to benefit from hardware and software reuse, the specialization of such systems is often achieved with corresponding control software along with various libraries or APIs. In fact, today's software aspect is so pervasive that even systems that have been traditionally mechanical in nature, such as automobiles, are integrating more and more control software to optimize such things as fuel consumption, cruise control, or sensor data processing.

The availability of such a rich spectrum of sub-systems has enabled faster avenues with regard to the development of future systems that already have the possibility of integrating available sub-components required for their operation. However, this corresponds to a higher level of system integration, where various components from a heterogeneous vendor pool participate in the realization of a new product or service. This, in turn, puts economic pressure on the various underpinning industry players that are competing to maintain or enlarge their market share. Thus, each vendor or service provider is required to achieve appropriate time-to-market as well as competitive pricing. These variables represent critical factors that can make or break a product. As a result, there is often a trade-off between business and engineering goals that can impact the time and expenditure allocated for the V&V process. In this context, undetected flaws in one of the building blocks of a highly integrated system may trickle into the functionality of the encompassing aggregate.

Consequently, this compounds the V&V process even more, forcing it to depend on the effectiveness of previous verification efforts. Also, technology forecasting, mainly underpinned by Moore's law, enable project planning based on the expected availability of certain products and services within a foreseeable time frame and with a reasonably accurate price estimate. These priorities are especially evident in areas where the information technology represents an instrumental factor. In this respect,

---

[1] Constant advancements have been made in fields such as mechanics, electronics, and manufacturing that have ramped up their respective industries.

M. Debbabi et al., *Verification and Validation in Systems Engineering*,
DOI 10.1007/978-3-642-15228-3_13, © Springer-Verlag Berlin Heidelberg 2010

we have witnessed the rapid proliferation of a myriad of gadgets, such as digital cameras, flash memory drives, GPS devices, cell phones, or audio/video players that are becoming more capable and less costly with each passing year. To that effect, increased capabilities, coupled with affordable prices, open the door for new products or services that were heretofore unmarketable to the ordinary consumers.[2] In addition, the trend toward an even higher level of integration is readily apparent. Indeed, our modern urban lifestyle requires a lot of portable gadgets, such as cell phones, GPS devices, flash memory drives. The very essence of these gadgets has called for their integration into aggregated systems, such as the modern smart phone, that can be more easily carried about while offering all the needed functionalities. In this situation, the reliability of a highly integrated system is all the more critical, since the user may depend solely on such system, and in a multitude of ways. Thus, a single point of failure can create multiple difficulties for the system users. Consequently, the case for adopting more comprehensive techniques and methodologies for the V&V of systems engineering products is even more compelling.

The increased challenges faced by modern system development, especially in the area of software-intensive systems design, led to the emergence of systems modeling languages such as UML 2.0 and SysML. Following an iterative process that benefited from industry feedback, these languages have been gradually endowed with the necessary expressiveness that can support the transition from document-based to model-based systems engineering (MBSE). This can bring along significant benefits in many areas by improving, among other aspects, design reuse and exchange, maintenance, and assessment.

In this pursuit, organizations such as INCOSE and OMG are representing very active drivers in the development of the aforementioned modeling languages meant to accommodate a broad range of systems engineering aspects. The present material aimed at providing the reader with relevant insights with respect to the process of V&V in model-driven systems engineering design and development. In this respect, it presented an overview of systems engineering, along with the relevance of modeling languages such as UML and SysML for the architecture and design of systems engineering design models. Moreover, it presented architectural concepts and V&V methodologies, along with their accompanying shortcomings, while detailing an emerging and more comprehensive V&V paradigm. The latter can enhance current approaches by synergistically applying formal methods, program analysis, and quality metrics on systems engineering design models.

Chapter 2 presented the paradigm of architecture frameworks that was adopted and extended by defense organizations, mainly the US Department of Defense in pursuit of defense systems' procurement and capability engineering. In the commercial field, the concept of architecture framework is known as enterprise architecture framework and is used by business and corporations for managing large scale

---

[2] As point in fact, the technological feasibility of modern personal entertainment devices can be tracked back to more than a decade but, at the time, the average person would hardly want to spend a whole month's earnings for such a gadget.

projects involving many design and development teams often spread nationwide or worldwide. Architecture frameworks ensure the commonality of views and enable effective information sharing and communication. The emergence of standardized modeling languages like SysML raised the need to use them in the context of architecture frameworks. In this respect, the corresponding features of interest have also been presented. In Chap. 3, an overview of the UML 2.0 modeling language was provided, describing the historical context of its emergence along with its corresponding structural and behavioral diagrams. Moreover, the UML profiling mechanism was also discussed. Chapter 4 presented the SysML modeling language along with a chronological account of its adoption process. The commonalities as well as the specific differences that are present between SysML and UML were detailed along with the features of SysML structural and behavioral diagrams. Moreover, specific details were given with respect to the informal syntax and semantics of the reused UML 2.0 behavioral models, namely the state machine, sequence, and activity diagrams.

Chapter 5 elaborated on the verification, validation and accreditation concepts. Relevant V&V methodologies were reviewed along with specific verification techniques for object-oriented designs, such as software engineering techniques, formal verification, and program analysis. Useful methodologies and relevant research initiatives were presented, including the state of the art in the verification and validation approaches targeting UML and SysML design models. Also, various tools targeting specific V&V aspects were presented, including formal verification environments and static program analyzers.

Chapter 6 presented an effective and synergistic approach for performing V&V on systems engineering design models expressed in standardized modeling languages such as UML and SysML. A number of established results were shown in support of the proposed synergistic verification and validation methodology, demonstrating its suitability for assessing systems engineering design models in a highly automated manner. In this respect, Chap. 7 demonstrated the usefulness of software engineering metrics for assessing structural aspects of design models captured by UML class and package diagrams. To that effect, a set of 15 metrics were discussed in the context of a relevant example. Moreover, Chap. 8 described the proposed verification methodology for behavioral diagrams. In this context, the concept of the configuration transition system (CTS) was detailed and shown as a valid semantic interpretation of design models expressed as state machine, sequence, or activity diagrams. The corresponding model-checking verification methodology was illustrated by using an appropriate model checker, namely NuSMV that can take as input the proposed semantic model. We showed the great potential for verifying systems engineering design models expressed in the considered behavioral diagrams. In this setting, the temporal logic CTL was introduced along with an illustrative description of its temporal operators, their expressiveness, and a related CTL macro-notation. Relevant case studies exemplifying the assessment of the state machine, sequence, and activity diagrams were also presented and discussed.

Chapter 9 presented the probabilistic verification of SysML activity diagrams. A translation algorithm was provided for mapping this type of diagram into an asynchronous probabilistic model, namely MDP, based on the input language of the probabilistic model checker PRISM. A case study demonstrated the proof of concept of the V&V approach for the performance analysis of asynchronous SysML activity diagram models. Furthermore, Chap. 10 detailed a transformation procedure for SysML activity diagrams annotated with time constraints and probability artifacts into a model consisting of a network of discrete-time Markov chains. Among other important performance aspects considered in the scope of a case study, we showed how the model can be analyzed by the probabilistic model checker PRISM for time-bounded reachability assessment.

Chapter 11 presented a probabilistic calculus that we called activity calculus (AC). It is used to capture the essence of SysML activity diagrams endowed with probabilistic features. The devised calculus was then used in order to build the underlying semantic foundations of SysML activity diagrams in terms of Markov decision processes using operational semantics framework.

Chapter 12 goal was to examine the soundness of the translation procedure described in Chap. 9 that maps SysML activity diagrams into MDP written in the input language of PRISM. This guarantees that the properties verified on the generated MDP PRISM model actually hold on the analyzed diagram. Accordingly, we formulated the soundness theorem based on a simulation pre-order upon Markov decision processes. The latter establishes a step-by-step unidirectional correspondence between the SysML activity diagram semantics and the semantics of the resulting MDP PRISM model generated by the translation algorithm. Thus, we also developed a formal syntax and semantics for the fragment of PRISM input language that has MDP semantics. The proof of soundness was derived using structural induction on the activity calculus syntax and the so-called weight function concept.

As final remarks, we can safely say that the trend toward model-based systems engineering (MBSE) is likely to continue unabated. In this respect, modeling languages like UML and SysML can bridge the many understanding and conceptual gaps by providing a rich yet precise expressiveness that can bring about a high degree of cohesion across the design, development, and verification teams. This is also relevant when considering today's competitive business environment that typically stimulates outsourcing, thus increasing the heterogeneity of the personnel involved in the processes of design, development, and V&V. The latter process can also draw significant benefits from MBSE since design models expressed in standardized modeling languages readily allow for the application of more comprehensive and rigorous design assessment procedures. Consequently, one can anticipate an improved level of harmonization between business and engineering objectives leading to higher quality products and services.

References

1. L. Aceto, W. J. Fokkink, and C. Verhoef. Structural Operational Semantics, chapter 3, pages 197–292. In Bergstra, J. A., Ponse, A., and Smolka, S. A., editors, *Handbook of Process Algebra*. Elsevier Science, Amsterdam, 2001.

2. D. Agnew, L. J. M. Claesen, and R. Camposano, editors. *Computer Hardware Description Languages and their Applications*, volume A-32 of *IFIP Transactions*. North-Holland, Amsterdam, 1993.

3. L. Alawneh, M. Debbabi, F. Hassaïne, Y. Jarraya, and A. Soeanu. A Unified Approach for Verification and Validation of Systems and Software Engineering Models. In *13th Annual IEEE International Conference and Workshop on the Engineering of Computer Based Systems (ECBS)*, Potsdam, Germany, March 2006.

4. H. Alla, R. David. *Discrete, Continuous, and Hybrid Petri Nets*. Springer, Berlin, 2005.

5. R. Alur and T. A. Henzinger. Reactive Modules. *Formal Methods in System Design*, 15(1): 7–48, 1999.

6. A. Artale. Formal Methods Lecture IV: Computation Tree Logic (CTL). http://www.inf. unibz.it/~artale/, 2009/2010. Faculty of Computer Science – Free University of Bolzano Lecture Notes.

7. ARTiSAN Software. ARTiSAN Real-time Studio. http://www.artisansw.com/pdflibrary/Rts_ 5.0_datasheet.pdf. Datasheet.

8. Averant Inc. Static Functional Verification with Solidify, a New Low-Risk Methodology for Faster Debug of ASICs and Programmable Parts. Technical report, Averant, Inc.s, 2001.

9. J. Bahuguna, B. Ravindran, and K. M. Krishna. MDP-Based Active Localization for Multiple Robots. In *the Proceedings of the Fifth Annual IEEE Conference on Automation Science and Engineering (CASE)*, Bangalore, India, pages 635–640, 2009. IEEE Press.

10. C. Baier. *On the Algorithmic Verification of Probabilistic Systems*. Habilitation, Universität Mannheim, Mannheim 1998.

11. C. Baier, B. Haverkort, H. Hermanns, and J.-P. Katoen. Model-Checking Algorithms for Continuous-Time Markov Chains. *IEEE Transactions on Software Engineering*, 29(7):2003, 2003.

12. C. Baier and M. Kwiatkowska. Domain Equations for Probabilistic Processes. *Mathematical Structures in Computer Science*, 10(6):665–717, 2000.

13. S. Balsamo and M. Marzolla. Performance Evaluation of UML Software Architectures with Multiclass Queueing Network Models. In *the Proceedings of the 5th International Workshop on Software and Performance (WOSP)*, pages 37–42, New York, USA, 2005. ACM Press.

14. J. Bansiya and C. G. Davis. A Hierarchical Model for Object-Oriented Design Quality Assessment. *IEEE Transactions on Software Engineering*, 28(1):4–17, 2002.

15. M. E. Beato, M. Barrio-Solrzano, and C. E. Cuesta. UML Automatic Verification Tool (TABU). In *SAVCBS 2004 Specification and Verification of Component-Based Systems, 12th ACM SIGSOFT Symposium on the Foundations of Software Engineering, Newport Beach, California, USA*. Department of Computer Science, Iowa State University, 2004.

M. Debbabi et al., *Verification and Validation in Systems Engineering*,
DOI 10.1007/978-3-642-15228-3, © Springer-Verlag Berlin Heidelberg 2010

16. L. Benini, A. Bogliolo, G. Paleologo, and G. De Micheli. Policy Optimization for Dynamic Power Management. *IEEE Transactions on Computer-Aided Design of Integrated Circuits and Systems*, 8(3):299–316, 2000.

17. A. Bennett and A. J. Field. Performance Engineering with the UML Profile for Schedulability, Performance and Time: a Case Study. In *the Proceedings of the 12th IEEE International Symposium on Modeling, Analysis, and Simulation of Computer and Telecommunications Systems (MASCOTS)*, Volendam, The Netherlands, pages 67–75, October 2004.

18. S. Bensalem, V. Ganesh, Y. Lakhnech, C. Mu noz, S. Owre, H. Rueß, J. Rushby, V. Rusu, H. Saïdi, N. Shankar, E. Singerman, and A. Tiwari. An Overview of SAL. In C. Michael Holloway, editor, *the Proceedings of the Fifth NASA Langley Formal Methods Workshop (LFM)*, pages 187–196, Hampton, VA, June 2000. NASA Langley Research Center.

19. E. Best, R. Devillers, and M. Koutny. *Petri Net Algebra*. Springer, New York, NY, USA, 2001.

20. A. Bianco and L. De Alfaro. Model Checking of Probabilistic and Nondeterministic Systems. In *Foundations of Software Technology and Theoretical Computer Science*, volume 1026 of *Lecture Notes in Computer Science*, pages 499–513. Springer, Berlin, 1995.

21. D. Binkley. The Application of Program Slicing to Regression Testing. In *Information and Software Technology Special Issue on Program Slicing*, pages 583–594. Elsevier, Amsterdam, 1999.

22. B. S. Blanchard and W. J. Fabrycky. *Systems Engineering and Analysis*. International Series in Industrial and Systems Engineering. Prentice Hall, Englewood Cliffs, NJ, 1981.

23. C. Bock. Systems Engineering in the Product Lifecycle. *International Journal of Product Development*, 2:123Ŭ137, 2005.

24. C. Bock. SysML and UML 2 Support for Activity Modeling. *Systems Engineering*, 9(2):160–186, 2006.

25. B. W. Boehm and V. R. Basili. Software Defect Reduction Top 10 List. *IEEE Computer*, 34(1):135–137, 2001.

26. G. Bolch, S. Greiner, H. de Meer, and K. S. Trivedi. *Queueing Networks and Markov Chains: Modeling and Performance Evaluation with Computer Science Applications*. Wiley, New York, NY, 2006.

27. A. Bondavalli, M. Dal Cin, G. Huszerl, K. Kosmidis, D. Latella, I. Majzik, M. Massink, and I. Mura. High-Level Integrated Design Environment for Dependability, Deliverable 2: Transformations. Report on the specification of analysis and transformation techniques, ESPRIT, December 1998. ESPRIT Project 27493.

28. A. Bondavalli, A. Fantechi, D. Latella, and L. Simoncini. Design Validation of Embedded Dependable Systems. *IEEE Micro*, 21(5):52–62, 2001.

29. A. Bondavalli, D. Latella, M. Dal Cin, and A. Pataricza. High-Level Integrated Design Environment for Dependability (HIDE). In *WORDS '99: Proceedings of the Fifth International Workshop on Object-Oriented Real-Time Dependable Systems*, page 87, Washington, DC, USA, 1999. IEEE Computer Society.

30. G. Booch. *Object-Oriented Analysis and Design with Applications*, Second Edition. Addison-Wesley, Reading, MA, 1997.

31. M. Bozga, J. C. Fernandez, L. Ghirvu, S. Graf, J. P. Krimm, and L. Mounier. IF: An Intermediate Representation and Validation Environment for Timed Asynchronous Systems. In Wing J. M., Woodcock J. and Davies J., editors, *World Congress on Formal Methods* in the Development of Computing Systems, Toulouse, France. Lecture Notes in Computer Science, vol. 1708, pages 307–327, Springer Berlin, 1999.

32. G. Brat and W. Visser. Combining Static Analysis and Model Checking for Software Analysis. In *the Proceedings of the 16th IEEE International Conference on Automated Software Engineering (ASE)*, page 262, Washington, DC, USA, 2001. IEEE Computer Society.

33. L. C. Briand, P. T. Devanbu, and W. L. Melo. An Investigation into Coupling Measures for C++. In *Proceedings of the 19th International Conference on Software Engineering*, Boston, MA, pages 412–421, ACM, New York, NY, 1997.

34. F. Brito, e Abreu, and W. Melo. Evaluating the Impact of Object-Oriented Design on Software Quality. In *the Proceedings of the 3rd International Software Metrics Symposium*, Berlin, Germany, pages 90–99, 1996.
35. M. Broy. Semantik der UML 2.0, October 2004.
36. J. Campos and J. Merseguer. On the Integration of UML and Petri Nets in Software Development. In *the Proceedings of the 27th International Conference on Applications and Theory of Petri Nets and Other Models of Concurrency (ICATPN)*, June 26–30, volume 4024 of *Lecture Notes in Computer Science*, pages 19–36. Springer, Berlin, 2006.
37. C. Canevet, S. Gilmore, J. Hillston, L. Kloul, and P. Stevens. Analysing UML 2.0 Activity Diagrams in the Software Performance Engineering Process. In *the Proceedings of the Fourth International Workshop on Software and Performance*, pages 74–78, Redwood Shores, CA, USA, January 2004. ACM Press.
38. C. Canevet, S. Gilmore, J. Hillston, M. Prowse, and P. Stevens. Performance Modelling with the Unified Modelling Language and Stochastic Process Algebras. *IEE Proceedings: Computers and Digital Techniques*, 150(2):107–120, 2003.
39. E. Carneiro, P. Maciel, G. Callou, E. Tavares, and B. Nogueira. Mapping SysML State Machine Diagram to Time Petri Net for Analysis and Verification of Embedded Real-Time Systems with Energy Constraints. In *the Proceedings of the International Conference on Advances in Electronics and Micro-electronics (ENICS'08)*, pages 1–6, Washington, DC, USA, 2008. IEEE Computer Society.
40. M. V. Cengarle and A. Knapp. UML 2.0 Interactions: Semantics and Refinement. In *3rd International Workshop on Critical Systems Development with UML (CSDUML '04, Proceedings)*, pages 85–99, München. Technische Universität München, 2004.
41. S. Ceri, P. Fraternali, and A. Bongio. Web Modeling Language (WebML): A Modeling Language for Designing Web Sites. *Computer Networks (Amsterdam, Netherlands: 1999)*, 33(1–6):137–157, 2000.
42. P. Chen, A. Tang, and J. Han. A Comparative Analysis of Architecture Frameworks. In *the Proceedings of the 11th Asia-Pacific Software Engineering Conference (APSEC'04)*, pages 640–647, Los Alamitos, CA, USA, 2004. IEEE Computer Society.
43. S. R. Chidamber and C. F. Kemerer. A Metrics Suite for Object Oriented Design. *IEEE Transactions on Software Engineering*, 20(6):476–493, 1994.
44. F. Ciesinski and M. Größer. On Probabilistic Computation Tree Logic. In Baier C., Haverkort B., Hermanns H., Katoen J-P. and Siegle M., editors, *Validation of Stochastic Systems*, vol. 2925 pages 147–188, Springer, Berlin, 2004.
45. A. Cimatti, E. Clarke, E. Giunchiglia, F. Giunchiglia, M. Pistore, M. Roveri, R. Sebastiani, and A. Tacchella. NuSMV Version 2: An OpenSource Tool for Symbolic Model Checking. In *the Proceedings of the International Conference on Computer-Aided Verification (CAV)*, volume 2404 of *LNCS*, Copenhagen, Denmark, July 2002. Springer.
46. A. Cimatti, E. Clarke, F. Giunchiglia, and M. Roveri. NuSMV: A New Symbolic Model Checker. *International Journal on Software Tools for Technology Transfer*, 2:2000, 2000.
47. A. Cimatti, E. M. Clarke, F. Giunchiglia, and M. Roveri. Nusmv: A New Symbolic Model Verifier. In *Proceeding of International Conference on Computer-Aided Verification (CAV'99)*, Trento, Italy. *Lecture Notes in Computer Science*, vol. 1633, pages 495–499. Springer, Berlin, 1999.
48. E. M. Clarke and E. A. Emerson. Design and Synthesis of Synchronization Skeletons Using Branching Time Temporal Logic. In *25 Years of Model Checking*, volume 5000 of *Lecture Notes in Computer Science*, pages 196–215. Springer, Berlin, 2008.
49. CNN. Unmanned European Rocket Explodes on First Flight. http://www.cnn.com/WORLD/ 9606/04/rocket.explode/, 1996. Last visited: January 2007.
50. Communications Committee. The International Council on Systems Engineering (INCOSE). http://www.incose.org/practice/whatissystemseng.aspx.
51. O. Constant, W. Monin, and S. Graf. A Model Transformation Tool for Performance Simulation of Complex UML Models. In *Companion of the 30th International Conference on Software Engineering*, pages 923–924, New York, NY, USA, 2008. ACM Press.

52. D.A Cook and J.M. Skinner. How to Perform Credible Verification, Validation, and Accreditation for Modeling and Simulation. In Special Systems & Software Technology conference Issue, *CrossTalk, The Journal of Defense Software Engineering*, vol. 18(5) May 2005. Software Technology Support Center (STSC), U.S. Air Force.

53. V. Cortellessa and R. Mirandola. Deriving a Queueing Network-Based Performance Model from UML Diagrams. In *the Proceedings of the 2nd International Workshop on Software and Performance (WOSP)*, pages 58–70, New York, NY, USA, 2000. ACM Press.

54. V. Cortellessa, P. Pierini, R. Spalazzese, and A. Vianale. MOSES: Modeling Software and Platform Architecture in UML 2 for Simulation-Based Performance Analysis. In *the Proceedings of the 4th International Conference on Quality of Software-Architectures*, pages 86–102, Berlin, Heidelberg, 2008. Springer.

55. P. Cousot, R. Cousot, J. Feret, and X. Rival L. Mauborgne, A. Miné. The ASTRÉE Static Analyzer. http://www.astree.ens.fr/. Last visited: May 2010.

56. Coverity. Coverity prevent static analysis. http://www.coverity.com/products/coverity-prevent.html. Last visited: May 2010.

57. M. L. Crane and J. Dingel. On the Semantics of UML State Machines: Categorization and Comparison. Technical Report 2005-501, School of Computing, Queen's University, 2005.

58. G. Csertan, G. Huszerl, I. Majzik, Z. Pap, A. Pataricza, and D. Varro. VIATRA: Visual Automated Transformations for Formal Verification and Validation of UML Models. In *ASE 2002: 17th IEEE International Conference on Automated Software Engineering,* Edinburgh, UK, September 23–27, 2002, 2002.

59. J. B. Dabney and T. L. Harman. *Mastering SIMULINK.* Prentice Hall PTR, Upper Saddle River, NJ, 1997.

60. J. S. Dahmann, R. M. Fujimoto, and R. M. Weatherly. The Department of Defense High Level Architecture. In *WSC '97: Proceedings of the 29th conference on Winter simulation*, pages 142–149, Washington, DC, USA, 1997. IEEE Computer Society.

61. P. Dasgupta, A. Chakrabarti, and P. P. Chakrabarti. Open Computation Tree Logic for Formal Verification of Modules. In *the Proceedings of the 2002 conference on Asia South Pacific Design Automation/VLSI Design (ASP-DAC'02)*, page 735, Washington, DC, USA, 2002. IEEE Computer Society.

62. R. Davis. Systems Engineering Experiences Growth as Emerging Discipline. http://www.nspe.org/etweb/1!-01systems.asp, November 2001. Engineering Times, National Society of Professional Engineers. Last Visited: September 7, 2006.

63. Defence Research and Development Canada. Suitability Study for Mapping Systems of Systems Architectures to Systems Engineering Modeling and Simulation Frameworks. Technical Report, Department of National Defence, Canada, 2007.

64. Defense Modeling and Simulation Office. Verification and Validation Techniques. http://vva.dmso.mil/Ref_Docs/VVTechniques/VVtechniques-pr.pdf, August 2001. Published as a Recommended Practices Guide (RPG).

65. V. Del Bianco, L. Lavazza, and M. Mauri. Model Checking UML Specifications of Real-Time Software. In *the Eighth IEEE International Conference on Engineering of Complex Computer Systems,* Greenbelt, Maryland, 2–4 December, 2002.

66. T. DeMarco. *Controlling Software Projects: Management, Measurement and Estimation.* Prentice Hall PTR, Upper Saddle River, NJ, 1986.

67. Department of Defense. *Instruction 5000.61: DoD Modeling and Simulation (M&S) Verification, Validation and Accreditation (VV&A),* May 2003.

68. Department of Defense Chief Information Officer. Department of Defense Net-Centric Services Strategy–Strategy for a Net-Centric, Service Oriented DOD Enterprise. Technical Report, Department of Defence, United States of America, The Pentagon Washington, DC, May 2007.

69. Department of Defense, United States of America. *Data Administration Procedures*, March 1994.

70. E. W. Dijkstra. Notes on Structured Programming. circulated privately, april 1970.

71. D. Djuric, D. Gasevic, and V. Devedzic. Adventures in Modeling Spaces: Close Encounters of the Semantic Web and MDA Kinds. In Kendall E.F., Oberle D., Pan J.Z. and Tetlow P., editors, *International Workshop on Semantic Web Enabled Software Engineering (SWESE)*, Galway, Ireland, 2005.

72. R. Dorfman. UML Examples: Elevator Simulation. http://www.web-feats.com/classes/dj/lessons/uml/elevator.htm. Last visited May 2010.

73. L. Doyle and M. Pennotti. Systems Engineering Experience with UML on a Complex System. In *CSER 2005: Conference on Systems Engineering Research*, Department of Systems Engineering and Engineering Management, Stevens Institute of Technology, 2005.

74. M. Duflot, M. Kwiatkowska, G. Norman, and D. Parker. A Formal Analysis of Bluetooth Device Discovery. *International Journal on Software Tools for Technology Transfer*, 8(6):621–632, 2006.

75. H. Eisner. *Essentials of Project and Systems Engineering Management*. Wiley, New York, NY 2002.

76. C. A. Ellis and G. J. Nutt. Modeling and Enactment of Workflow Systems. In *the Proceedings of the 14th International Conference on Application and Theory of Petri Nets*, Chicago, Illinois, USA, pages 1–16. 1993. Springer.

77. G. Engels, C. Soltenborn, and H. Wehrheim. Analysis of UML Activities Using Dynamic Meta Modeling. In M. M. Bonsangue and E. B. Johnsen, editors, *the Proceedings of the International Conference on Formal Methods for Open Object-Based Distributed Systems (FMOODS)*, volume 4468 of *Lecture Notes in Computer Science*, pages 76–90. Springer, New York, NY 2007.

78. R. Eshuis. *Semantics and Verification of UML Activity Diagrams for Workflow Modelling*. PhD thesis, University of Twente, 2002.

79. R. Eshuis. Symbolic Model Checking of UML Activity Diagrams. *ACM Transactions on Software Engineering and Methodology*, 15(1):1–38, 2006.

80. R. Eshuis and R. Wieringa. Tool Support for Verifying UML Activity Diagrams. *IEEE Transactions Software Engineering*, 30(7):437–447, 2004.

81. H. Fecher, M. Kyas, and J. Schönborn. Semantic Issues in UML 2.0 State Machines. Technical Report 0507, Christian-Albrechts-Universität zu Kiel, 2005.

82. D. Flater, P. A. Martin, and M. L. Crane. Rendering UML Activity Diagrams as Human-Readable Text. Technical Report NISTIR 7469, National Institute of Standards and Technology (NIST), November 2007.

83. Fortify. Fortify Source Code Analyzer (SCA) in Development. http://www.fortify.com/products/detect/in_development.jsp. Last visited: May 2010.

84. C. Fournet and G. Gonthier. The Join Calculus: A Language for Distributed Mobile Programming. In *the Applied Semantics Summer School (APPSEM)*, September 2000. Draft available from http://research.microsoft.com/ fournet.

85. S. Friedenthal, A. Moore, and R. Steiner. *A Practical Guide to SysML: The Systems Modeling Language*. Elsevier Science & Technology Books, July 2008.

86. S. Friedenthal, A. Moore, and R. Steiner. OMG Systems Modeling Language (OMG SysML) Tutorial. www.omgsysml.org/INCOSE-OMGSysML-Tutorial-Final-090901.pdf, 2009.

87. S. Gallotti, C. Ghezzi, R. Mirandola, and G. Tamburrelli. Quality Prediction of Service Compositions through Probabilistic Model Checking. In *the Proceedings of the 4th International Conference on Quality of Software-Architectures (QoSA'08)*, pages 119–134, Berlin, Heidelberg, 2008. Springer.

88. V. Garousi, L. C. Briand, and Y. Labiche. Control Flow Analysis of UML 2.0 Sequence Diagrams. In *Model Driven Architecture - Foundations and Applications, First European Conference, ECMDA-FA 2005, Nuremberg, Germany, November 7–10, 2005, Proceedings*, volume 3748 of *Lecture Notes in Computer Science*, pages 160–174. Springer, 2005.

89. M. Genero, M. Piattini, and C. Calero. Early Measures for UML Class Diagrams. *L'OBJET*, 6(4), 2000.

90. G. K. Gill and C. F. Kemerer. Cyclomatic Complexity Density and Software Maintenance Productivity. *IEEE Transactions on Software and Engineering*, 17(12):1284–1288, 1991.

91. S. Gnesi and F. Mazzanti. Mu-UCTL: A Temporal Logic for UML Statecharts. Technical report, ISTI, http://www.pst.ifi.lmu.de/projekte/agile/papers/2004-TR-68.pdf, 2004.

92. S. Gnesi and F. Mazzanti. On the Fly Model Checking of Communicating UML State Machines. In IEE INSPEC, editor, *SERA 2004 conference*, 2004.

93. S. Gnesi and F. Mazzanti. A Model Checking Verification Environment for UML Statecharts. In *XLIII AICA Annual Conference, University of Udine – AICA 2005*, October 2005.

94. J. O. Grady. *System Validation and Verification*. Systems engineering series. CRC, Boca Raton FL, 1998.

95. GRaphs for Object-Oriented VErification (GROOVE). http://groove.sourceforge.net/groove-index.html. Last Visited: January 2010.

96. R. Gronback. Model Validation: Applying Audits and Metrics to UML Models. In *BorCon 2004 Proceedings*, 2004.

97. R. Grosu and S. A. Smolka. Safety-Liveness Semantics for UML 2.0 Sequence Diagrams. In *the Proceedings of the 5th International Conference on Applications of Concurrency to System Design (ACSD'05)*, Saint Malo, France, June 2005.

98. N. Guelfi and A. Mammar. A Formal Semantics of Timed Activity Diagrams and its PROMELA Translation. In *the 12th Asia-Pacific Software Engineering Conference (APSEC'05)* Taiwan, pages 283–290. IEEE Computer Society, 2005.

99. P. J. Haas. *Stochastic Petri Nets: Modelling, Stability, Simulation*. Operations Research and Financial Engineering. Springer, New York, NY, 2002.

100. R. Haijema and J. Van der wal. An MDP Decomposition Approach for Traffic Control at Isolated Signalized Intersections. *Probability in the Engineering and Informational Sciences*, 22(4):587–602, 2008.

101. R. Harper. *Programming in Standard ML*. Online working draft, February 13, 2009.

102. Hewlett-Packard Development Company L.P. HP Code Advisor Version C.02.15-User's Guide. http://h21007.www2.hp.com/portal/download/files/unprot/codeadvisor/Cadvise_UG.pdf. Last visited: May 2010.

103. J. Hillston. Process Algebras for Quantitative Analysis. In *the Proceedings of the 20th Annual IEEE Symposium on Logic in Computer Science (LICS)*, pages 239–248, Washington, DC, USA, 2005. IEEE Computer Society.

104. R. C. Hite. Enterprise Architecture: Leadership Remains Key to Establishing and Leveraging Architectures for Organizational Transformation. Technical Report Report GAO-06-831, United States Government Accountability Office, August 2006. Report to the Chairman, Committee on Government Reform, House of Representatives.

105. C. A. R. Hoare. Communicating Sequential Processes. *Communications of the ACM*, 26(1):100–106, 1983.

106. H.P. Hoffmann. UML 2.0-Based Systems Engineering Using a Model-Driven Development Approach. *CROSSTALK The Journal of Defense Software Engineering*, November 2005.

107. A. Hohl. HDL for System Design. In H. Schwärtzel and I. Mizin, editors, *Advanced Information Processing: Proceedings of a Joint Symposium Information Processing and Software Systems Design Automation*, pages 313–326. Springer, Berlin, Heidelberg, 1990.

108. J. K. Hollingsworth. Critical Path Profiling of Message Passing and Shared-Memory Programs. *IEEE Transactions on Parallel and Distributed Systems*, 09(10):1029–1040, 1998.

109. G.J. Holzmann. The model checker spin. *IEEE Transactions on Software Engineering*, 23(5):279–295, May 1997. Special issue on Formal Methods in Software Practice.

110. Z. Hu and S. M. Shatz. Mapping UML Diagrams to a Petri Net Notation for System Simulation. In *the Proceedings of the Sixteenth International Conference on Software Engineering and Knowledge Engineering (SEKE'04)*, Banff, Alberta, Canada, pages 213–219, 2004.

111. Q. Hu and W. Yue. *Markov Decision Processes with their Applications* . Springer, New York, NY 2008.

112. E. Huang, R. Ramamurthy, and L. F. McGinnis. System and Simulation Modeling Using SysML. In *the Proceedings of the 39th conference on Winter simulation (WSC'07)*, pages 796–803, Piscataway, NJ, USA, 2007. IEEE Press.

113. IEEE Std. 1220-1998. *IEEE Standard for Application and Management of the Systems Engineering Process*, 1998.
114. *IEEE Std 1320.2-1998, IEEE Standard for Conceptual Modeling Language Syntax and Semantics for $IDEF1X_{97}$ ($IDEF_{object}$)*, 1998.
115. *IEEE Std 1012-2004, IEEE Standard for Software Verification and Validation*, 2005.
116. INCOSE. Overview of the ISO System. http://www.iso.org/iso/en/aboutiso/introduction/index.html. Last visited: December 2006.
117. INCOSE. Systems Engineering Vision 2020. Technical Report TP-2004-004-02, International Council on Systems Engineering (INCOSE), September 2007.
118. Institute of Electrical and Electronics Engineers. *IEEE Std 1278.1a-1998, IEEE Standard for Distributed Interactive Simulation – Application Protocols*, New York, NY, 1998.
119. Institute of Electrical and Electronics Engineers. *IEEE Std 1516-2000, IEEE Standard for Modeling and Simulation (M&S) High Level Architecture (HLA) – Framework and Rules*, New York, NY, 2000.
120. International Council on Systems Engineering (INCOSE) Website. http://www.incose.org/. Last Visited: February 2010.
121. ISO. TC184/SC4, Setting the Standards for Industrial Data. http://www.tc184-sc4.org/. Last visited May 2010.
122. ISO. *Industrial Automation Systems and Integration: Product Data Representation and Exchange*, 1994.
123. I. Jacobson. *Object-Oriented Software Engineering*. ACM Press, New York, NY, USA, 1992.
124. M. Janeba. The Pentium Problem. http://www.willamette.edu/~mjaneba/pentprob.html, 1995. Last visited: January 2007.
125. Y. Jarraya, A. Soeanu, M. Debbabi, and F. Hassaïne. Automatic Verification and Performance Analysis of Time-Constrained SysML Activity Diagrams. In *the Proceedings of the 14th Annual IEEE International Conference and Workshop on the Engineering of Computer Based Systems (ECBS)*, Tucson, AZ, USA, March 2007.
126. K. Jensen. *Coloured Petri Nets. Basic Concepts, Analysis Methods and Practical Use*, volume 1 of *Monographs in Theoretical Computer Science*. Springer, New York, NY 1997.
127. C. Johnson and P. Gray. Assessing the Impact of Time on User Interface Design. *SIGCHI Bull.*, 28(2):33–35, 1996.
128. B. Jonsson and K. G. Larsen. Specification and Refinement of Probabilistic Processes. In *the Proceedings of the 6th Annual IEEE Symposium on Logic in Computer Science (LICS)*, Amsterdam, Holland, pages 266–277. IEEE Computer Society, 1991.
129. P. S. Kaliappan, H. Koenig, and V. K. Kaliappan. Designing and Verifying Communication Protocols Using Model Driven Architecture and SPIN Model Checker. In *the Proceedings of the International Conference on Computer Science and Software Engineering (CSSE'08)*, pages 227–230, Washington, DC, USA, 2008. IEEE Computer Society.
130. M. Kattenbelt and M. Huth. Abstraction Framework for Markov Decision Processes and PCTL via Games. Technical Report RR-09-01, Oxford University Computing Laboratory, 2009.
131. S. K. Kim and D. A Carrington. A Formal V&V Framework for UML Models Based on Model Transformation Techniques. In *2nd MoDeVa Workshop – Model Design and validation*, Inria, France, 2005.
132. P. J. B. King and R. Pooley. Derivation of Petri Net Performance Models from UML Specifications of Communications Software. In *the Proceedings of the 11th International Conference on Computer Performance Evaluation: Modelling Techniques and Tools (TOOLS)*, pages 262–276, London, UK, 2000. Springer.
133. A. Kirshin, D. Dotan, and A. Hartman. A UML Simulator Based on a Generic Model Execution Engine. *Models in Software Engineering*, pages 324–326, 2007.
134. Klocwork. Klocwork Truepath. http://www.klocwork.com/products/insight/klocwork-truepath/. Last visited: May 2010.
135. A. Knapp, S. Merz, and C. Rauh. Model Checking - Timed UML State Machines and Collaborations. In *FTRTFT '02: Proceedings of the 7th International Symposium on Formal*

Techniques in Real-Time and Fault-Tolerant Systems, Oldenburg, Germany, pages 395–414. Springer, 2002.

136. C. Kobryn. Will UML 2.0 be Agile or Awkward? *Commun. ACM*, 45(1):107–110, 2002.

137. K. Korenblat and C. Priami. Extraction of PI-calculus specifications from UML sequence and state diagrams. Technical Report DIT-03-007, Informatica e Telecomunicazioni, University of Trento, Trento, Italy, February 2003.

138. A. Kossiakoff and W. N. Sweet. *Systems Engineering Principles and Practice*. Wiley, New York, NY, 2003.

139. D. Kroening. Application Specific Higher Order Logic Theorem Proving. In Autexier S. and Mantel H., editors, *Proceedings of the Verification Workshop (VERIFY'02)*, Copenhagen, Denmark, pages 5–15, July 2002.

140. M. Kwiatkowska, G. Norman, and D. Parker. Quantitative Analysis with the Probabilistic Model Checker PRISM. *Electronic Notes in Theoretical Computer Science*, 153(2):5–31, 2005.

141. D. Latella, I. Majzik, and M. Massink. Automatic Verification of a Behavioural Subset of UML Statechart Diagrams Using the SPIN Model-Checker. *Formal Aspects in Computing*, 11(6):637–664, 1999.

142. D. Latella, I. Majzik, and M. Massink. Towards a Formal Operational Semantics of UML Statechart Diagrams. In *Proceedings of the IFIP TC6/WG6.1 Third International Conference on Formal Methods for Open Object-Based Distributed Systems (FMOODS)*, page 465, Deventer, The Netherlands, The Netherlands, 1999. Kluwer, B.V.

143. W. Li and S. Henry. Maintenance Metrics for the Object Oriented Paradigm. In *First International Software Metrics Symposium*, pages 52–60, 1993.

144. W. Li and S. Henry. Object-Oriented Metrics that Predict Maintainability. *Journal of Systems and Software*, Baltimore, MD, USA, 23(2):111–122, 1993.

145. X. Li, Z. Liu, and J. He. A formal semantics of UML sequence diagrams. In *Proc. of Australian Software Engineering Conference (ASWEC'2004), 13–16 April 2004*, Melbourne, Australia, 2004. IEEE Computer Society.

146. C. Lindemann, A. Thümmler, A. Klemm, M. Lohmann, and O. P. Waldhorst. Performance Analysis of Time-Enhanced UML Diagrams Based on Stochastic Processes. In *the Proceedings of the 3rd International Workshop on Software and Performance (WOSP)*, pages 25–34, New York, NY, USA, 2002. ACM Press.

147. J. Long. Relationships Between Common Graphical Representations in Systems Engineering. Technical Report, Vitech Corporation, 2002.

148. M. Lonsdale and J. Kasser. Memorandum of Understanding: The Systems Engineering Society of Australia (SESA) and the Australian Chapter of the INCOSE. http://www.sesa.org.au/sesa_incose_mou.htm. November 2004, the SETE'04 Conference, Adelaide.

149. J.P. López-Grao, J. Merseguer, and J. Campos. Performance Engineering Based on UML and SPN: A Software Performance Tool. In *the Proceedings of the Seventeenth International Symposium on Computer and Information Sciences*, pages 405–409. CRC Press, Boca Raton, FL, October 2002.

150. M. Lorenz and J. Kidd. *Object-Oriented Software Metrics: A Practical Guide*. Prentice Hall, Upper Saddle River, NJ, 1994.

151. R. C. Martin. OO Design Quality Metrics, 1994.

152. Maude system. http://maude.cs.uiuc.edu/. Last Visited: January 2010.

153. R. J. Mayer, J. W. Crump, R. Fernandes, A. Keen, and M. K. Painter. Information Integration for Concurrent Engineering (IICE) Compendium of Methods Report. Technical Report, Knowledge-Based Systems, Inc., 1995.

154. R. J. Mayer, M. K. Painter, and P. S. Dewitte. IDEF Family of Methods for Concurrent Engineering and Business Re-engineering Applications. Technical Report, Knowledge-Based Systems, Inc., 1992.

155. S. Mazzini, D. Latella, and D. Viva. PRIDE: An Integrated Software Development Environment for Dependable Systems. In *DASIA 2004: Data Systems in Aerospace, Nice, France.* ESA Publications Division, 2004.

156. T. J. McCabe. A Complexity Measure. *IEEE Transactions on Software Engineering*, 2:308–320, 1976.
157. K. L. McMillan. The SMV System. Technical Report CMU-CS-92-131, Carnegie Mellon University, 1992.
158. K. L. McMillan. Getting Started with SMV. Technical Report, Cadence Berkeley Labs, 1999.
159. S. Mehta, S. Ahmed, S. Al-Ashari, Dennis Chen, Dev Chen, S. Cokmez, P. Desai, R. Eltejaein, P. Fu, J. Gee, T. Granvold, A. Iyer, K. Lin, G. Maturana, D. McConn, H. Mohammed, J. Moudgal, S. Nori, N. Parveen, G. Peterson, M. Splain, and T. Yu. Verification of the Ultrasparc Microprocessor. In *40th IEEE Computer Society International Conference (COMPCON'95)*, San Francisco, California, USA, pages 452–461, 1995.
160. J. Merseguer and J. Campos. Software Performance Modelling Using UML and Petri Nets. *Lecture Notes in Computer Science*, 2965:265–289, 2004.
161. E. Mikk, Y. Lakhnech, M. Siegel, and G. J. Holzmann. Implementing Statecharts in PROMELA/SPIN. In *WIFT '98: Proceedings of the Second IEEE Workshop on Industrial Strength Formal Specification Techniques*, page 90. IEEE Computer Society, Boca Raton, FL, USA, 1998.
162. D. Miller. Higher-Order Logic Programming. In *the Proceedings of the Eighth International Conference on Logic Programming (ICLP)*, Jerusalem, Israel, page 784, 1990.
163. R. Milner. An Algebraic Definition of Simulation Between Programs. In *the Proceedings of the 2nd International Joint Conference on Artificial Intelligence (IJCAI)*, London, UK, pages 481–489, San Francisco, CA, 1971. William Kaufmann.
164. R. Milner. *Communicating and Mobile Systems: The Pi-Calculus*. Cambridge University Press, Cambridge, 1999.
165. MODAF. The Ministry of Defence Architecture Framework. http://www.mod.uk/modaf. Last visited: May 2010.
166. F. Mokhati, P. Gagnon, and M. Badri. Verifying UML Diagrams with Model Checking: A Rewriting Logic Based Approach. In *The Proceedings of the Seventh International Conference on Quality Software, (QSIC'07)*, Portland, Oregon, USA, pages 356–362, October 2007.
167. Nasa. Software Quality Metrics for Object-Oriented System Environments. Technical Report SATC-TR-95-1001, National Aeronautics and Space Administration, Goddard Space Flight Center, Greenbelt, Maryland, June 1995.
168. Navy Modeling and Simulation Management Office. Modeling and Simulation Verification, Validation, and Accreditation Implementation Handbook. Technical Report, Department of the Navy, US, March 2004.
169. D. M. Nicol. Special Issue on the Telecommunications Description Language. *SIGMETRICS Performance Evaluation Review*, 25(4):3, 1998.
170. H.R. Nielson, F. Nielson, and C. Hankin. *Principles of Program Analysis*. Springer, New York, NY 1999.
171. Northrop Grumman Corp. and NASA ARC. *V&V of Advanced Systems at NASA*, 2002.
172. G. Norman and V. Shmatikov. Analysis of Probabilistic Contract Signing. *Journal of Computer Security*, 14(6):561–589, 2006.
173. I. Ober, S. Graf, and D. Lesens. A Case Study in UML Model-Based Validation: The Ariane-5 Launcher Software. In *FMOODS'06*, volume 4037 of *Lecture Notes in Computer Science*. Springer, Berlin, 2006.
174. I. Ober, S. Graf, and I. Ober. Validating Timed UML Models by Simulation and Verification. In *Workshop on Specification and Validation of UML models for Real Time and Embedded Systems (SVERTS 2003), A Satellite Event of UML 2003,* San Francisco, October 2003, October 2003. Downloadable Through http://www- verimag.imag.fr/EVENTS/SVERTS/.
175. Object Management Group. Meta-Object Facility (MOF) Specification, 2002.
176. Object Management Group. XML Metadata Interchange (XMI) Specification, 2003.
177. Object Management Group. *UML for Systems Engineering, Request For Proposal*, March 2003.

178. Object Management Group. *MDA Guide Version 1.0.1*, June 2003.

179. Object Management Group. *UML Profile for Schedulability, Performance and Time*, January 2005.

180. Object Management Group. *Unified Modeling Language: Infrastructure Version 2.0*, March 2005.

181. Object Management Group. *Unified Modeling Language: Superstructure Version 2.0*, March 2005.

182. Object Management Group. What is omg-uml and why is it important? http://www.omg.org/news/pr97/umlprimer.html. Last Visited April 2006.

183. Object Management Group. About the Object Management Group (OMG). http://www.omg.org/gettingstarted/gettingstartedindex.htm. Visited: December 2006.

184. Object Management Group. Introduction to OMG's Unified Modeling Language(UML). http://www.omg.org/gettingstarted/what_is_uml.htm. Last visited: December 2006.

185. Object Management Group. *Unified Modeling Language: Infrastructure Version 2.1.1*, February 2007.

186. Object Management Group. *Unified Modeling Language: Superstructure Version 2.1.1*, February 2007.

187. Object Management Group. *OMG Systems Modeling Language (OMG SysML) Specification v1.0*, September 2007. OMG Available Specification.

188. Object Management Group. *OMG Unified Modeling Language: Superstructure 2.1.2*, November 2007.

189. Object Management Group. *A UML Profile for MARTE: Modeling and Analysis of Real-Time Embedded Systems, Beta 2*, June 2008. OMG Adopted Specification.

190. Object Management Group. *OMG Systems Modeling Language (OMG SysML) Specification v 1.1*, November 2008.

191. Object Management Group. *Unified Profile for DoDAF and MODAF (UPDM), Version 1.0*, December 2009.

192. Object Management Group. Systems Engineering Domain Special Interest Group Website. http://syseng.omg.org/syseng_info.htm. Last visited: May 2010.

193. H. A. Oldenkamp. Probabilistic Model Checking – A Comparison of Tools. Master's Thesis, University of Twenty, The Netherlands, May 2007.

194. Open Group. The Open Group Architecture Forum. http://www.opengroup.org/architecture. Last visited: May 2010.

195. Open Group. TOGAF. http://www.opengroup.org/togaf/. Last visited: May 2010.

196. Optimyth. Checking. http://www.optimyth.com/en/products/checking-qa.html. Last Visited: May 2010.

197. C. J. J. Paredis and T. Johnson. Using OMG's SysML to Support Simulation. In *the Proceedings of the 40th Conference on Winter Simulation (WSC'08)*, pages 2350–2352. Winter Simulation Conference, Miami, Florida, 2008.

198. T. Pender. *UML Bible*. Wiley, New York, NY, 2003.

199. D. C. Petriu and H. Shen. Applying the UML Performance Profile: Graph Grammar-Based Derivation of LQN Models from UML Specifications. In *the Proceedings of the 12th International Conference on Computer Performance Evaluation, Modelling Techniques and Tools (TOOLS)*, pages 159–177, London, UK, 2002. Springer.

200. D. Pilone and N. Pitman. *UML 2.0 in a Nutshell*. O'Reilly, 2005.

201. G. D. Plotkin. A Structural Approach to Operational Semantics. Technical Report DAIMI FN-19, University of Aarhus, 1981.

202. R. Pooley. Using UML to Derive Stochastic Process Algebra Models. In Davies and Bradley, editors, *the Proceedings of the Fifteenth Performance Engineering Workshop*, Department of Computer Science, The University of Bristol, UK, pages 23–33, July 1999.

203. PRISM Team. The PRISM Language – Semantics. Last Visited: March 2009.

204. PRISM Team. PRISM – Probabilistic Symbolic Model Checker. http://www.prismmodelchecker.org/index.php. Last Visited: September 2009.

205. G. Quaranta and P. Mantegazza. Using Matlab-Simulink RTW to Build Real Time Control Applications in User Space with RTAI-LXRT, In the Third Real-Time Linux Workshop, Milano, Italy, 2001.
206. W. Reisig. *Petri Nets, An Introduction*. Springer, Berlin, 1985.
207. J. Rumbaugh, I. Jacobson, and G. Booch. *The Unified Modeling Language Reference Manual*, Second Edition. Addison-Wesley, Reading, MA, 2005.
208. J. Rutten, M. Kwiatkowska, G. Norman, and D. Parker. *Mathematical Techniques for Analyzing Concurrent and Probabilistic Systems*, volume 23 of *CRM Monograph Series*. American Mathematical Society, Providence, RI, 2004.
209. J. Rutten, M. Kwiatkowska, G. Norman, and D. Parker. *Mathematical Techniques for Analyzing Concurrent and Probabilistic Systems*. In Panangaden P., and van Breugel F., editors, volume 23 of *CRM Monograph Series*. American Mathematical Society, Providence, RI, 2004.
210. W. H. Sanders and J. F. Meyer. Stochastic Activity Networks: Formal Definitions and Concepts. *Lecture Notes in Computer Science*, pages 315–343. Springer, Berlin, 2002.
211. M. Sano and T. Hikita. Dynamic Semantic Checking for UML Models in the IIOSS System. In *the Proceedings of the International Symposium on Future Software Technology (ISFST)*, Xian, China, October 2004.
212. T. Schäfer, A. Knapp, and S. Merz. Model Checking UML State Machines and Collaborations. *Electronic Notes in Theoretical Computer Science*, 55(3):13, 2001.
213. Ph. Schnoebelen. The Verification of Probabilistic Lossy Channel Systems. In *Validation of Stochastic Systems – A Guide to Current Research*, volume 2925 of *Lecture Notes in Computer Science*, pages 445–465. Springer, Berlin, 2004.
214. J. Schumann. Automated Theorem Proving in High-Quality Software Design. In Hölldobler S., editor, *Intellectics and Computational Logic*, Applied Logic Series, vol. 19, pages 295–312, Kluwer Academic Publishers, Dordrecht, 2000.
215. Scientific Toolworks. Understand: Source code analysis & metrics. http://www.scitools.com/index.php. Last Visited: May 2010.
216. F. Scuglík. Relation Between UML2 Activity Diagrams and CSP Algebra. *WSEAS Transactions on Computers*, 4(10):1234–1240, 2005.
217. R. Segala and N. A. Lynch. Probabilistic Simulations for Probabilistic Processes. In *the Proceedings of the Concurrency Theory (CONCUR'94)*, pages 481–496, London, UK, 1994. Springer.
218. Semantic Designs Inc. The dms software reengineering toolkit. http://www.semdesigns.com/products/DMS/DMSToolkit.html. Last visited: May 2010.
219. B. Selic. On the Semantic Foundations of Standard UML 2.0. In *SFM*, pages 181–199, 2004.
220. R. Shannon. Introduction to the Art and Science of Simulation. In *Proceedings of the 1998 Winter Simulation Conference*, volume 1, Washington, Washington DC, pages 7–14. IEEE, 1998.
221. G. Smith. *The Object-Z Specification Language*. Kluwer Academic Publishers, Norwell, MA, USA, 2000.
222. SofCheck. Sofcheck inspector. http://www.sofcheck.com/products/inspector.html. Last Visited: May 2010.
223. H. Störrle. Semantics of Interactions in UML 2.0. In *Proceedings of the 2003 IEEE Symposium on Human Centric Computing Languages and Environments (HCC'03)*, Auckland, New Zealand, pages 129–136, IEEE Computer Society, Washington, DC, 2003.
224. H. Störrle. Semantics of Control-Flow in UML 2.0 Activities. In *2004 IEEE Symposium on Visual Languages and Human-Centric Computing (VL/HCC 2004)*, pages 235–242, Rome, Italy, 2004. IEEE Computer Society.
225. H. Störrle. Semantics of Exceptions in UML 2.0 Activities. Technical Report 0403, Ludwig-Maximilians-Universität München, Institut für Informatik, Munich, Germany, 2004.
226. H. Störrle. Semantics and Verification of Data Flow in UML 2.0 Activities. *Electrical Notes in Theoretical Computer Science*, 127(4):35–52, 2005.

227. SysML Forum. SysML Forum-Frequently Asked Questions. http://www.sysmlforum.com/FAQ.htm. Last visited: December 2009.

228. N. Tabuchi, N. Sato, and H. Nakamura. Model-Driven Performance Analysis of UML Design Models Based on Stochastic Process Algebra. In *the Proceedings of the First European Conference on Model Driven Architecture – Foundations and Applications (ECMDA-FA)*, volume 3748 of *Lecture Notes in Computer Science*, pages 41–58, 2005. Springer, Berlin.

229. Technical Board. Systems Engineering Handbook: A "What To" Guide For All SE Practitioners. Technical Report INCOSE-TP-2003-016-02, Version 2a, International Council on Systems Engineering, June 2004.

230. Technical Board. Systems Engineering Handbook: A Guide for System Life Cycle Processes and Activities. Technical Report INCOSE-TP-2003-002-03, Version 3, International Council on Systems Engineering, June 2006.

231. The MathWorks Inc. PolySpace Embedded Software Verification. http://www.mathworks.com/products/polyspace/. Last visited: May 2010.

232. F. Tip. A Survey of Program Slicing Techniques. *Journal of Programming Languages*, 3:121–189, 1995.

233. M. Tribastone and S. Gilmore. Automatic Extraction of PEPA Performance Models from UML Activity Diagrams Annotated with the MARTE Profile. In *the Proceedings of the 7th International Workshop on Software and Performance (WOSP)*, pages 67–78, New York, NY, 2008. ACM.

234. M. Tribastone and S. Gilmore. Automatic Translation of UML Sequence Diagrams into PEPA Models. In *the Proceedings of the Fifth International Conference on Quantitative Evaluation of Systems September 2008 (QEST)*, St Malo, France, pages 205–214. IEEE Press, 2008.

235. J. Trowitzsch, A. Zimmermann, and G. Hommel. Towards Quantitative Analysis of Real-Time UML Using Stochastic Petri Nets. In *the Proceedings of the 19th IEEE International Workshop on Parallel and Distributed Processing Symposium (IPDPS)*, page 139.b, Washington, DC, USA, 2005. IEEE Computer Society.

236. G. C. Tugwell, J. D. Holt, C. J. Neill, and C. P. Jobling. Metrics for Full Systems Engineering Lifecycle Activities (MeFuSELA). In *Proceedings of the Ninth International Symposium of the International Council on Systems Engineering (INCOSE 99)*, Brighton, UK, 1999.

237. C. Turrel, R. Brown, J.-L. Igarza, K. Pixius, F. Renda, and C. Rouget. Federation Development and Execution Process (fedep) Tools in Support of NATO Modelling & Simulation (m&s) Programmes. Technical Report TR-MSG-005, North Atlantic Treaty Organisation and Research AND Technology Organisation, May 2004.

238. Universitat Bremen. udraw(graph)tool. http://www.informatik.uni-bremen.de/uDrawGraph/en/index.html.

239. University of Birmingham. http://www.bham.ac.uk/. Last Visited: January 2010.

240. University of Oxford. http://www.ox.ac.uk/. Last Visited: January 2010.

241. UPDM Group. UPDM Group Website. http://www.updmgroup.org/. Last visited: May 2010.

242. U.S. Bureau of Land Management. IDEF Model. http://www.blm.gov/ba/bpr/idef.htm. Last Visited February 21, 2006.

243. US Department of Defence. *DoD Architecture Framework Version 1.5, Volume I: Definitions and Guidelines*, April 2007.

244. J. URen. An Overview of AP233, STEPŠs Systems Engineering Standard. http://www.dtic.mil/ndia/2003systems/slides.ppt, October 2003.

245. USAF Research Group. Object-Oriented Model Metrics. Technical report, The United States Air Force Space and Warning Product-Line Systems, Pernambuco - Brasil, 1996.

246. F. Vahid. *Digital Design with RTL Design, Verilog and VHDL*, Second Edition, 2010 Wiley, New York, NY.

247. W. M. P. van der Aalst. The Application of Petri Nets to Workflow Management. *Journal of Circuits, Systems, and Computers*, 8(1):21–66, 1998.

248. M. Y. Vardi. Branching vs. Linear Time: Final Showdown. In *the Proceedings of the 7th International Conference on Tools and Algorithms for the Construction and Analysis of Systems (TACAS)*, pages 1–22, London, UK, 2001. Springer.

249. D. Verton. Software Failure Cited in August Blackout Investigation. http://www.computerworld.com/securitytopics/security/recovery/story/0,10801,87400,00.html, 2003. Last Visited: January 2007.

250. A. Viehl, T. Schänwald, O. Bringmann, and W. Rosenstiel. Formal Performance Analysis and Simulation of UML/SysML Models for ESL Design. In *DATE '06: Proceedings of the Conference on Design, Automation and Test in Europe*, pages 242–247, Belgium, 2006. European Design and Automation Assoc.

251. V. Vitolins and A. Kalnins. Semantics of UML 2.0 Activity Diagram for Business Modeling by Means of Virtual Machine. In *Proceedings of the Ninth IEEE International EDOC Enterprise Computing Conference (EDOC'05)*, Enschede, The Netherlands, pages 181–194, IEEE Computer Society, Los Alamitos, CA, 2005.

252. E. Wandeler, L. Thiele, M. Verhoef, and P. Lieverse. System Architecture Evaluation Using Modular Performance Analysis: A Case Study. *International Journal on Software Tools for Technology Transfer*, 8(6):649–667, 2006.

253. R. Wang and C. H. Dagli. An Executable System Architecture Approach to Discrete Events System Modeling Using SysML in Conjunction with Colored Petri Net. In *the Proceedings of the 2nd Annual IEEE Systems Conference*, Montreal, Quebec, Canada, pages 1–8. IEEE, April 2008.

254. C. S. Wasson. *System Analysis, Design, and Development: Concepts, Principles, and Practices*. Wiley Series in Systems Engineering and Management. Wiley-Interscience, Hoboken, NJ, 2006.

255. T. Weilkiens. *Systems Engineering with SysML/UML: Modeling, Analysis, Design*. Morgan Kaufmann Publishers Inc., Burlington, MA, 2008.

256. S. White, M. Cantor, S. Friedenthal, C. Kobryn, and B. Purves. Panel: Extending UML from Software to Systems Engineering. In *the Proceedings of the 10th IEEE International Conference on Engineering of Computer-Based Systems (ECBS)*, pages 271. IEEE Computer Society, Huntsville, AL, USA, April 2003.

257. World Wide Web Consortium. *Extensible Markup Language (XML) 1.0 (Fifth Edition)*, W3C Recommendation edition, November 2008. Online Resource http://www.w3.org/TR/xml/.

258. D. Xu, H. Miao, and N. Philbert. Model Checking UML Activity Diagrams in FDR. In *the Proceedings of the ACIS International Conference on Computer and Information Science*, pages 1035–1040, Los Alamitos, CA, USA, 2009. IEEE Computer Society.

259. J. A. Zachman. A Framework for Information Systems Architecture. *IBM Systems Journal*, 26:276–292, 1987.

260. X. Zhan and H. Miao. An Approach to Formalizing the Semantics of UML Statecharts. In *Conceptual Modeling – ER 2004, 23rd International Conference on Conceptual Modeling*, Shanghai, China, November 2004, Proceedings, pages 753–765, 2004.

261. A. W. Zinn. The Use of Integrated Architectures to Support Agent Based Simulation: an Initial Investigation. Master of Science in Systems Engineering, Air Force Institute of Technology, Air University, Air Education and Training Command, Wright-Patterson Air Force Base, Ohio, March 2004.

Index